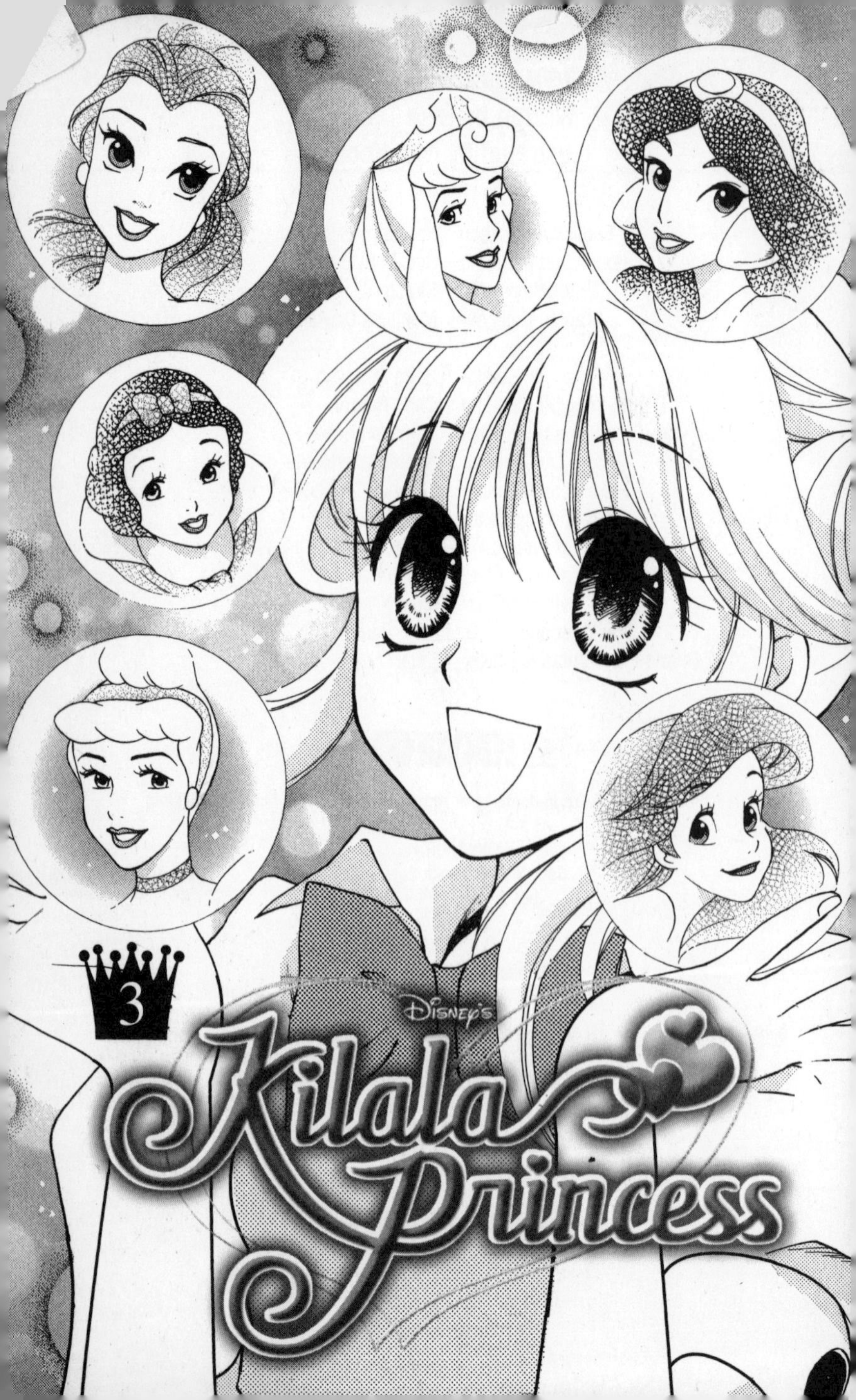
3
Disney's
Kilala Princess

Kilala Princess Volume 3
Written by Rika Tanaka
Illustrated by Nao Kodaka

English Adaptation - Katherine Schilling
Retouch and Lettering - Star Print Brokers
Production Artist - Skooter
Graphic Designer - Monalisa De Asis

Editor - Hope Donovan
Digital Imaging Manager - Chris Buford
Pre-Production Supervisor - Erika Terriquez
Art Director - Anne Marie Horne
Production Manager - Elisabeth Brizzi
Managing Editor - Vy Nguyen
VP of Production - Ron Klamert
Editor-in-Chief - Rob Tokar
Publisher - Mike Kiley
President and C.O.O. - John Parker
C.E.O. and Chief Creative Officer - Stuart Levy

A  Manga

TOKYOPOP and 🐭 are trademarks or registered trademarks of TOKYOPOP Inc.

TOKYOPOP Inc.
5900 Wilshire Blvd. Suite 2000
Los Angeles, CA 90036

E-mail: info@TOKYOPOP.com
Come visit us online at www.TOKYOPOP.com

Original Manga Comic by Kodansha / Nao Kodaka
© Disney
All rights reserved.

ISBN: 978-1-4278-0276-7

First TOKYOPOP printing: September 2007
10 9 8 7 6 5 4 3 2
Printed in the USA

Disney's

Kilala Princess

Volume 3

Art by Nao Kodaka
Story by Rika Tanaka

TOKYOPOP®

HAMBURG // LONDON // LOS ANGELES // TOKYO

MEET Kilala AND FRIENDS

Kilala:
An ordinary girl who loves all the Disney princesses. Kilala's parents have gone to a faraway land called Paradiso because her mother is sick.

Tippe:
Kilala's pet flying mouse.

Kilala's on an adventure to find a princess!

With help from Snow White, Kilala and Rei rescued Kilala's best friend Erica from kidnappers. Now they've left Snow White's world, and Kilala and Rei are at a ball, where they must say goodbye.

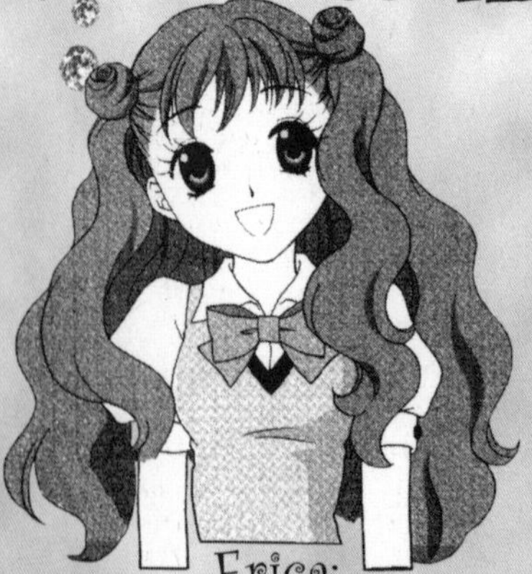

Erica:
Kilala's best friend. Erica was kidnapped because she won the Princess Contest at school.

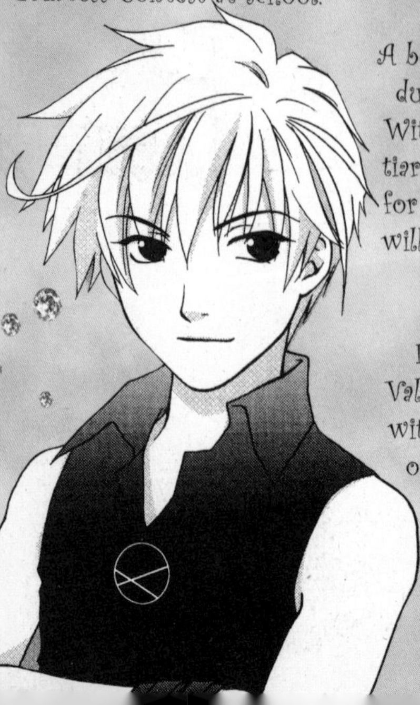

Rei:
A boy who met Kilala during his journey. With the help of the tiara, Rei is searching for the princess who will save his country.

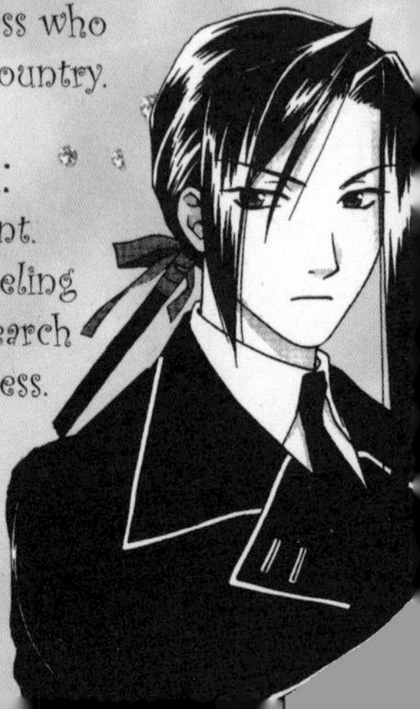

Valdou:
Rei's assistant. Valdou is traveling with Rei in search of the princess.

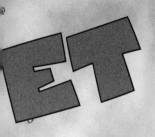

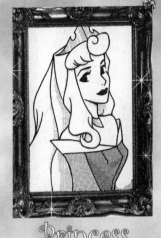

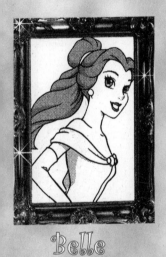

Princess
Aurora

Belle

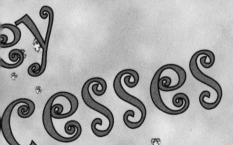

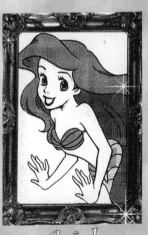

Ariel

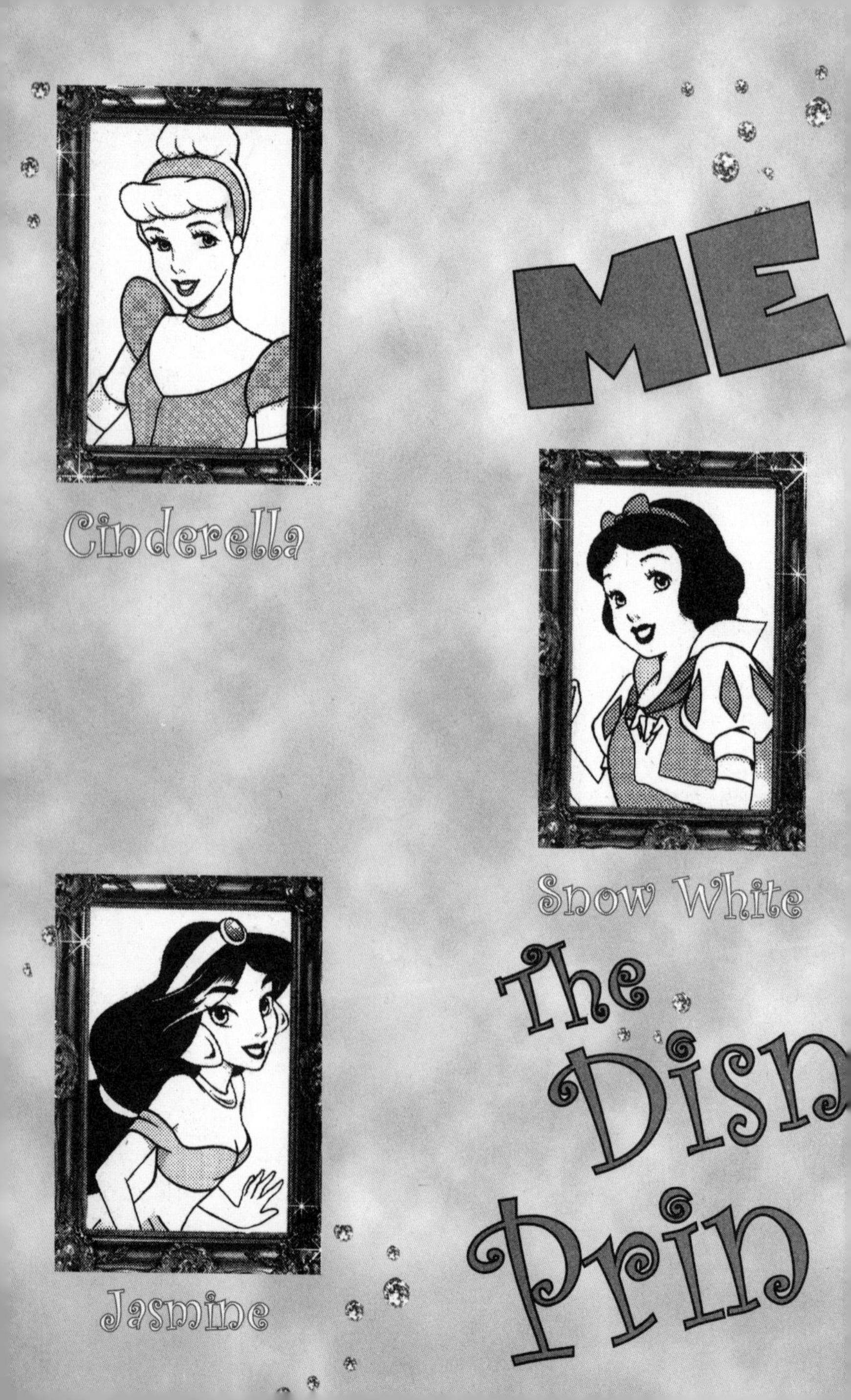
ME
Snow White
The
Disn
Prin
Cinderella
Jasmine

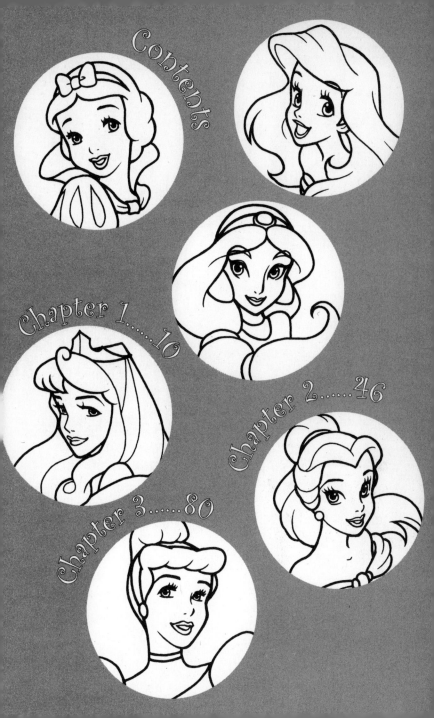

Contents

Chapter 1.....10

Chapter 2.....46

Chapter 3.....80

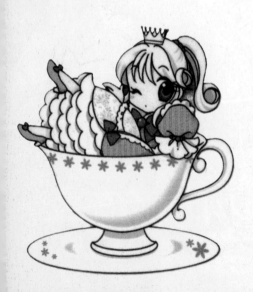

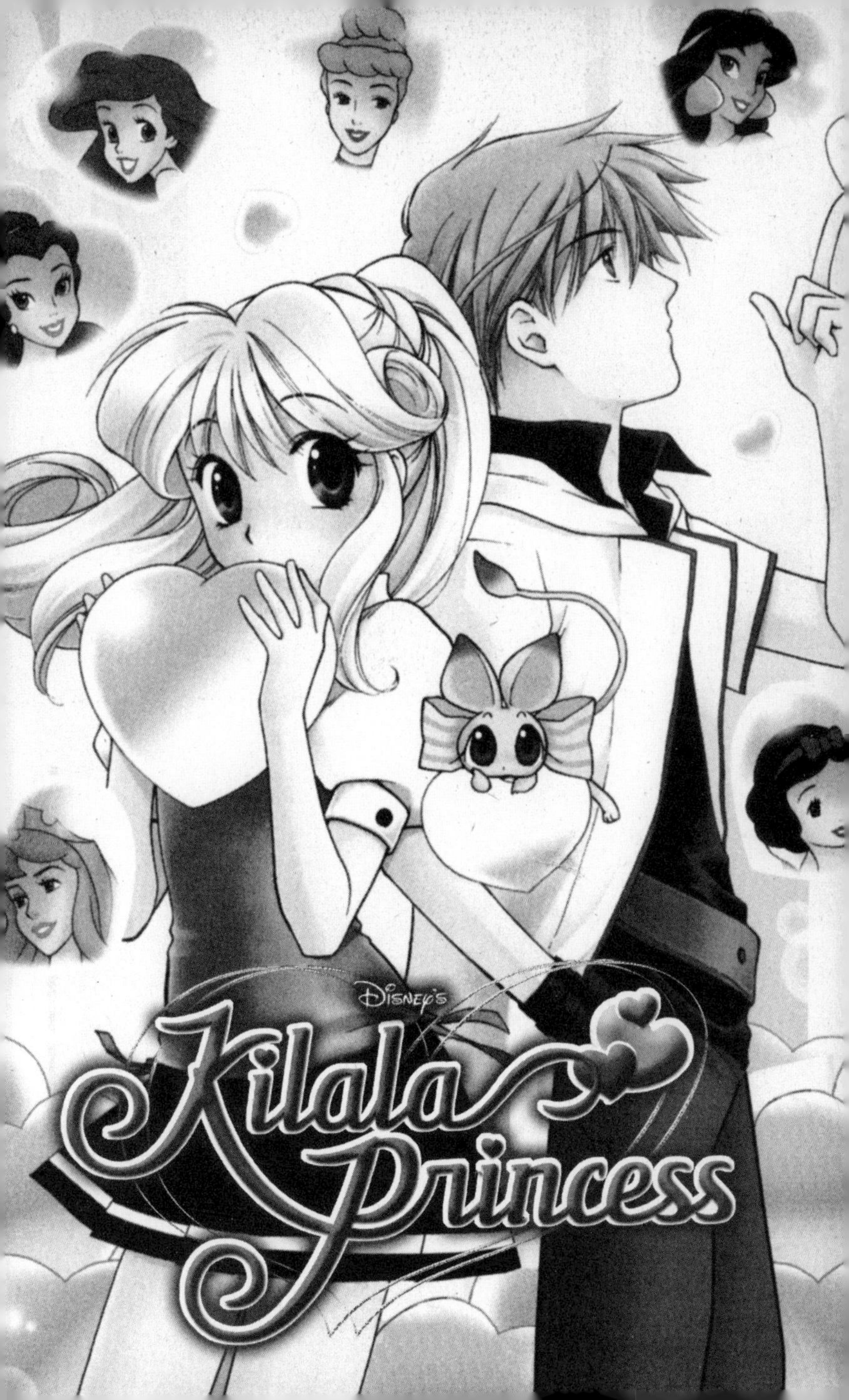
Disney's
Kilala Princess

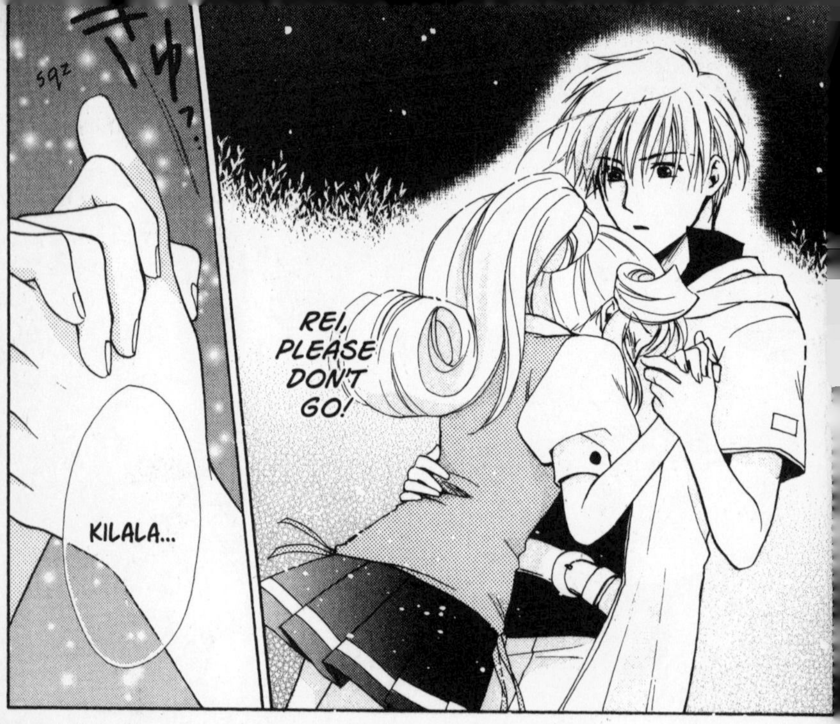
REI, PLEASE DON'T GO!
きゅっ
sqz
KILALA...

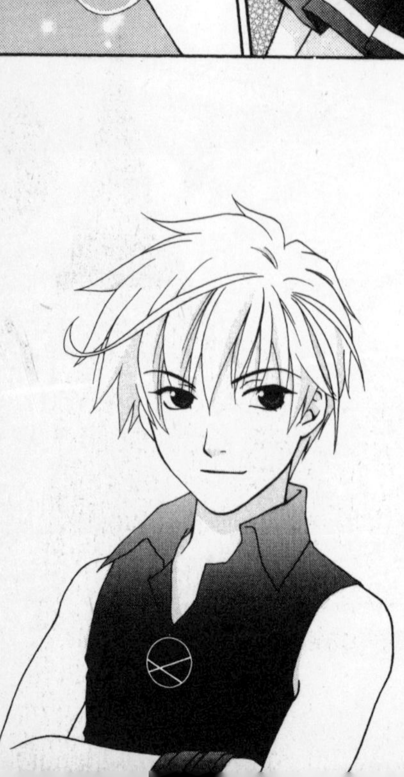

Rei

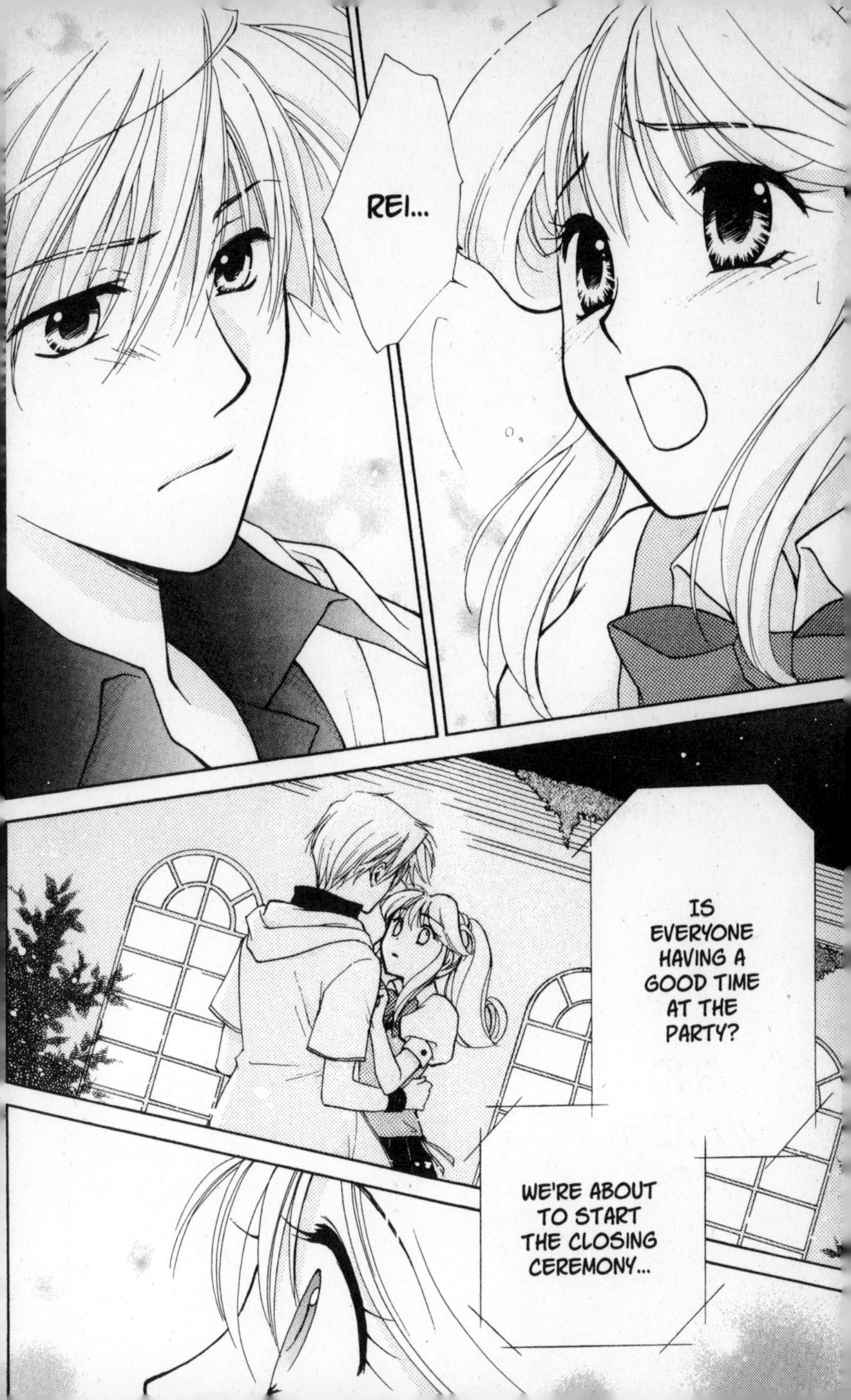
REI...
IS EVERYONE HAVING A GOOD TIME AT THE PARTY?
WE'RE ABOUT TO START THE CLOSING CEREMONY...

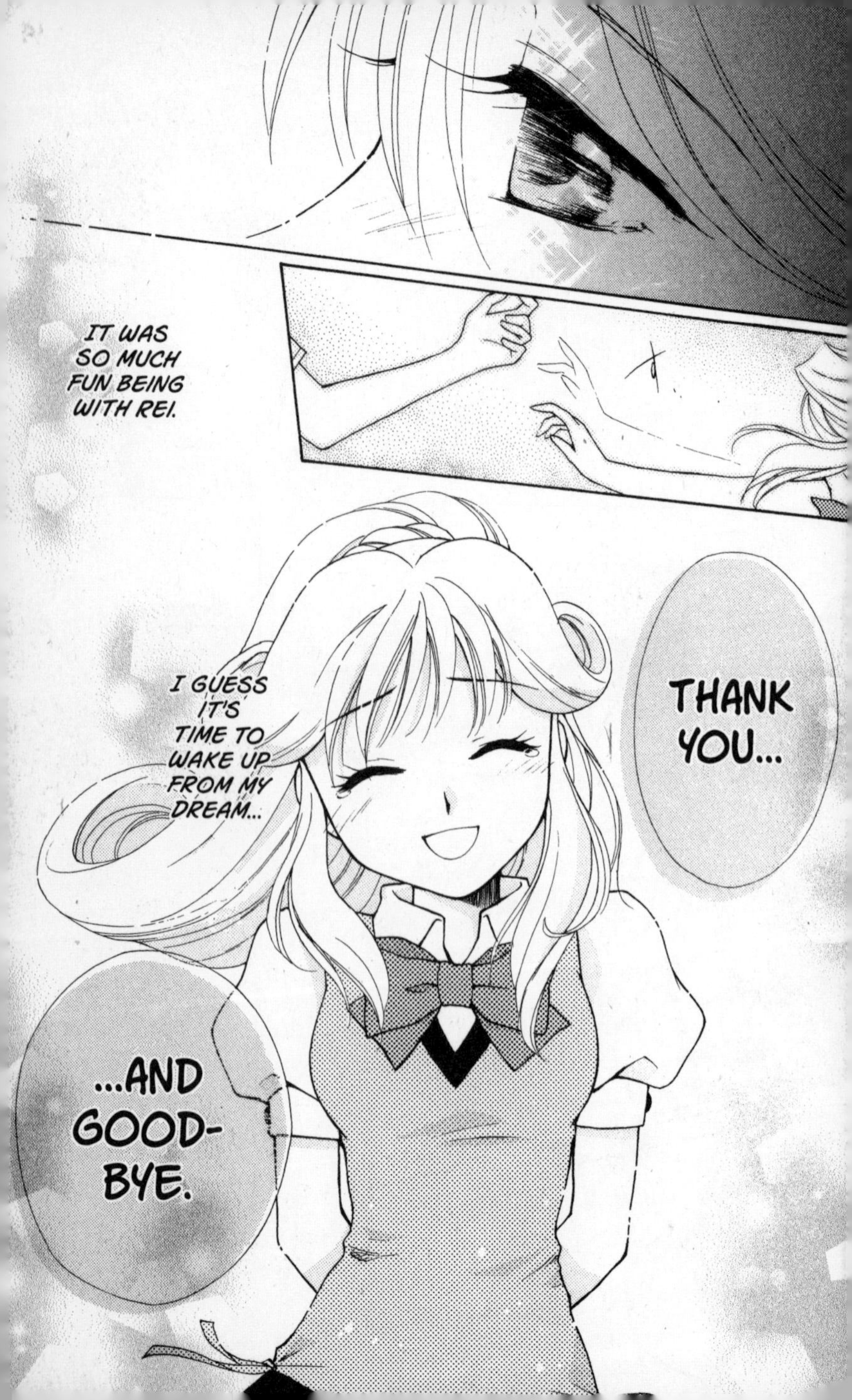
IT WAS SO MUCH FUN BEING WITH REI.
THANK YOU...
I GUESS IT'S TIME TO WAKE UP FROM MY DREAM...
...AND GOOD-BYE.

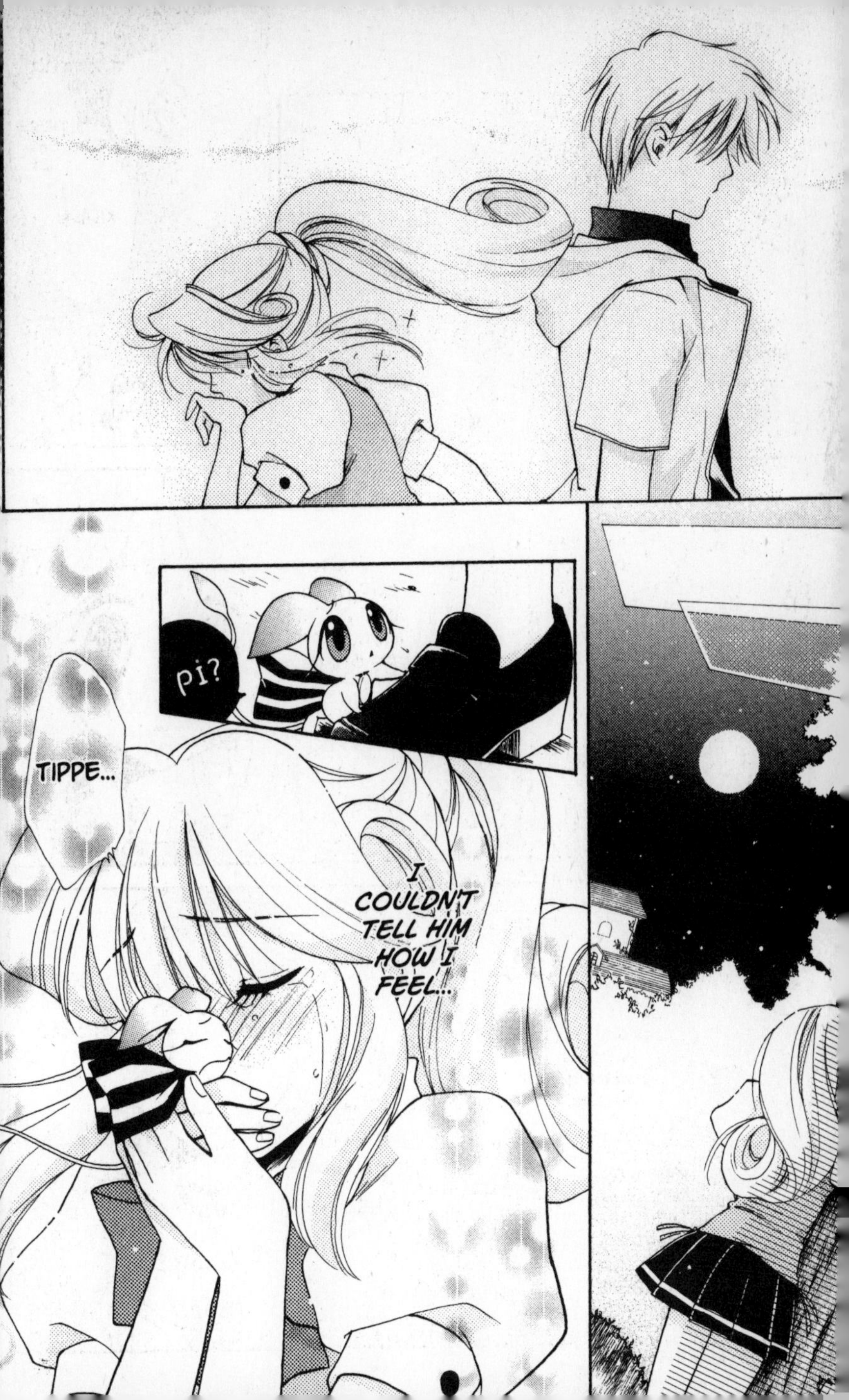
pi?
I COULDN'T TELL HIM HOW I FEEL...
TIPPE...

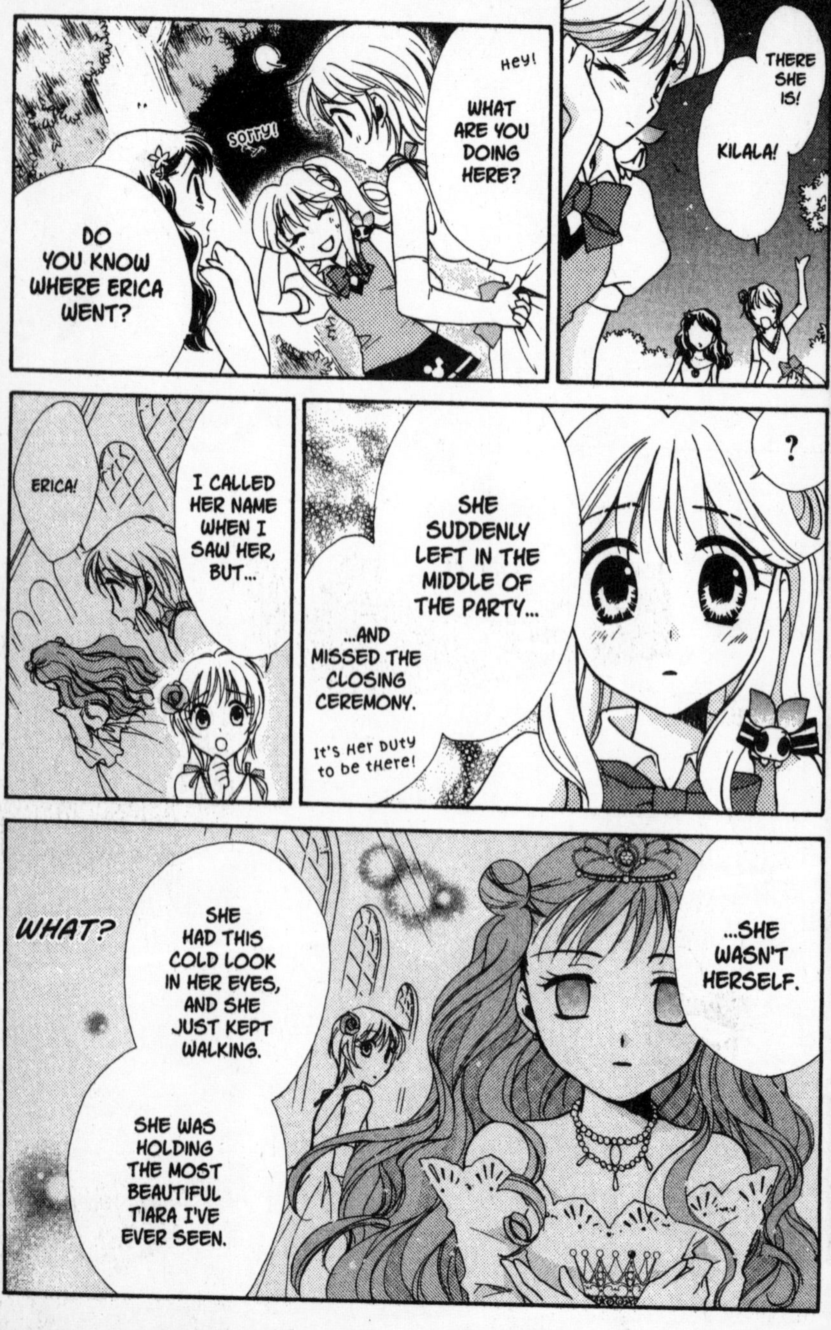
THERE SHE IS!
KILALA!
Hey!
WHAT ARE YOU DOING HERE?
SORRY!
DO YOU KNOW WHERE ERICA WENT?
?
SHE SUDDENLY LEFT IN THE MIDDLE OF THE PARTY...
...AND MISSED THE CLOSING CEREMONY.
It's Her Duty to be there!
I CALLED HER NAME WHEN I SAW HER, BUT...
ERICA!
...SHE WASN'T HERSELF.
SHE HAD THIS COLD LOOK IN HER EYES, AND SHE JUST KEPT WALKING.
SHE WAS HOLDING THE MOST BEAUTIFUL TIARA I'VE EVER SEEN.
WHAT?

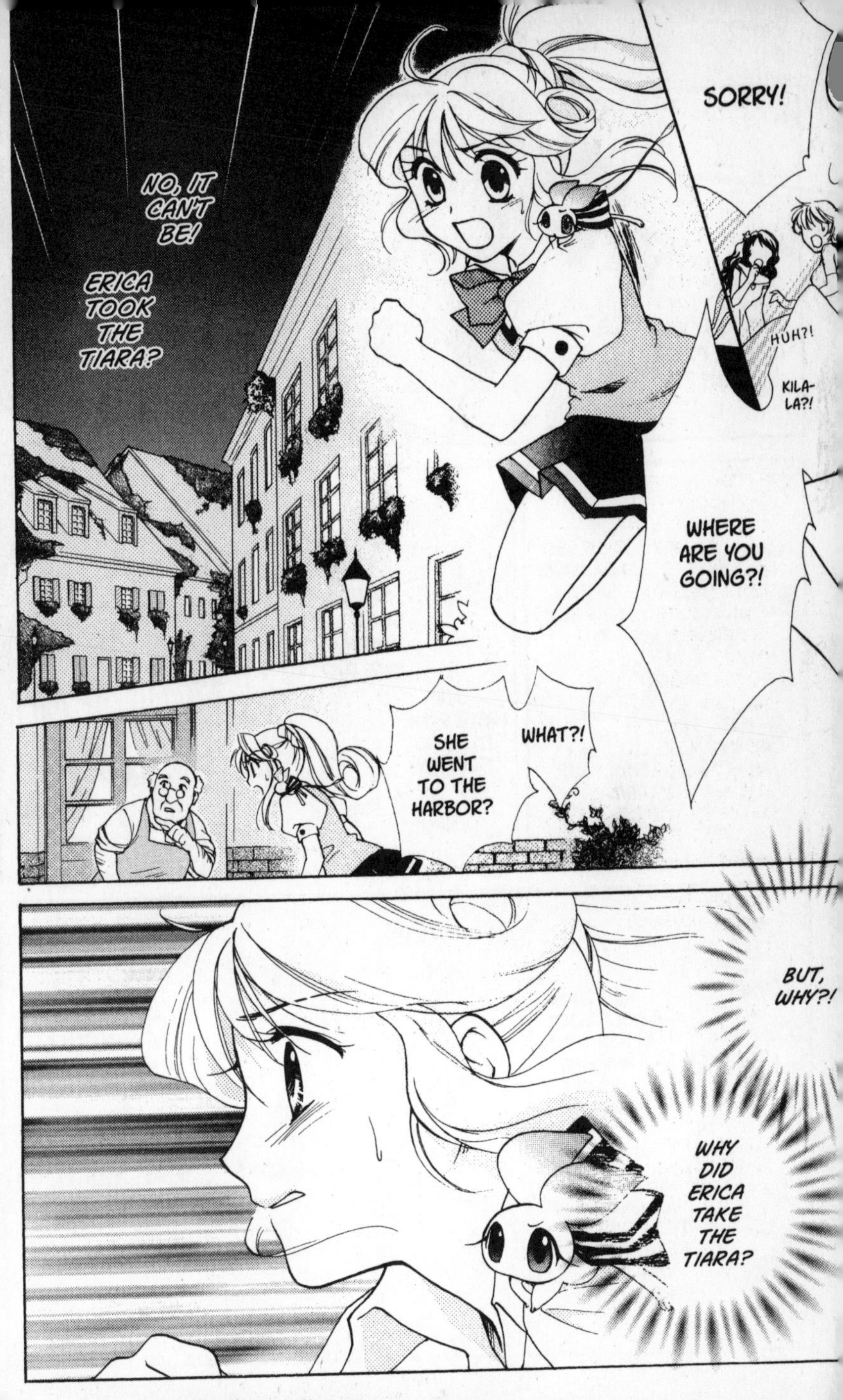
SORRY!
HUH?!
KILA-LA?!
WHERE ARE YOU GOING?!
NO, IT CAN'T BE!
ERICA TOOK THE TIARA?
WHAT?!
SHE WENT TO THE HARBOR?
BUT, WHY?!
WHY DID ERICA TAKE THE TIARA?

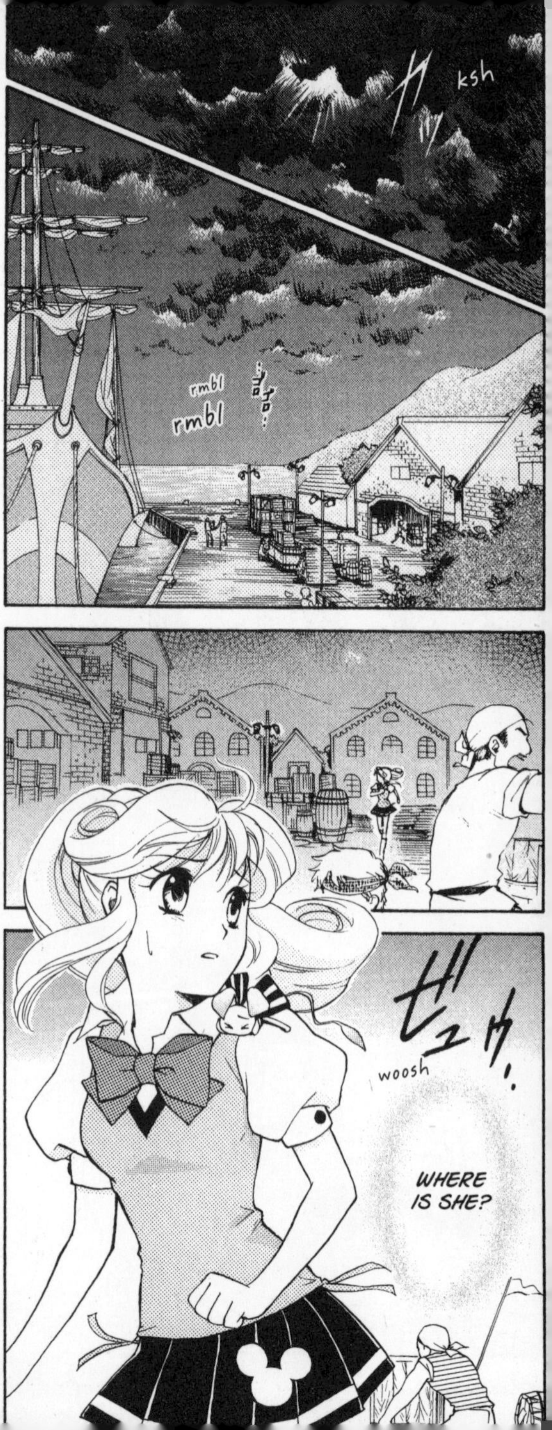
ksh
rmbl
rmbl
woosh
WHERE IS SHE?

Rika Tanaka

HELLO! MY NAME IS RIKA TANAKA, AND I'M WRITING THE STORY FOR *KILALA PRINCESS*. I'VE LOVED DISNEY ANIMATION EVER SINCE I WAS A CHILD, AND I'M EXCITED TO WRITE THIS STORY.

ENTERING THE LOVELY WORLDS OF THE DISNEY PRINCESSES, BECOMING FRIENDS AND GOING ON ADVENTURES TOGETHER... IT'S A DREAM COME TRUE FOR ME! WHEN I'M WRITING THIS STORY, I FEEL LIKE I'M KILALA, AND I CRY WITH HER, LAUGH WITH HER, AND FALL IN LOVE WITH REI. MY DESK IS ALWAYS A MESS. HA HA!

BY THE WAY, YOU'RE PROBABLY WONDERING WHAT'S GOING TO HAPPEN TO KILALA. WHAT ABOUT KILALA AND REI? ACTUALLY, I DON'T EVEN KNOW YET. HA HA! I HOPE TO WRITE THE REST OF THE STORY AND REACH A WONDERFUL ENDING--LEAVING BUTTERFLIES IN YOUR STOMACH DURING THE JOURNEY!

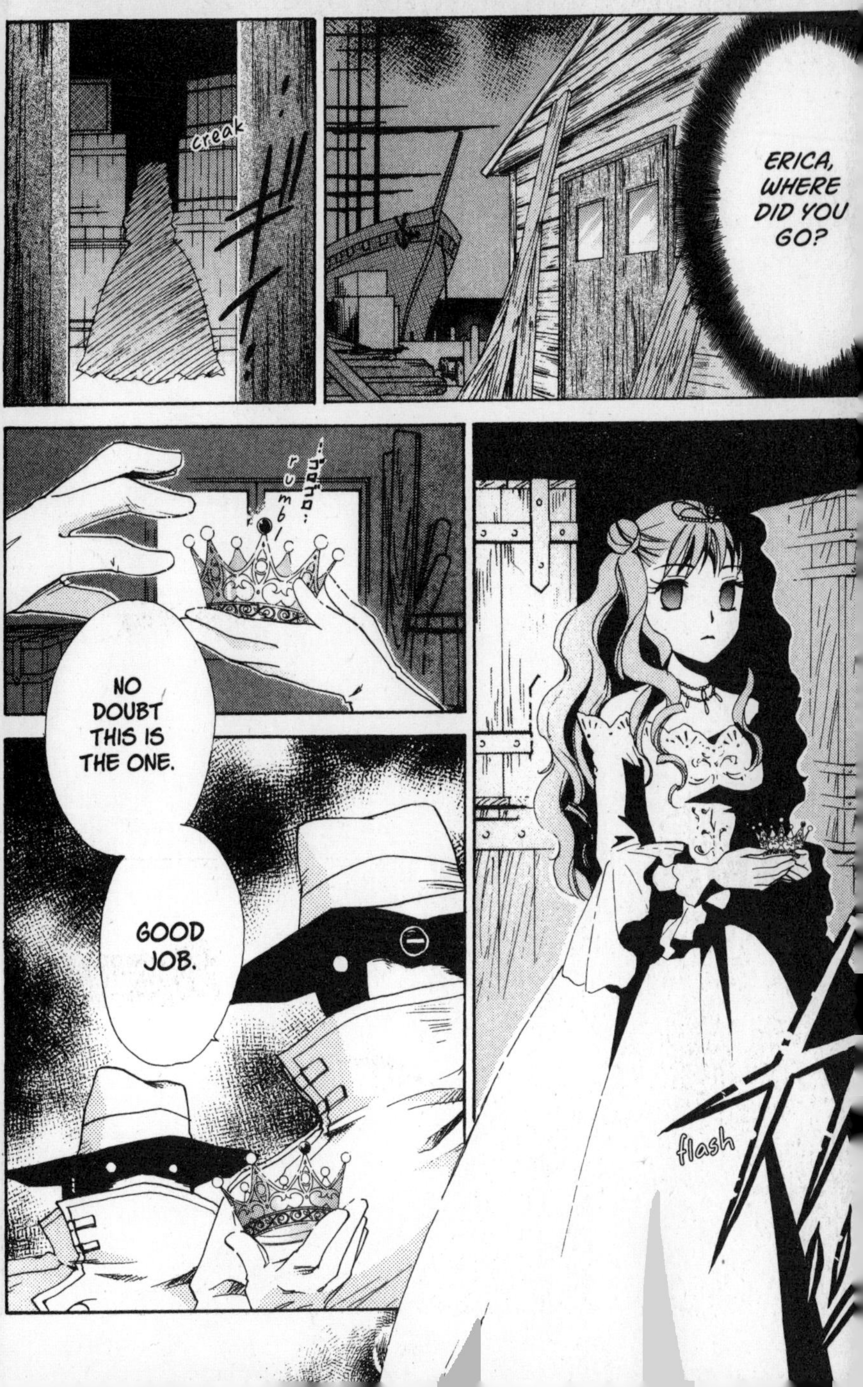
ERICA, WHERE DID YOU GO?
creak
flash
rumble
NO DOUBT THIS IS THE ONE.
GOOD JOB.

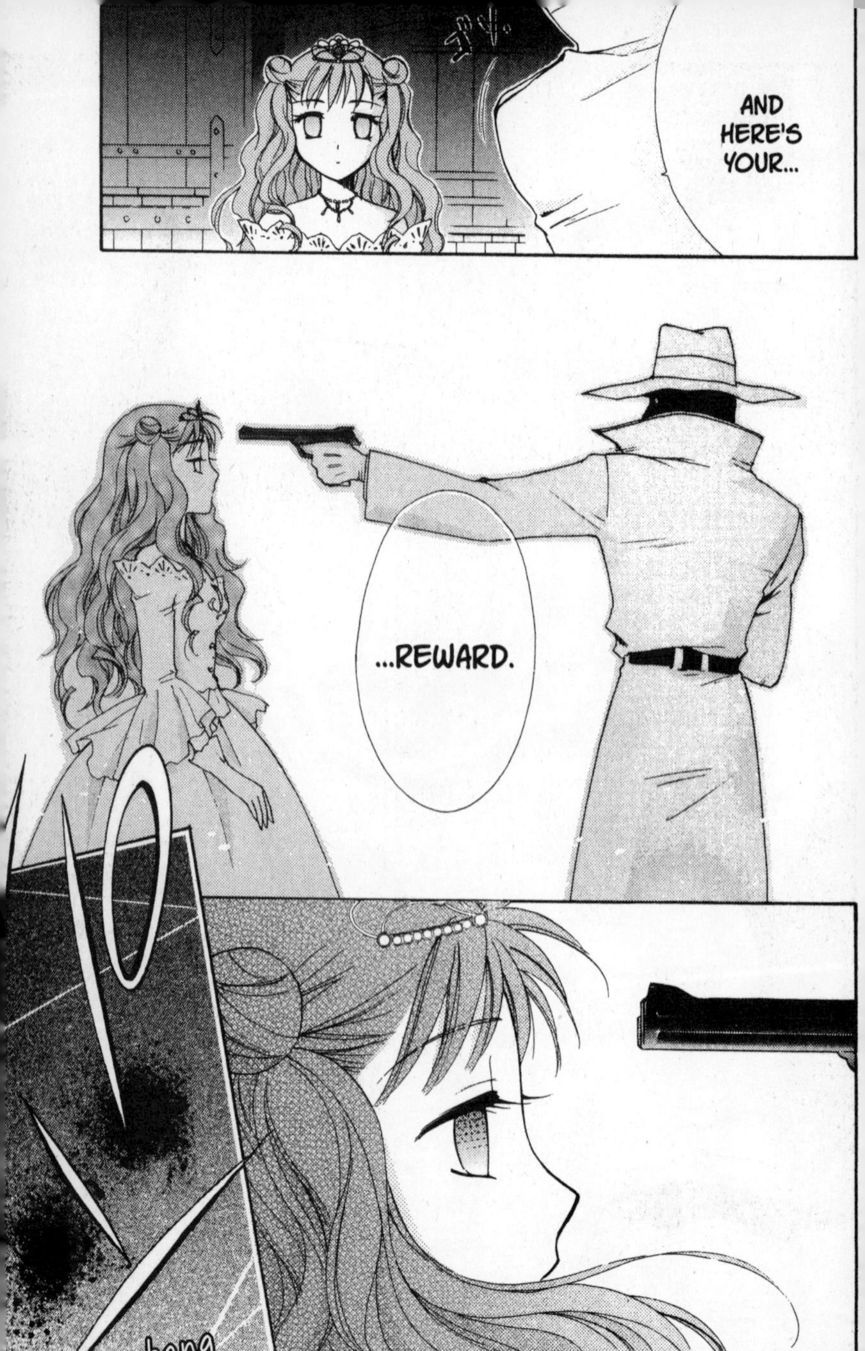
AND HERE'S YOUR...
...REWARD.
bang

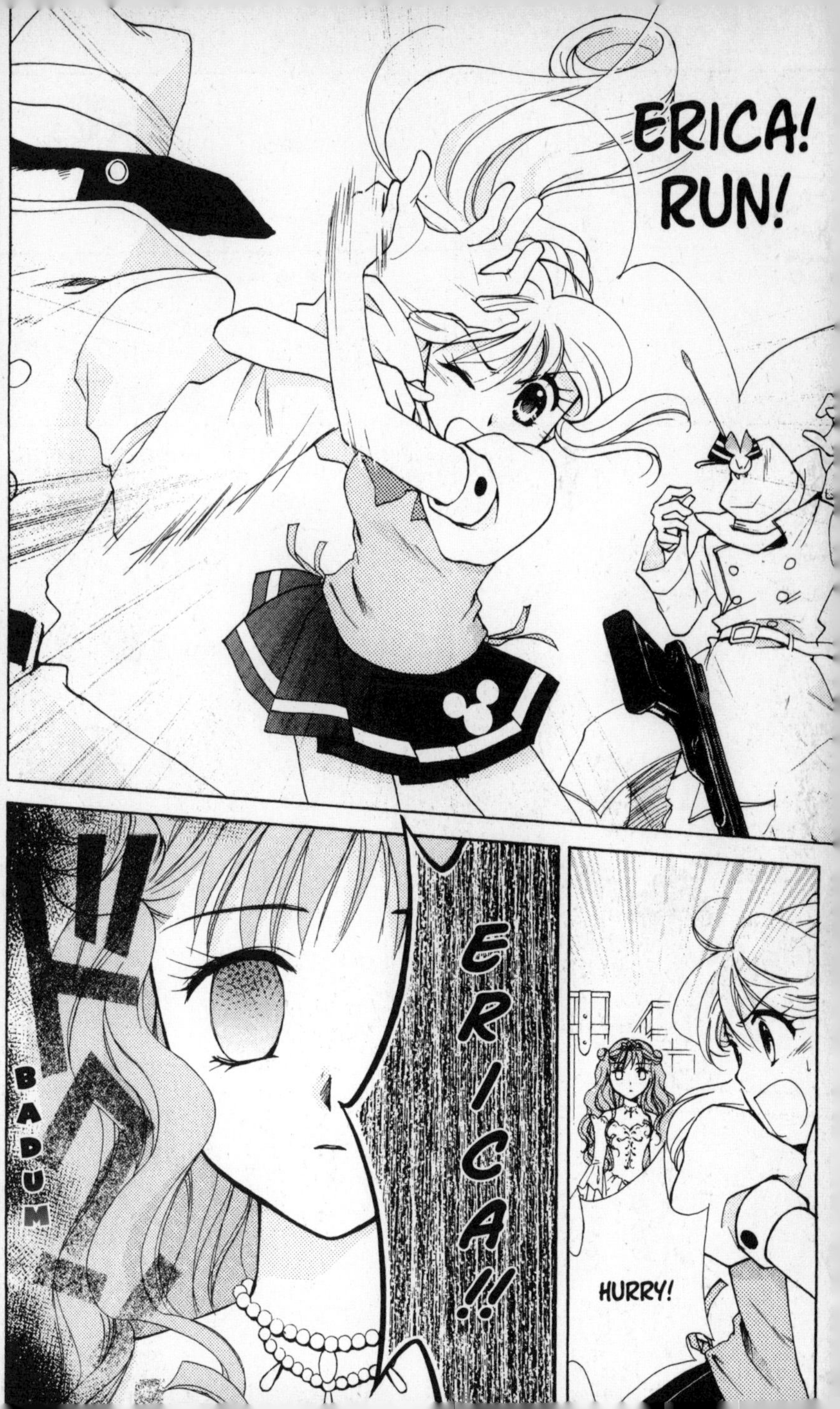
ERICA!
RUN!
HURRY!
ERICA!!
BADUM

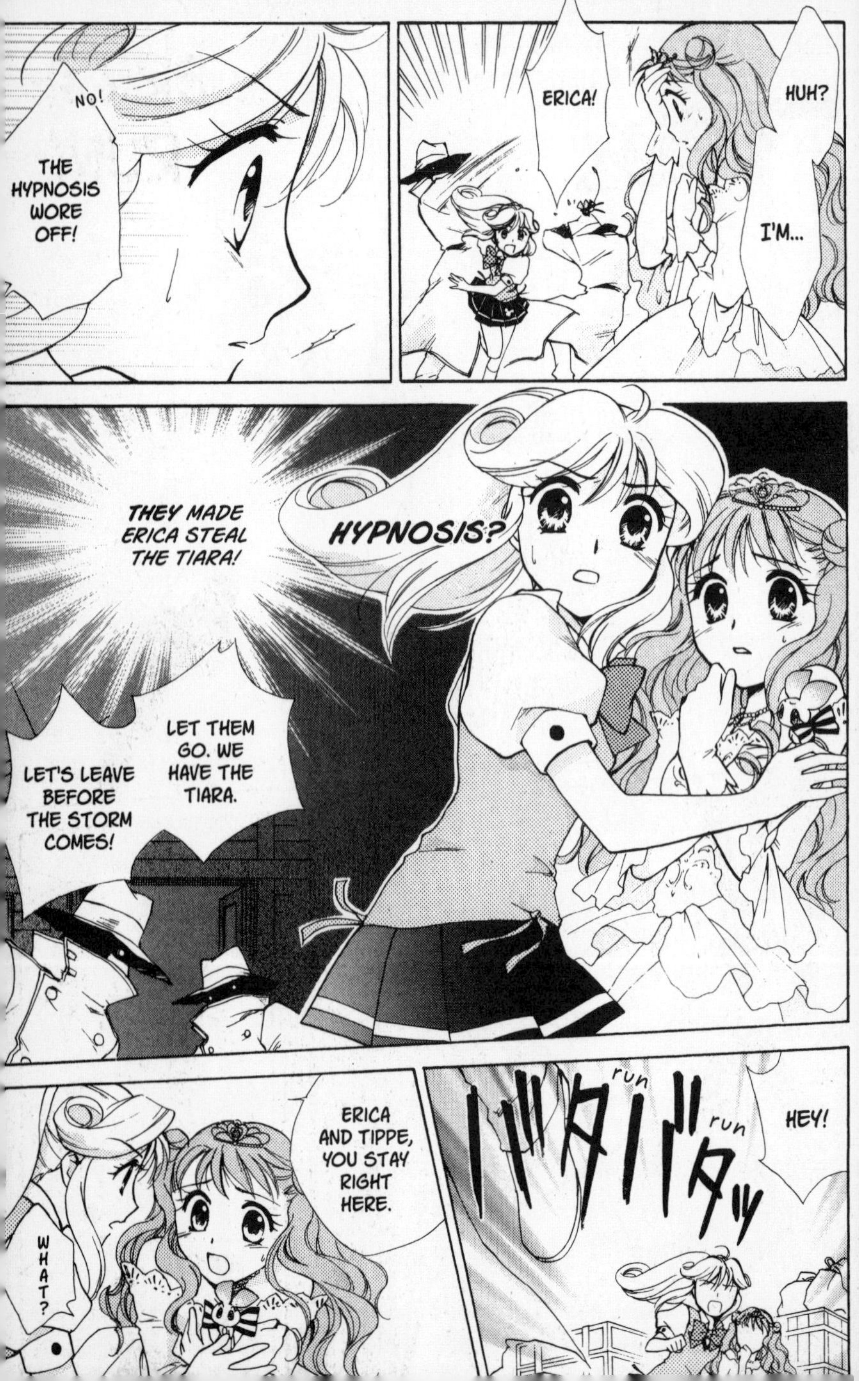
ERICA!
HUH?
I'M...
NO!
THE HYPNOSIS WORE OFF!
HYPNOSIS?
THEY MADE ERICA STEAL THE TIARA!
LET THEM GO. WE HAVE THE TIARA.
LET'S LEAVE BEFORE THE STORM COMES!
HEY!
バタバタッ
run run
ERICA AND TIPPE, YOU STAY RIGHT HERE.
WHAT?

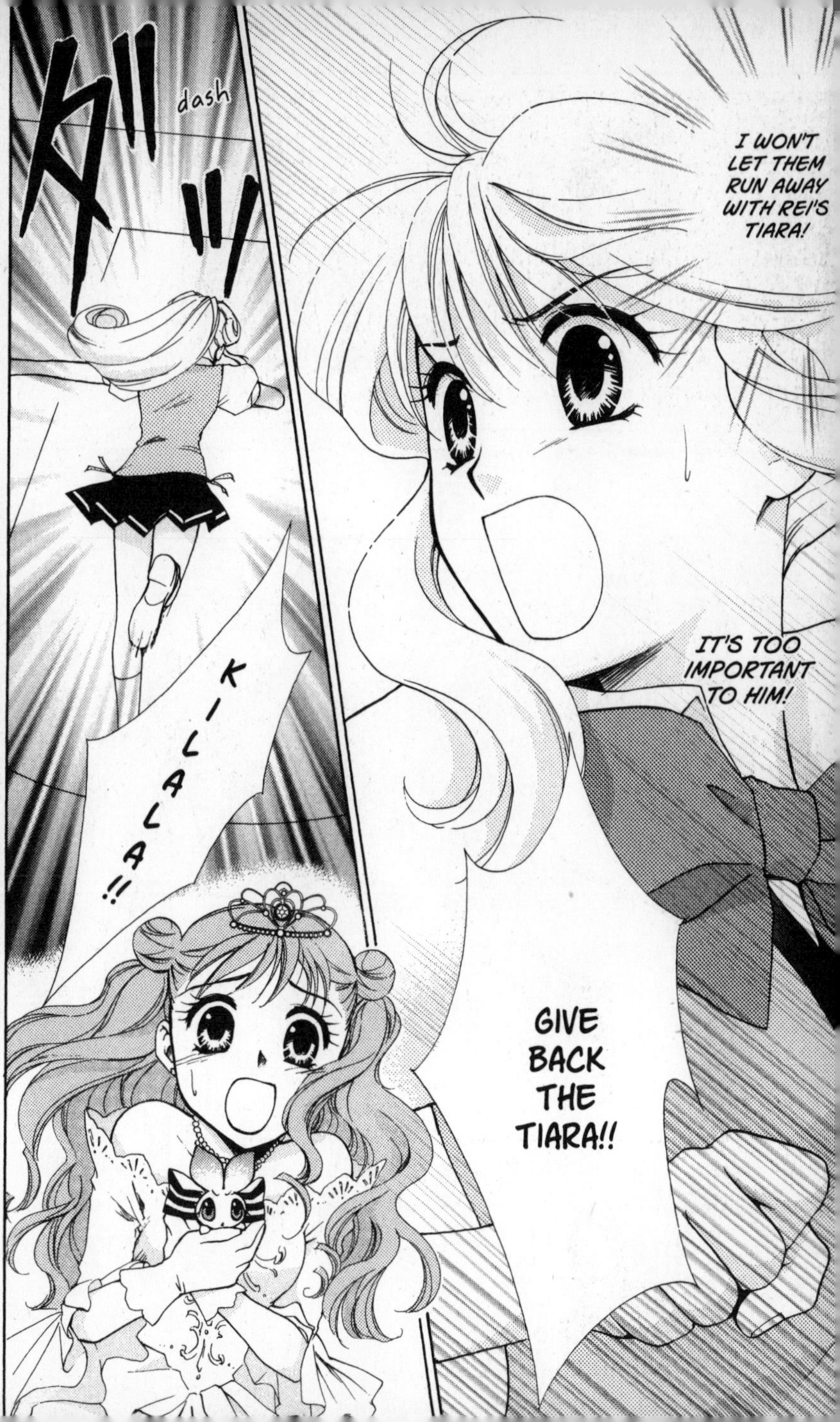
I WON'T LET THEM RUN AWAY WITH REI'S TIARA!
IT'S TOO IMPORTANT TO HIM!
GIVE BACK THE TIARA!!
ダッ
dash
KILALA!!

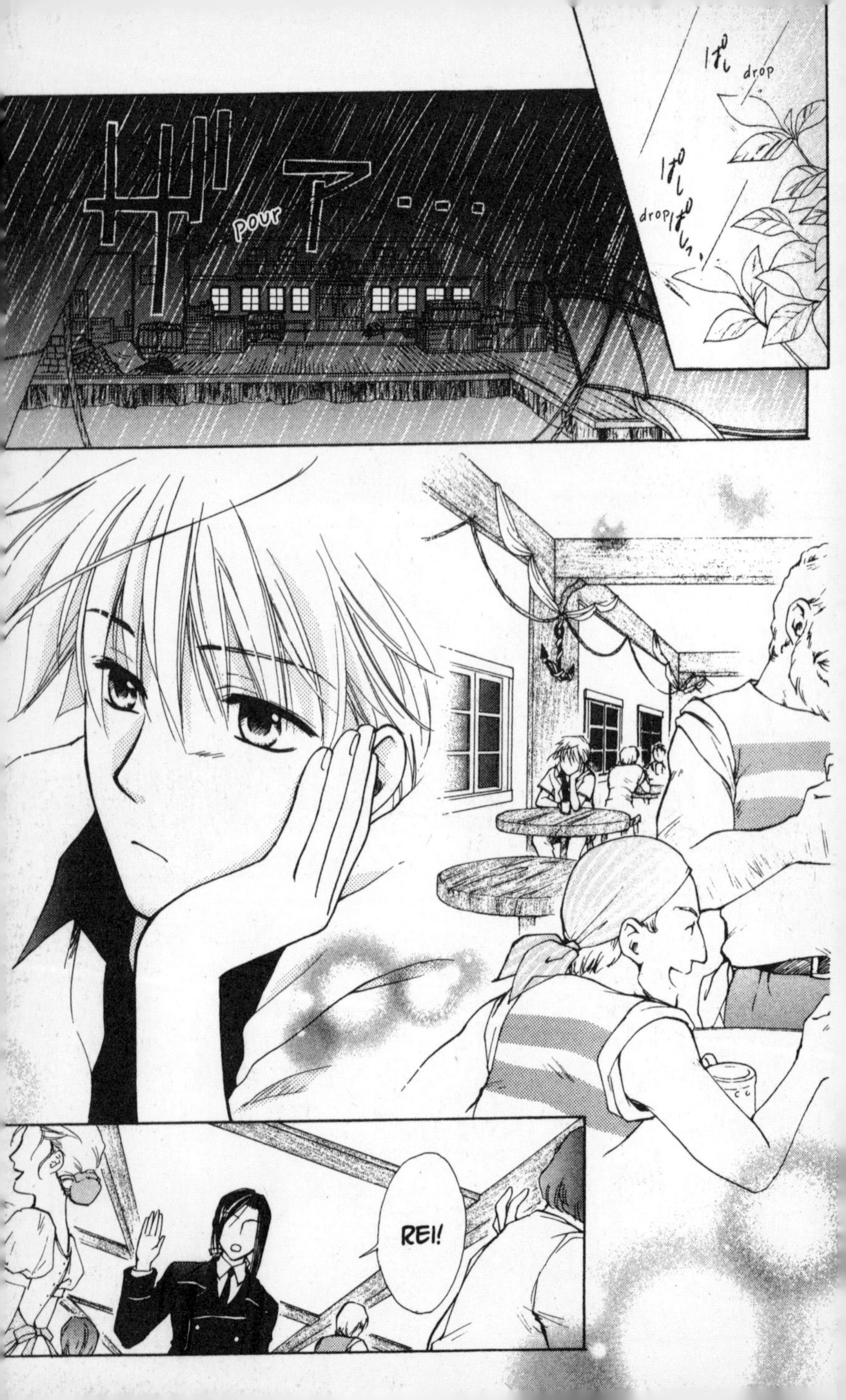

drop
drop
ザァ・・・
pour
REI!

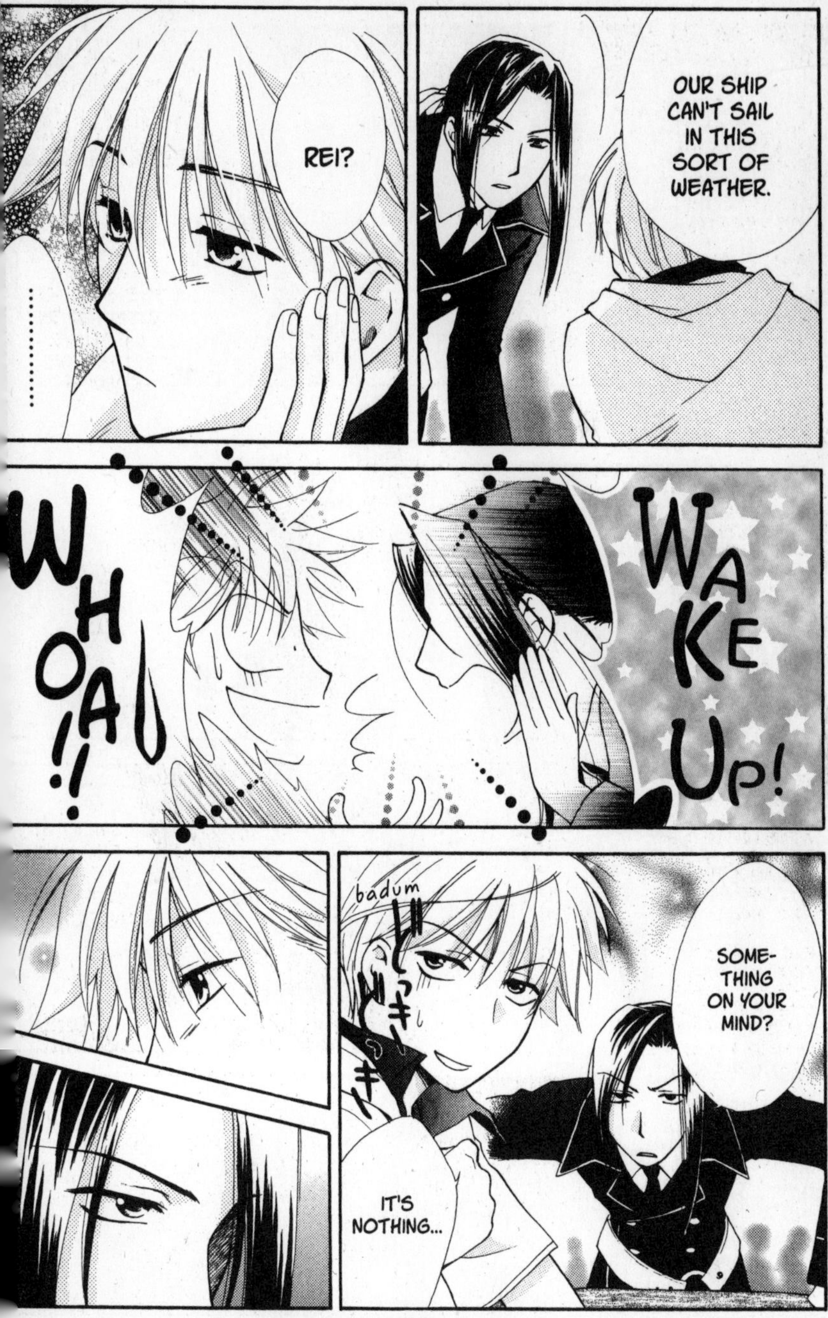
OUR SHIP CAN'T SAIL IN THIS SORT OF WEATHER.
REI?
......
WAKE UP!
WHOA!!
SOME-THING ON YOUR MIND?
badum
IT'S NOTHING...

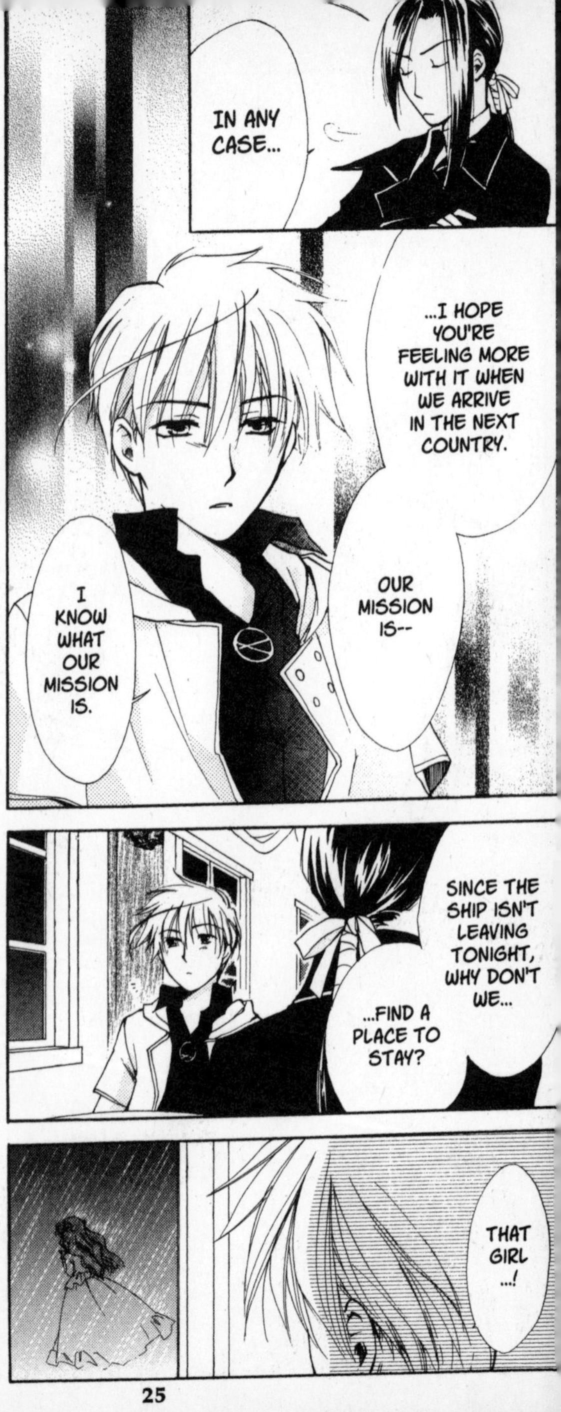
IN ANY CASE...
...I HOPE YOU'RE FEELING MORE WITH IT WHEN WE ARRIVE IN THE NEXT COUNTRY.
OUR MISSION IS--
I KNOW WHAT OUR MISSION IS.
SINCE THE SHIP ISN'T LEAVING TONIGHT, WHY DON'T WE...
...FIND A PLACE TO STAY?
THAT GIRL ...!

Nao Kodaka

HELLO! MY NAME IS NAO KODAKA, AND THE FIRST VOLUME OF *KILALA PRINCESS* IS THE FIRST COMIC BOOK I'VE EVER DRAWN!

SINCE I WAS A CHILD, I'VE BEEN SURROUNDED BY DISNEY BOOKS. THE CINDERELLA ART BOOK WAS MY MOST PRIZED POSSESSION. AND I HAD NO IDEA THAT I'D BE DRAWING HER IN MY MANGA. LIFE CAN BE STRANGE SOMETIMES...

TO DRAW THE SIX PRINCESSES RIGHT, I PLAY THE DVDS ALL DAY IN MY ROOM. I CAN'T COUNT HOW MANY TIMES I'VE WATCHED THE MOVIES, BUT I CAN TELL YOU WHICH SCENE OF *SNOW WHITE* IS PLAYING JUST BY THE AUDIO ALONE (I'M NOT SURE THIS IS SOMETHING I SHOULD BRAG ABOUT...).

KILALA AND REI ARE MY ORIGINAL CHARACTERS, BUT IT WASN'T EASY ARRIVING AT THEIR CURRENT FORM. THERE'S A FINE LINE BETWEEN THE DETAILED STYLE USED FOR GIRLS' COMICS AND THE SIMPLIFIED DRAWING OF DISNEY COMICS!

THIS MANGA IS THE CROWNING ACHIEVEMENT OF EVERYONE'S HARD WORK AND EFFORTS, AND I WAS NEARLY IN TEARS WHEN I FIRST HELD THE FIRST COMIC BOOK.

AND LAST BUT NOT LEAST, I THANK YOU, THE READERS, FOR TAKING THE TIME TO READ *KILALA PRINCESS*!

★ ★ ★

special thanks to my big sister!

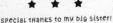

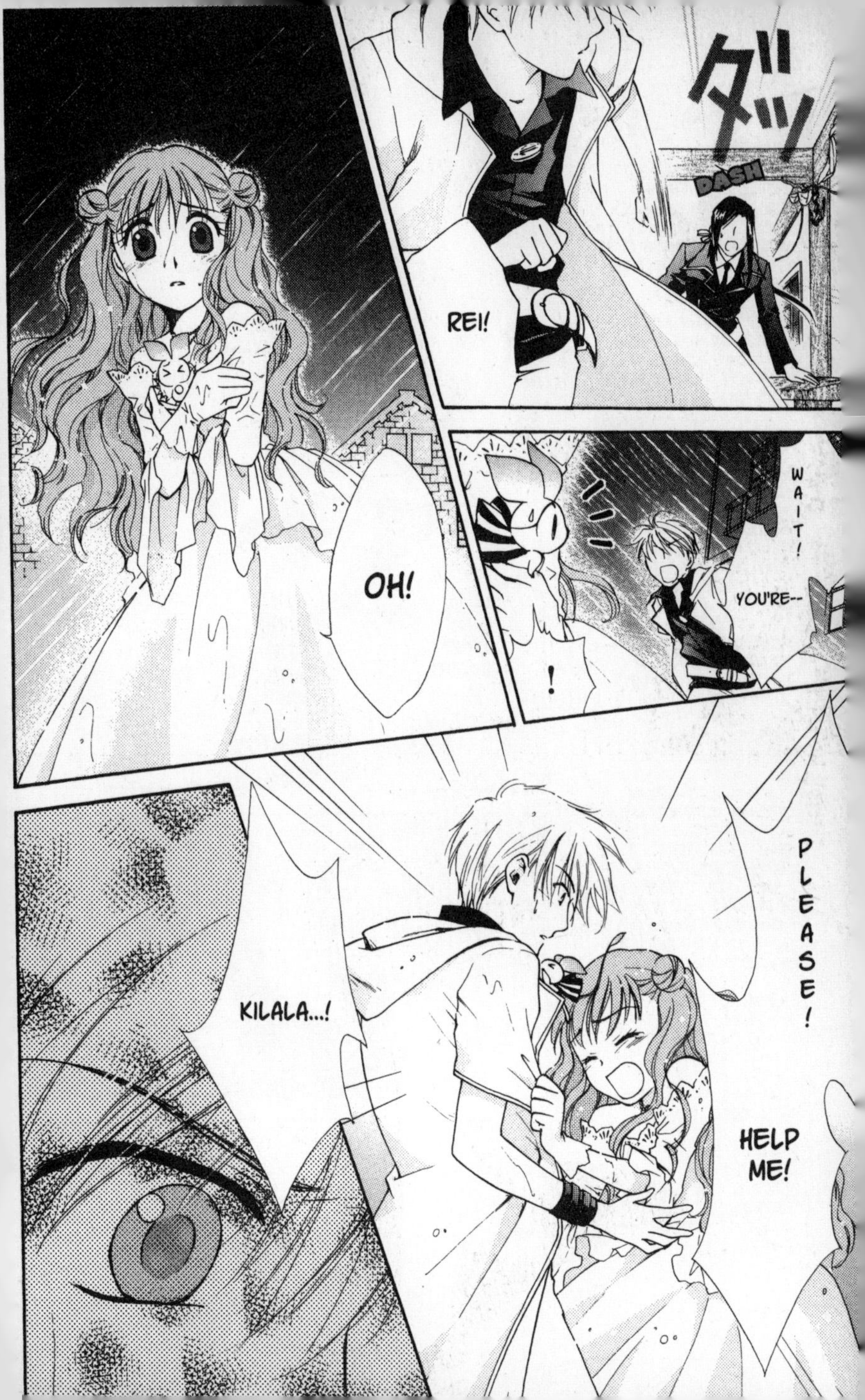
ダッ
DASH
REI!
WAIT!
YOU'RE--
!
OH!
PLEASE!
HELP ME!
KILALA...!

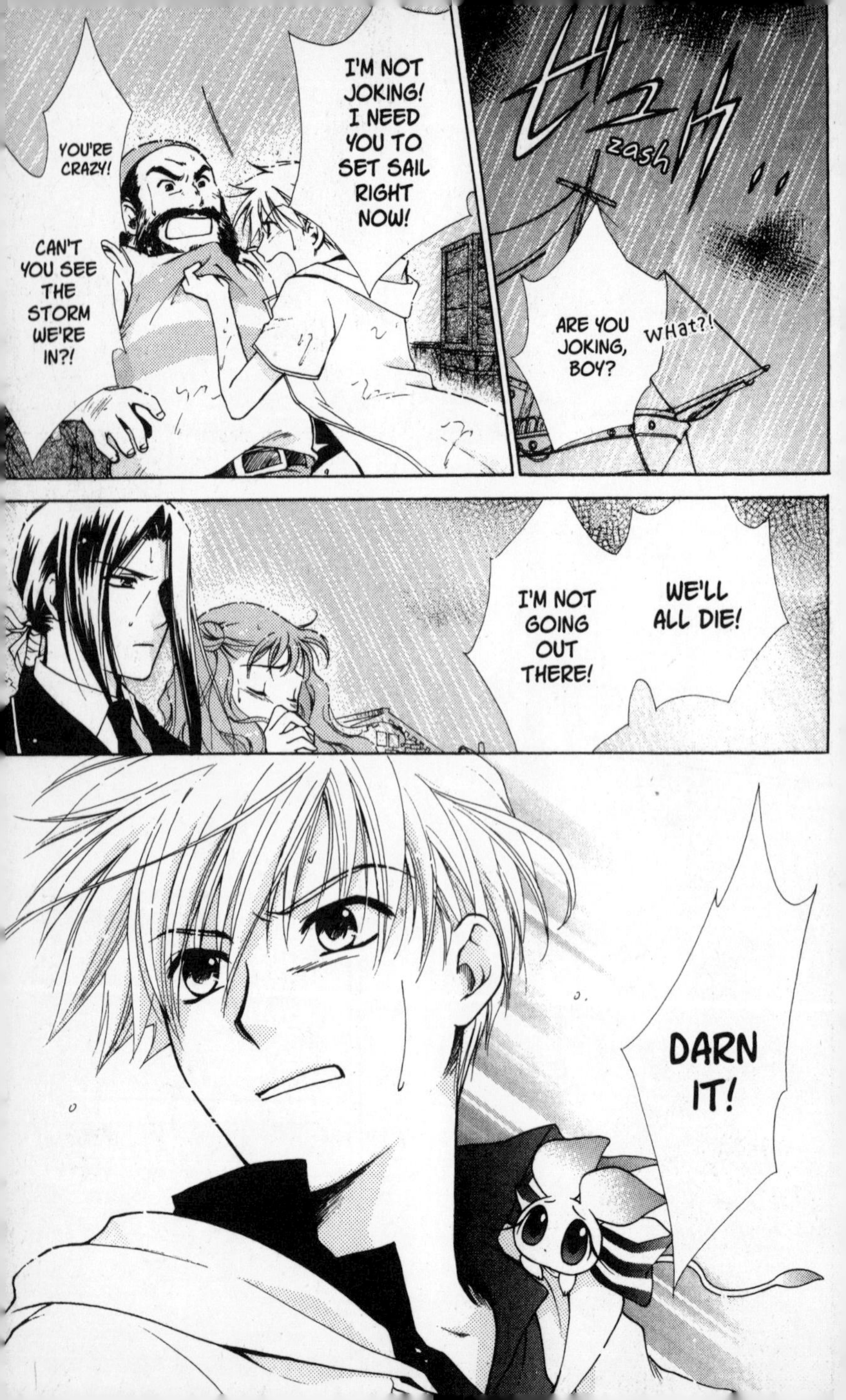
zash
WHAT?!
ARE YOU JOKING, BOY?
I'M NOT JOKING! I NEED YOU TO SET SAIL RIGHT NOW!
YOU'RE CRAZY!
CAN'T YOU SEE THE STORM WE'RE IN?!
WE'LL ALL DIE!
I'M NOT GOING OUT THERE!
DARN IT!

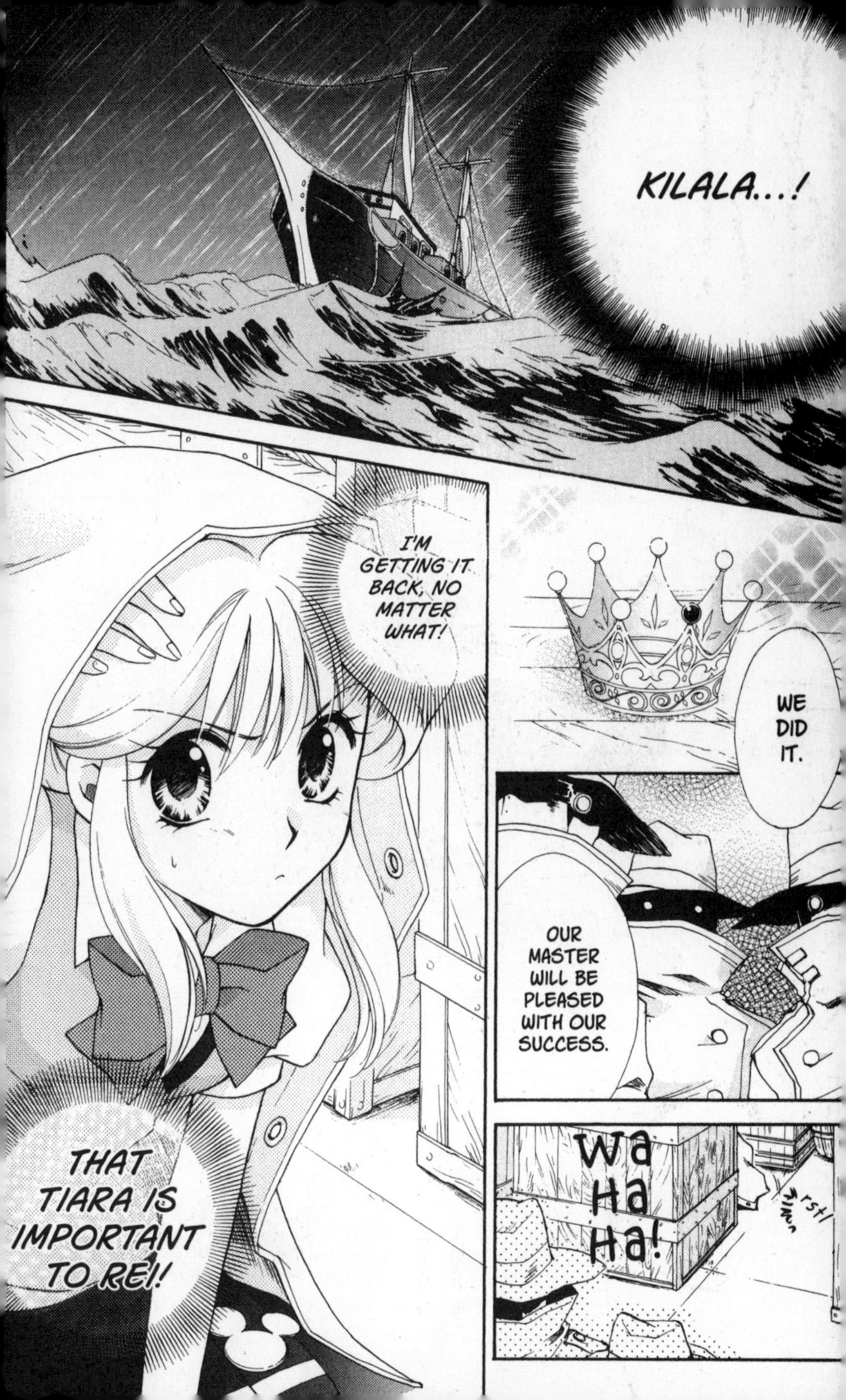
KILALA...!
WE DID IT.
OUR MASTER WILL BE PLEASED WITH OUR SUCCESS.
WA HA HA!
rstl
I'M GETTING IT BACK, NO MATTER WHAT!
THAT TIARA IS IMPORTANT TO REI!

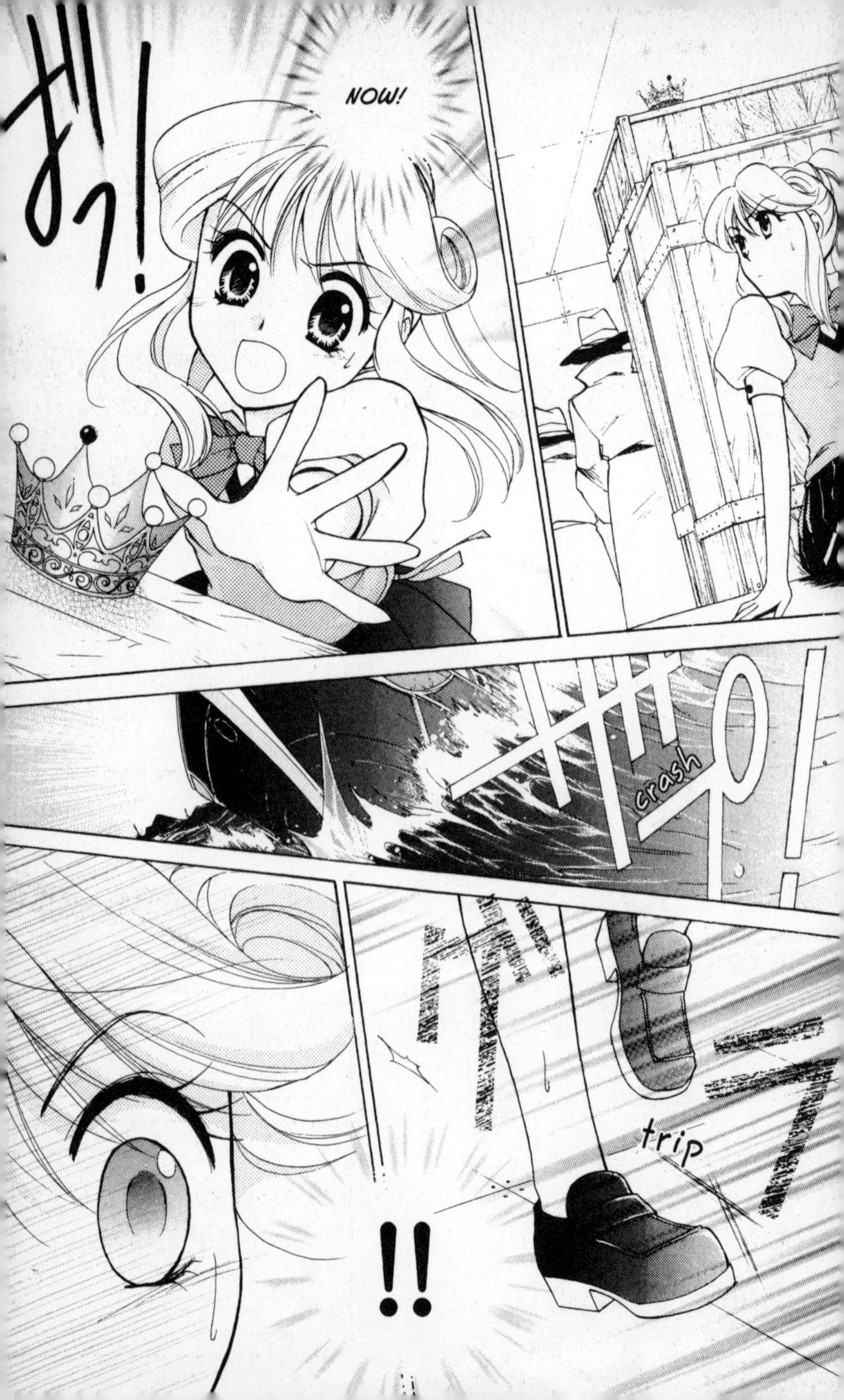
NOW!
crash
trip
!!

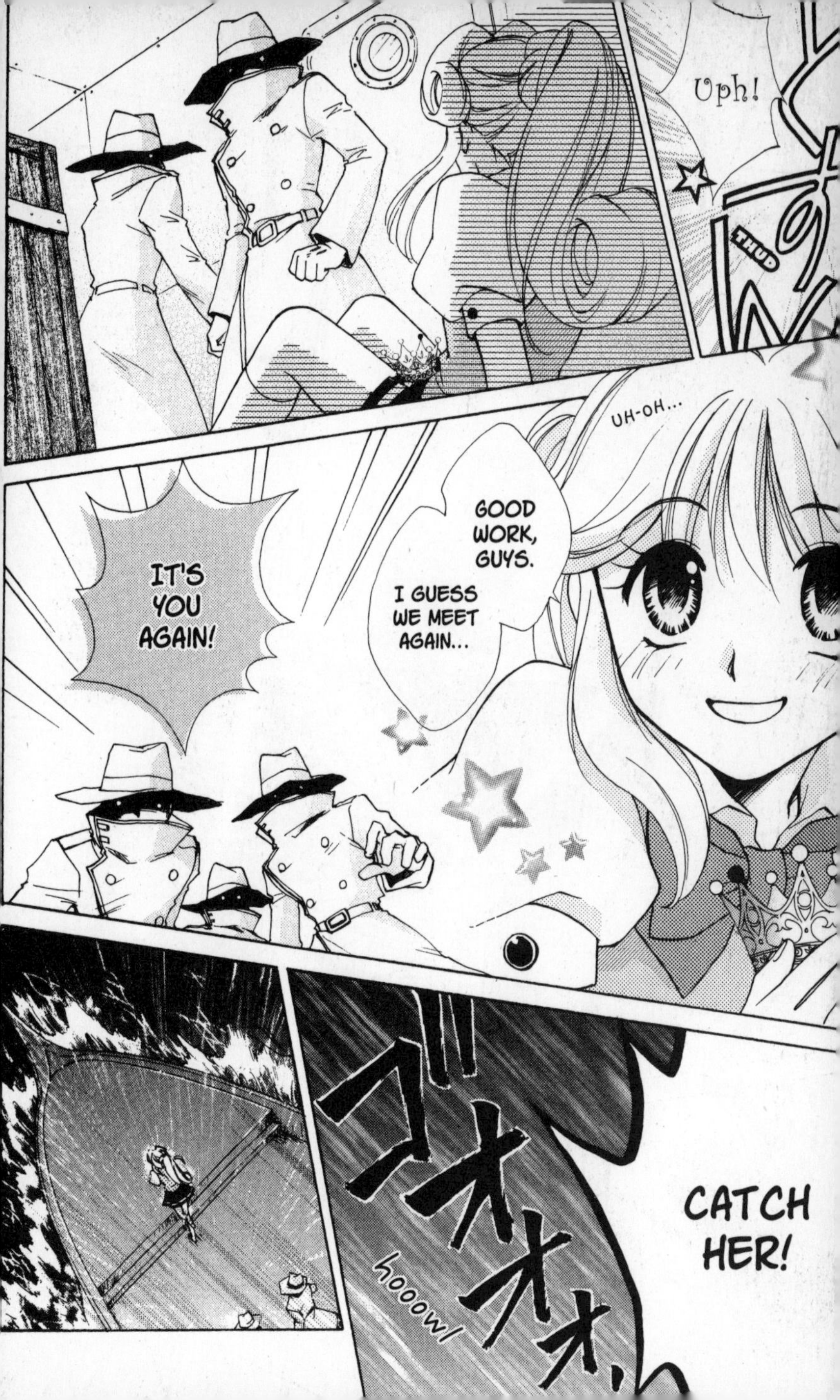
Uph!
THUD
UH-OH...
GOOD WORK, GUYS.
I GUESS WE MEET AGAIN...
IT'S YOU AGAIN!
CATCH HER!
hooow!

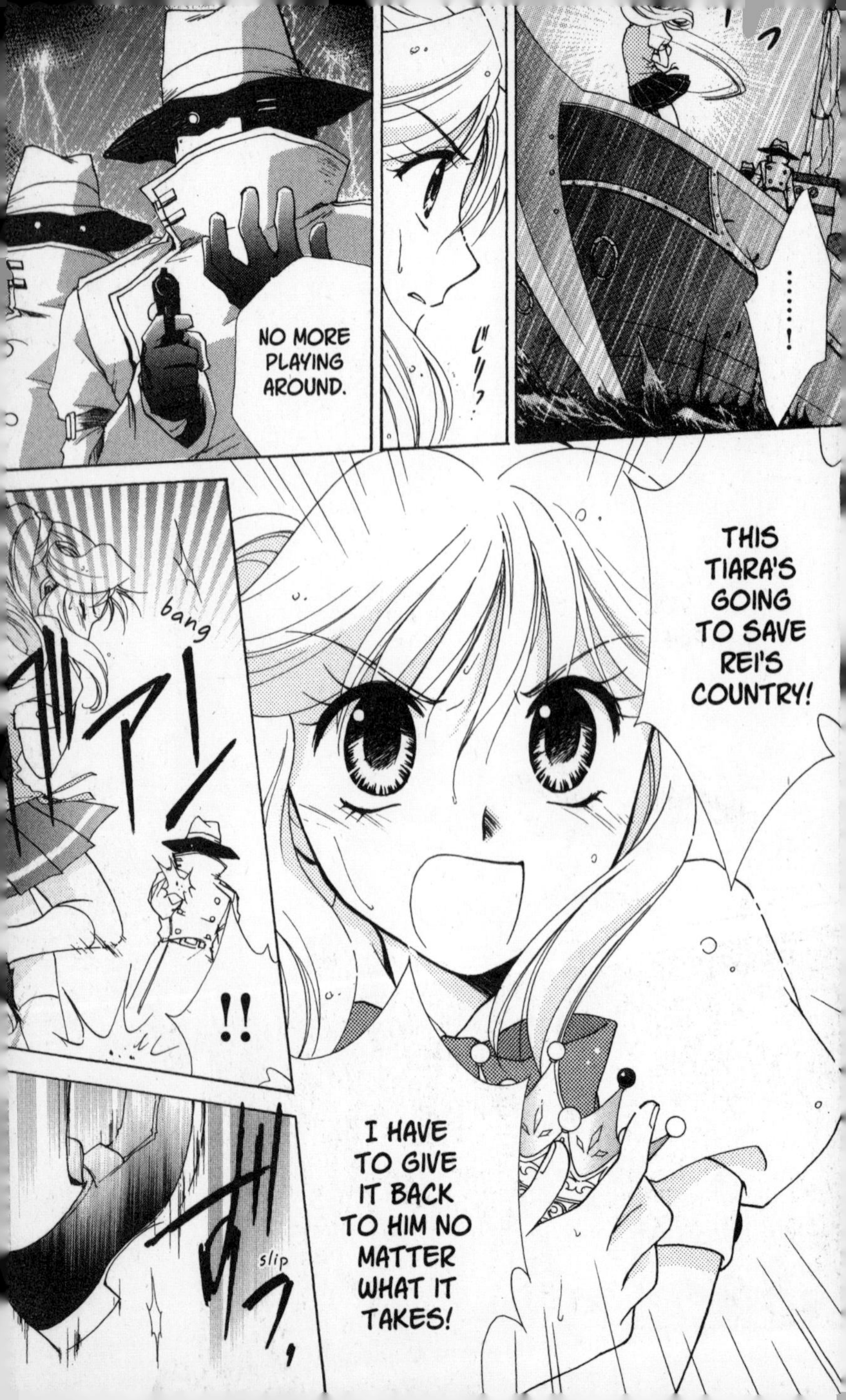
......!
NO MORE PLAYING AROUND.
THIS TIARA'S GOING TO SAVE REI'S COUNTRY!
I HAVE TO GIVE IT BACK TO HIM NO MATTER WHAT IT TAKES!
bang
!!
slip

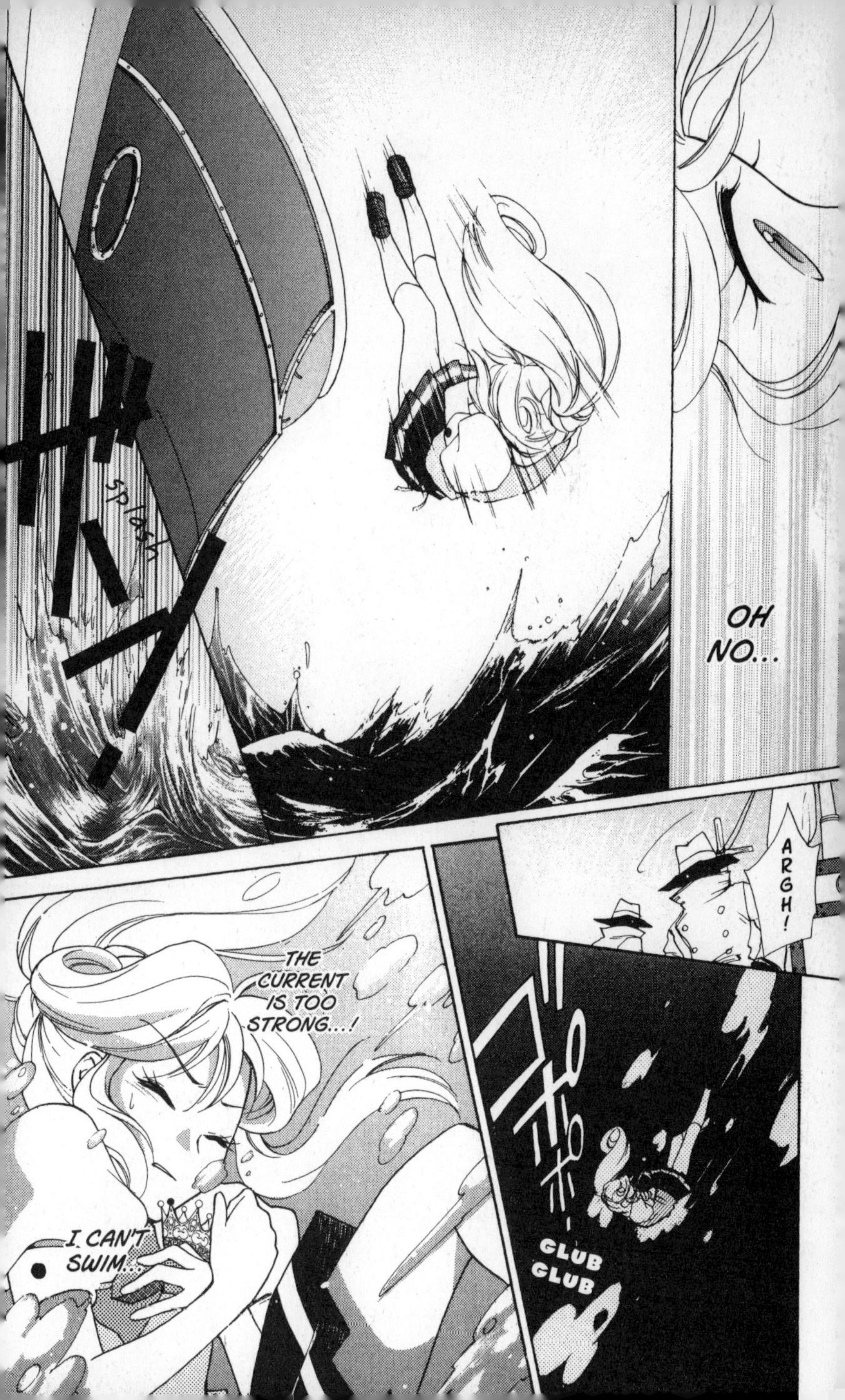
OH NO...
splash
ARGH!
GLUB GLUB
THE CURRENT IS TOO STRONG...!
I CAN'T SWIM...

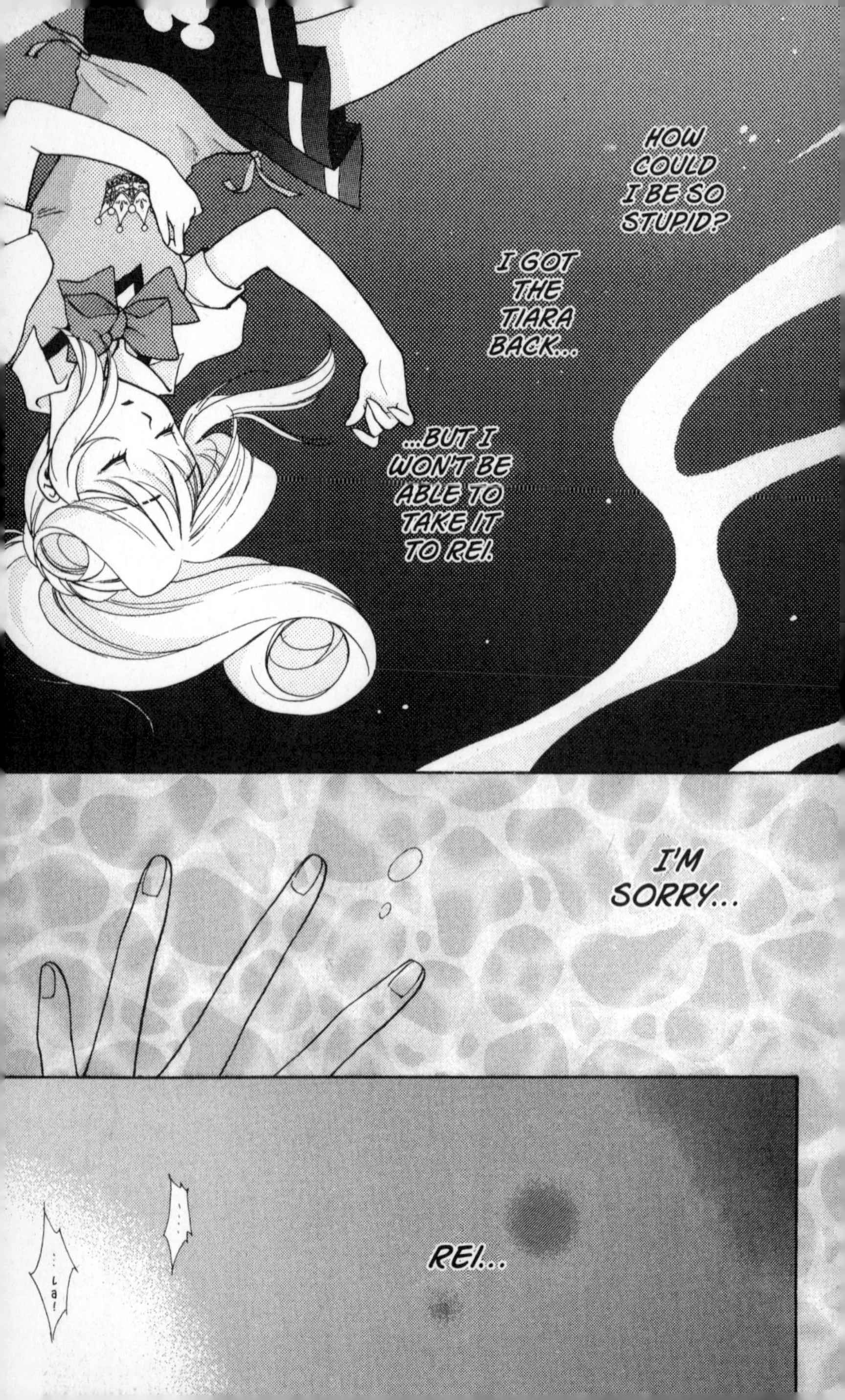
HOW COULD I BE SO STUPID?
I GOT THE TIARA BACK...
...BUT I WON'T BE ABLE TO TAKE IT TO REI.
I'M SORRY...
REI...
...
...La!

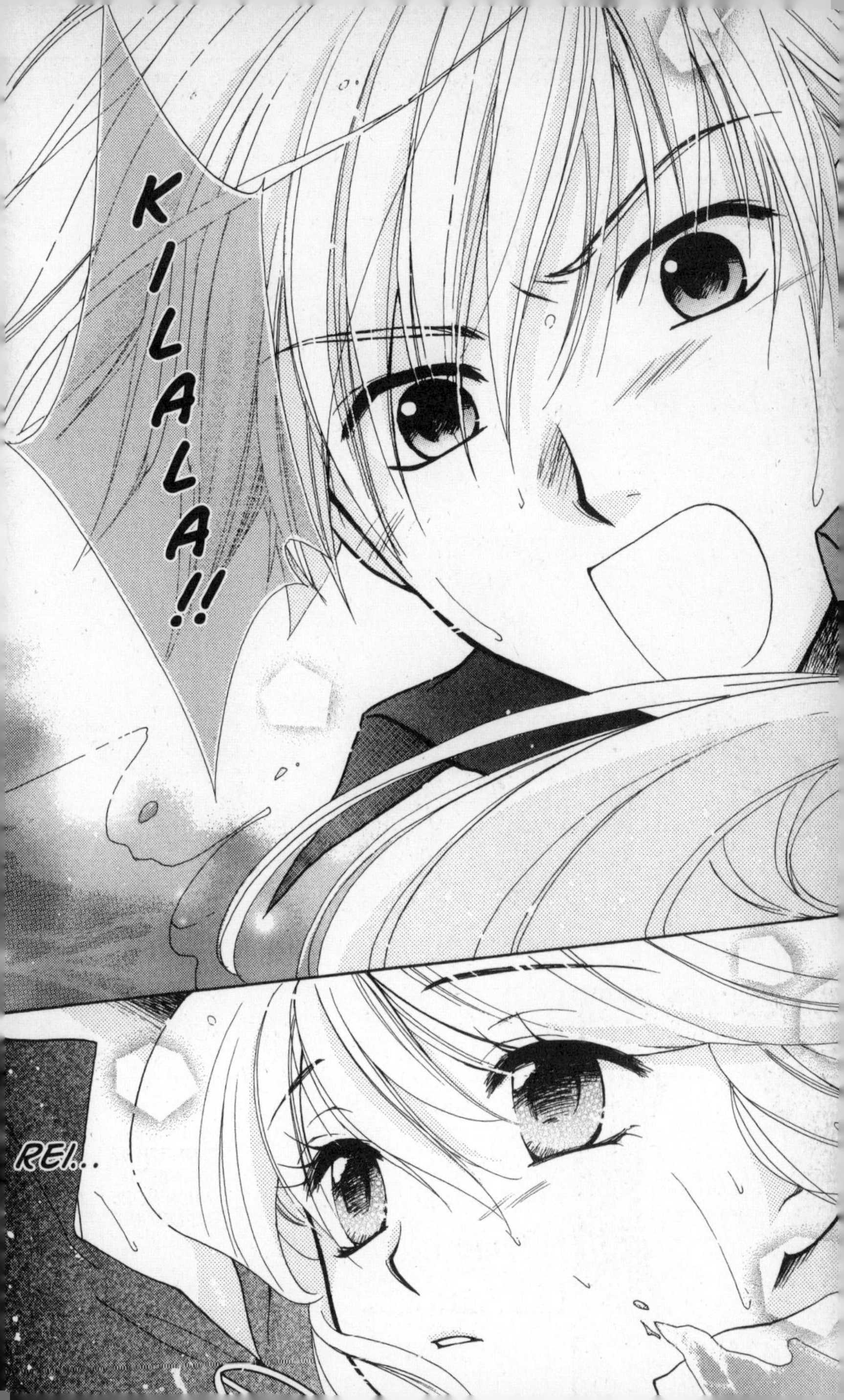
KILALA!!
REI...

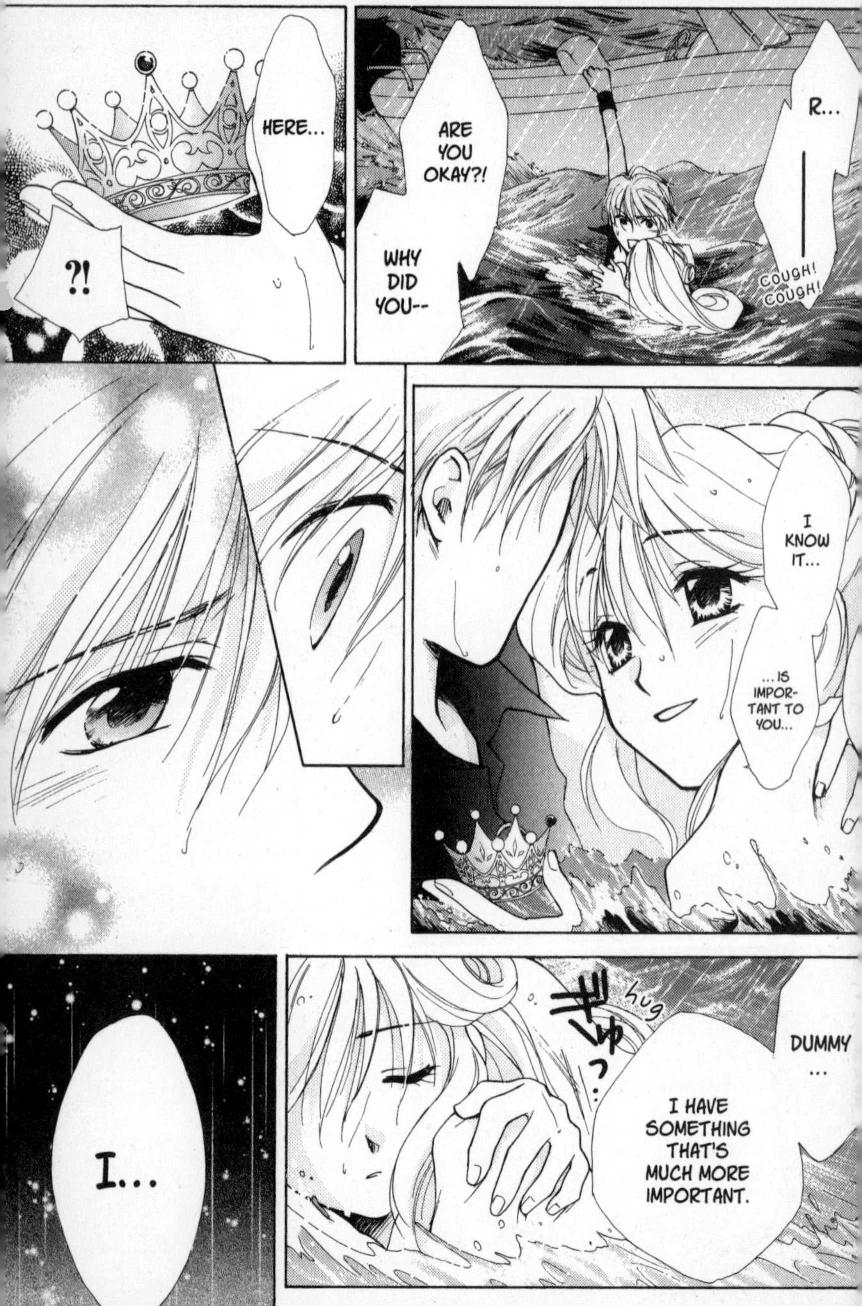
R...
COUGH! COUGH!
ARE YOU OKAY?!
WHY DID YOU--
HERE...
?!
I KNOW IT...
...IS IMPORTANT TO YOU...
hug
ぎゅっ
DUMMY...
I HAVE SOMETHING THAT'S MUCH MORE IMPORTANT.
I...

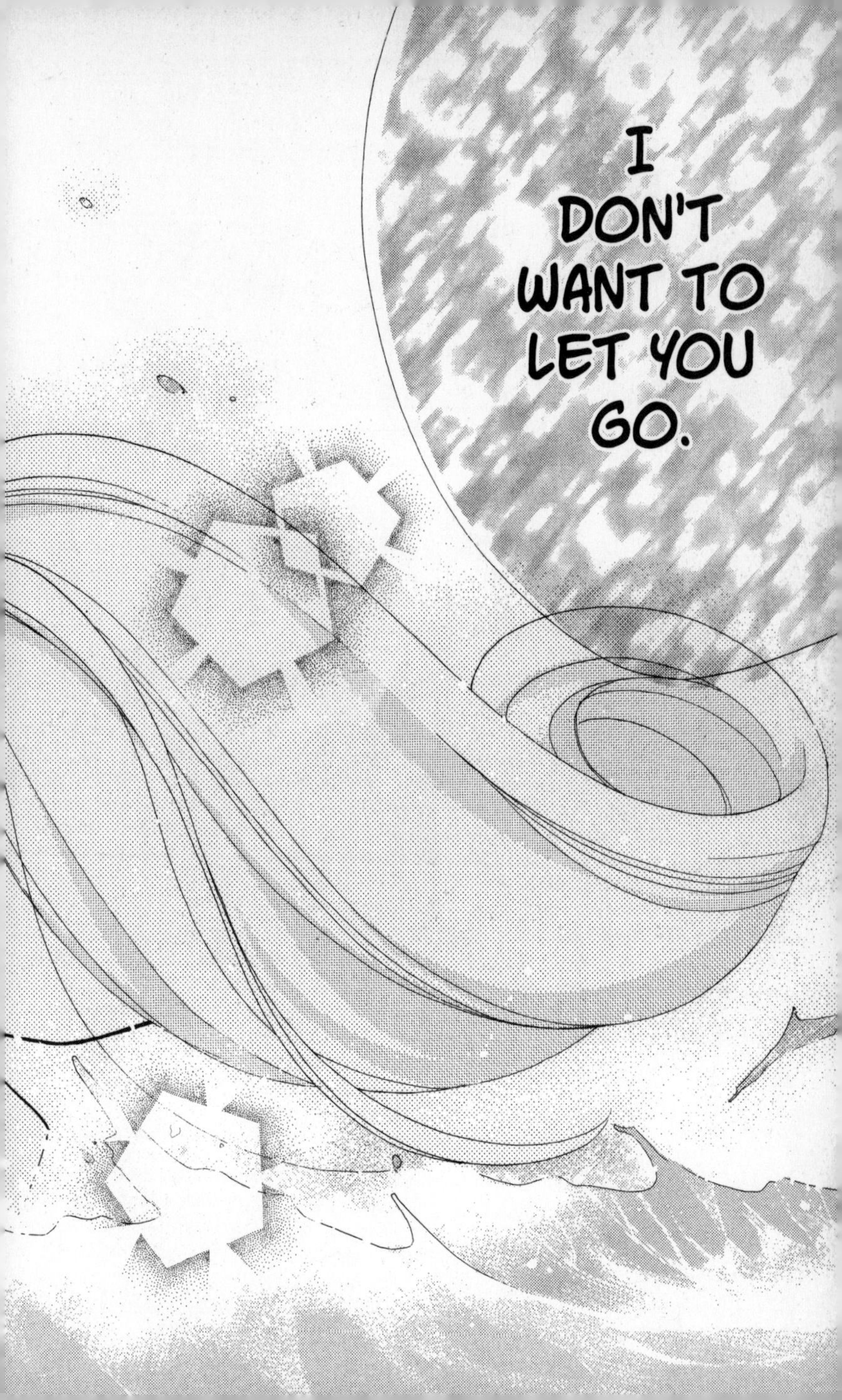
I DON'T WANT TO LET YOU GO.

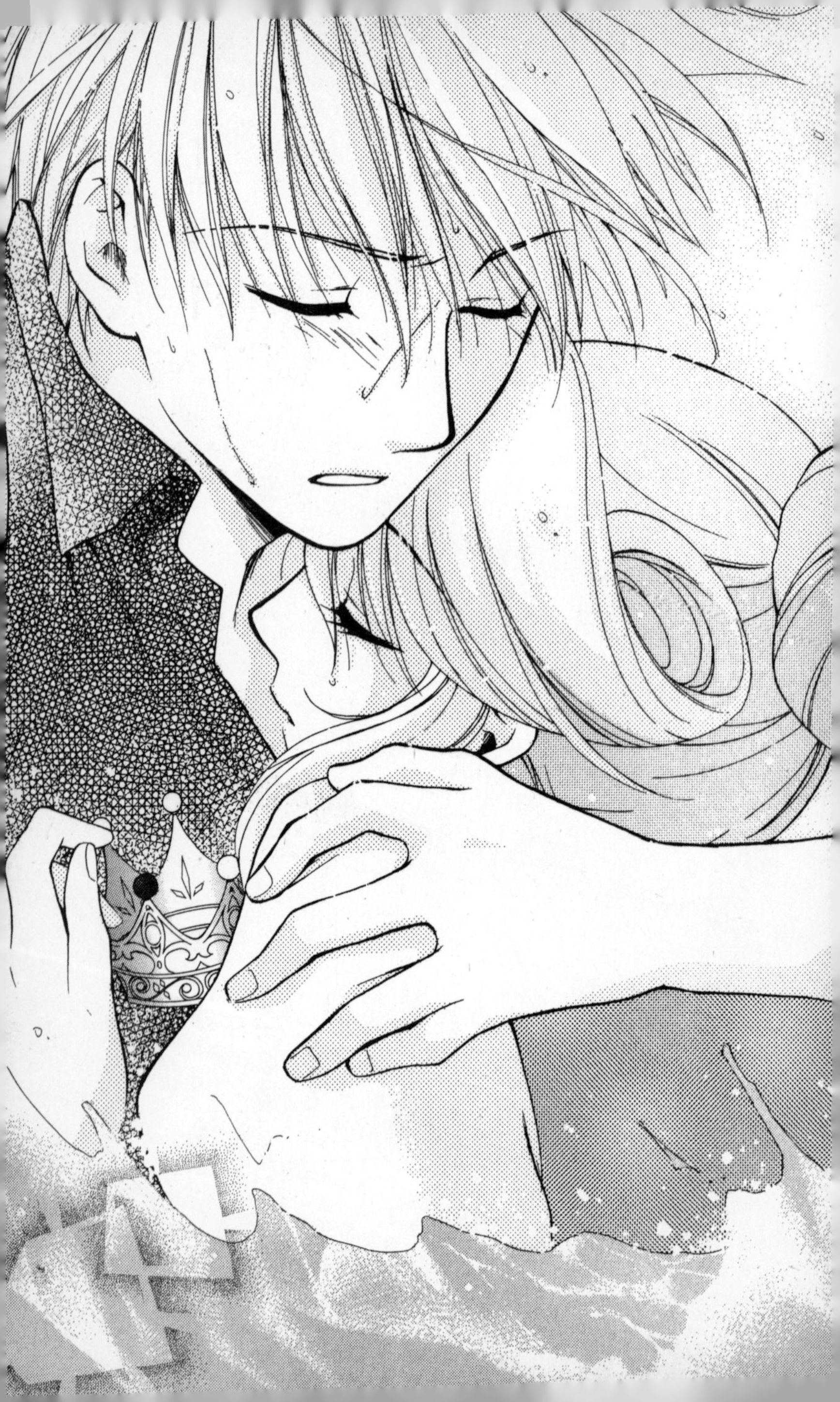

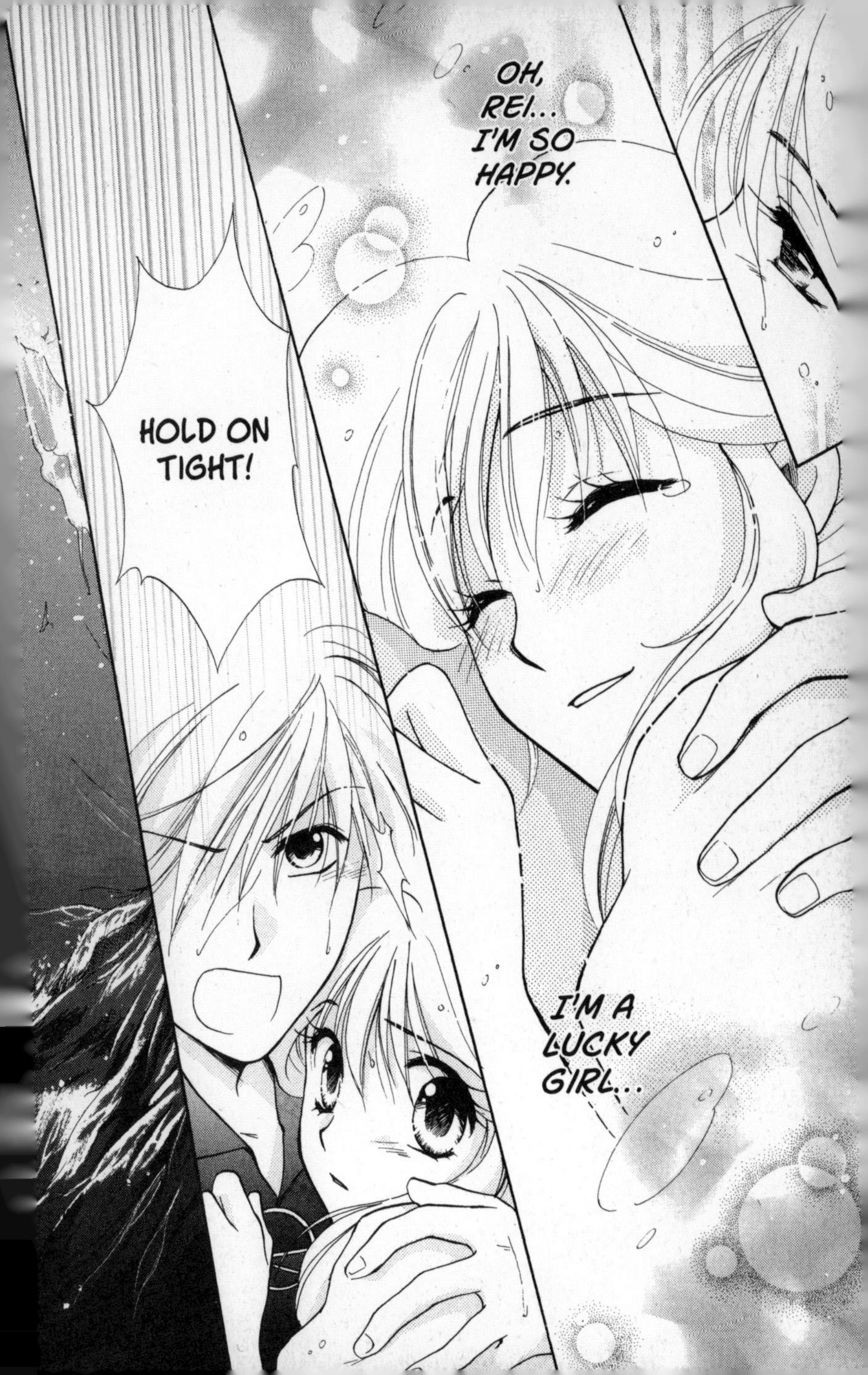
OH, REI... I'M SO HAPPY.
I'M A LUCKY GIRL...
HOLD ON TIGHT!

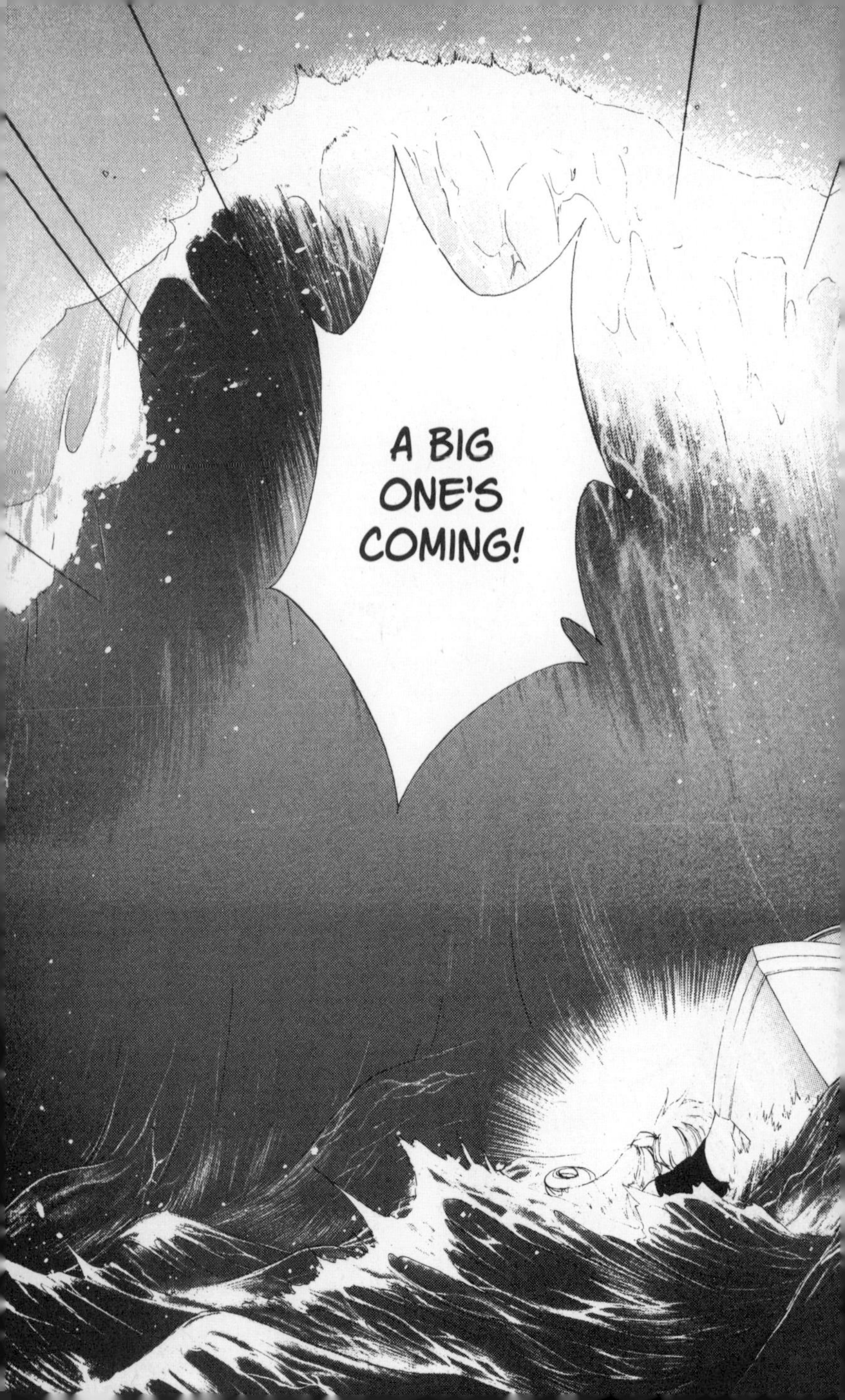
A BIG ONE'S COMING!

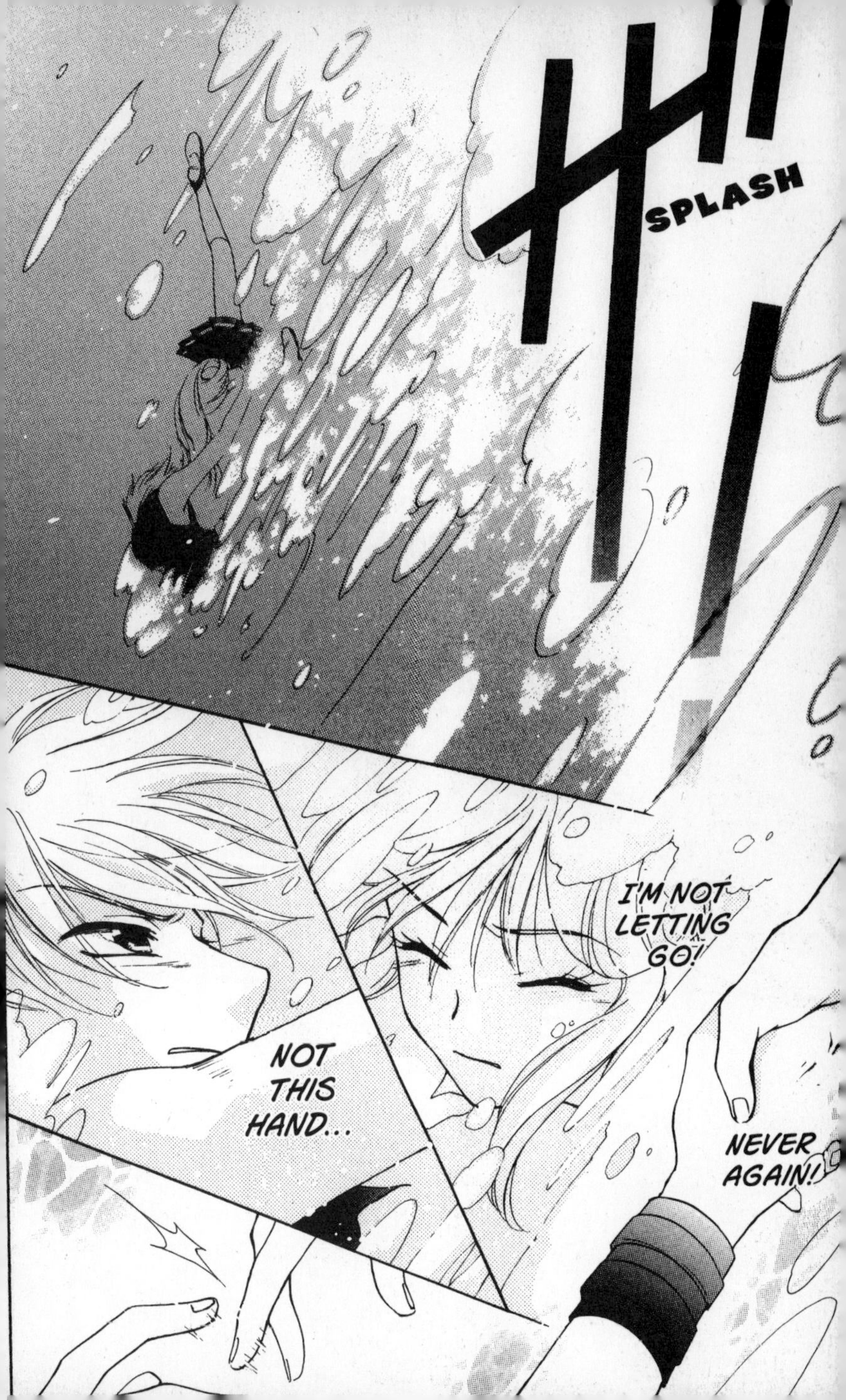
SPLASH
I'M NOT LETTING GO!
NOT THIS HAND...
NEVER AGAIN!

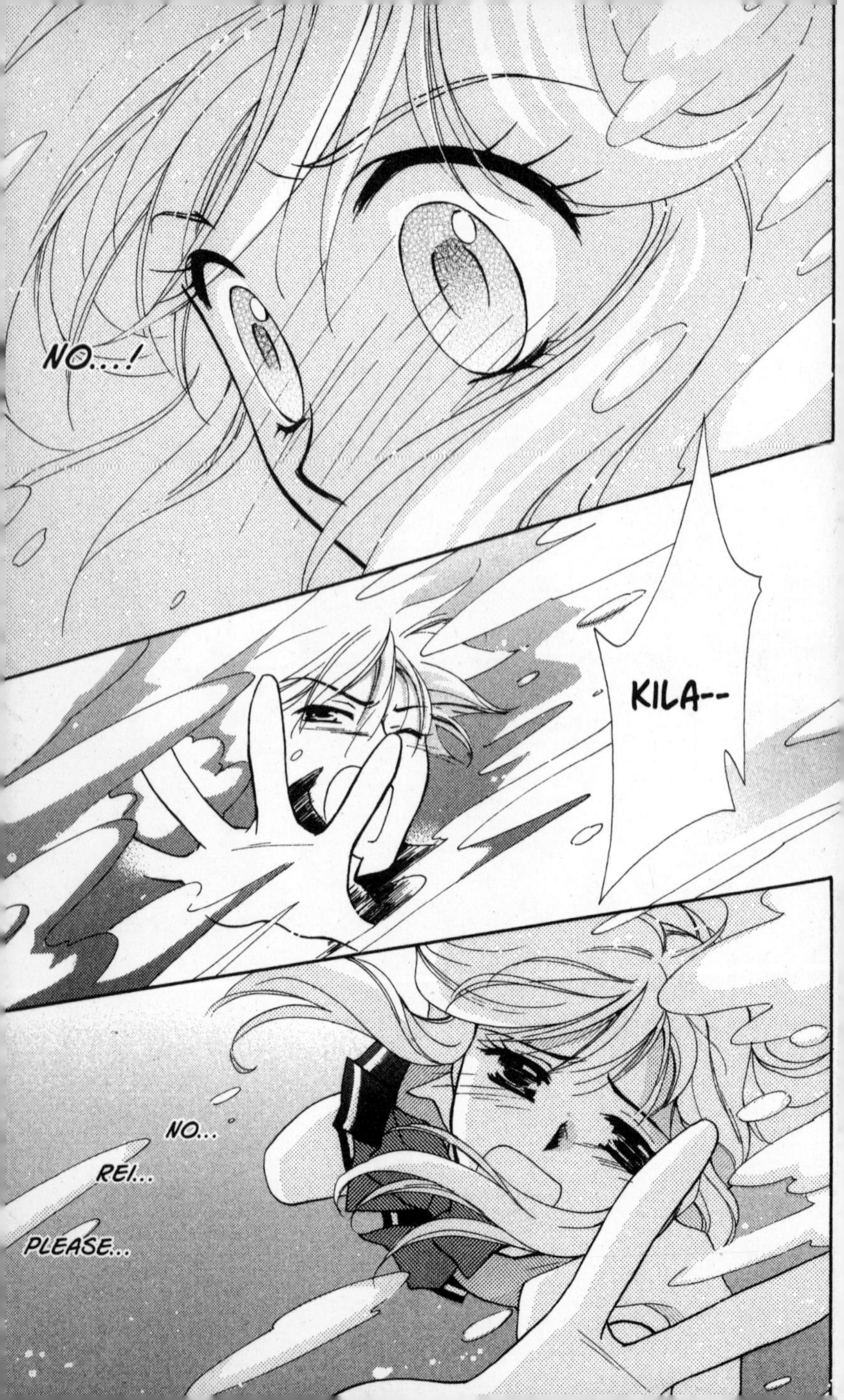
NO...!
KILA--
NO...
REI...
PLEASE...

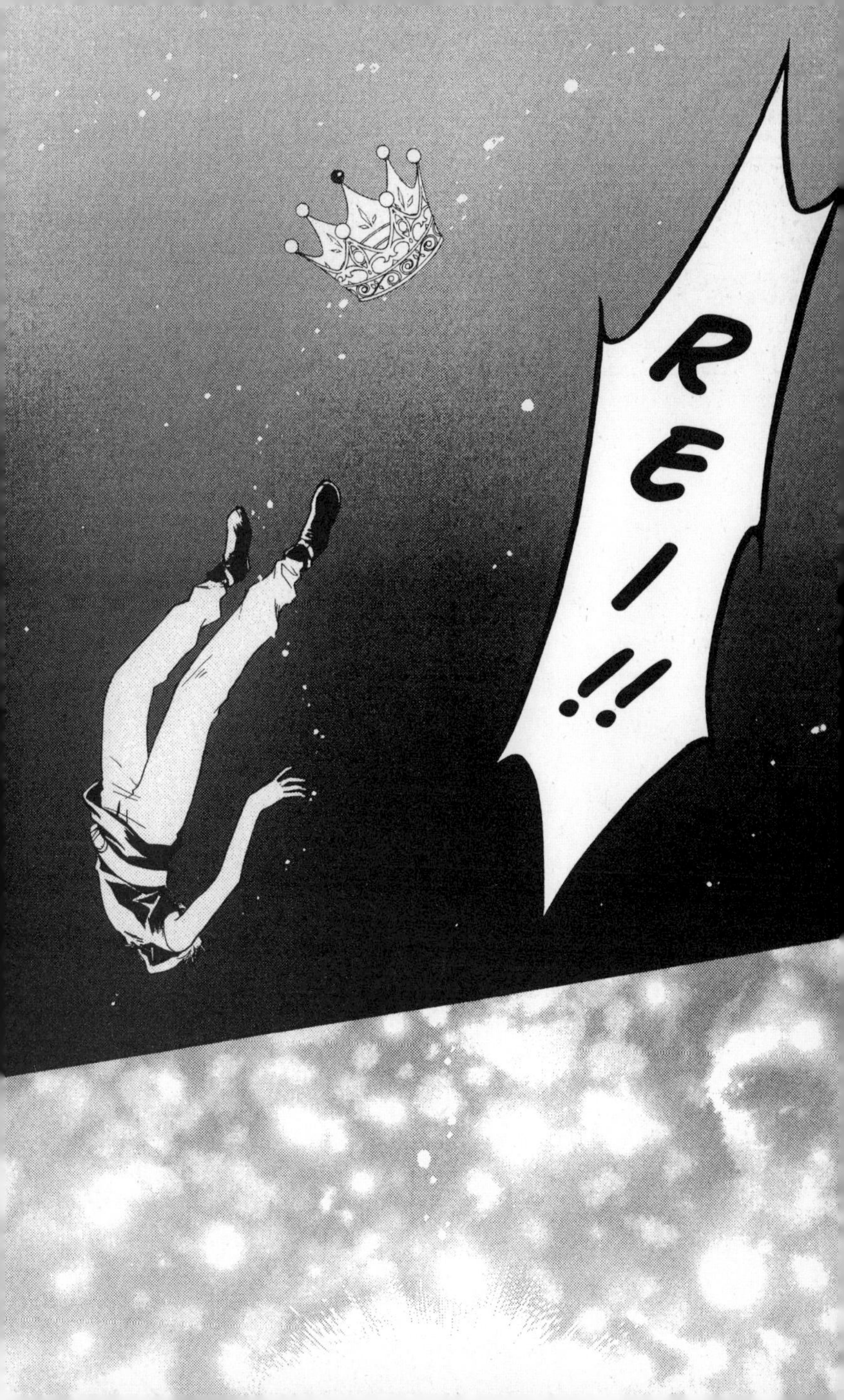
REI!!

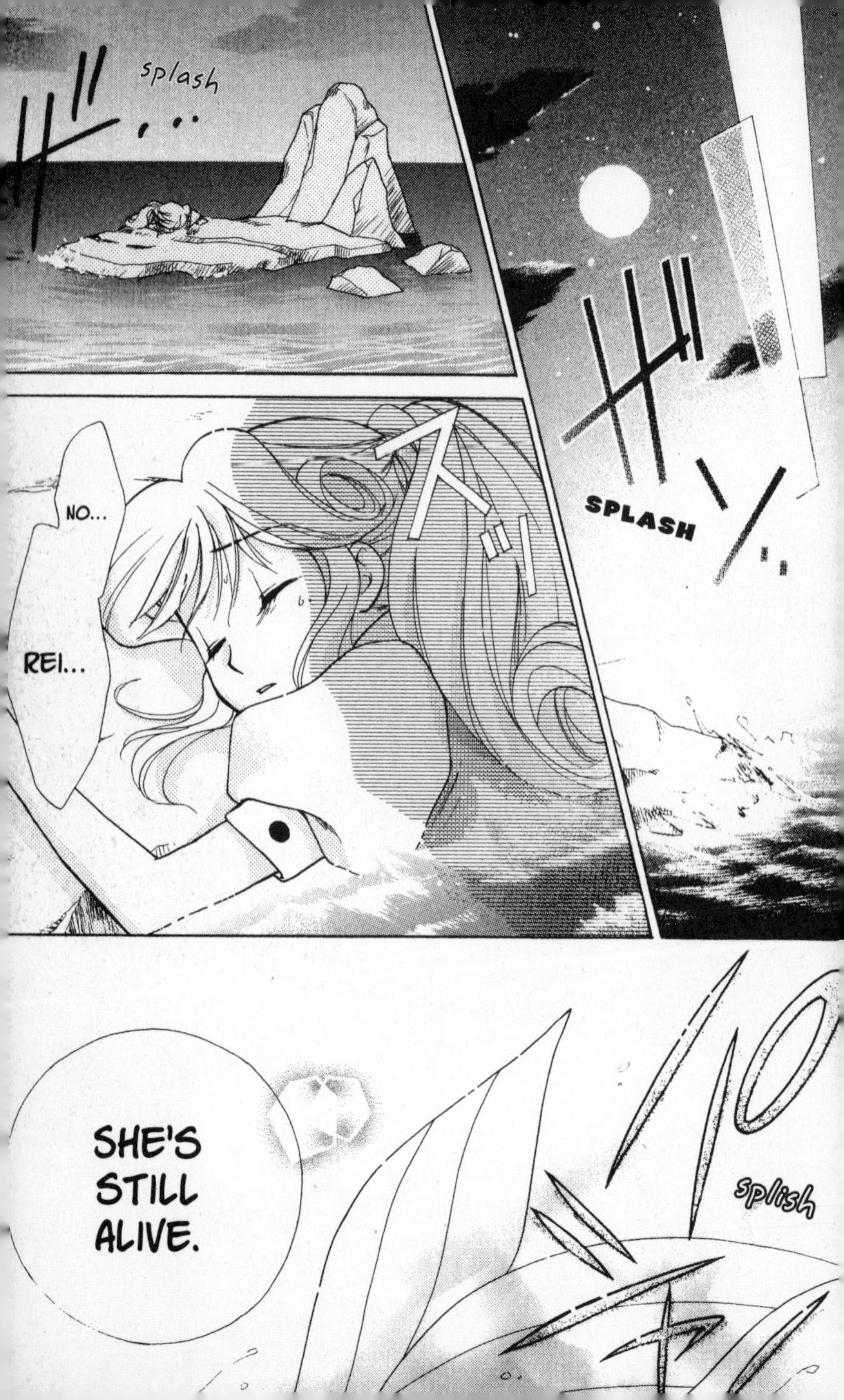
SPLASH
splash
NO...
REI...
splish
SHE'S STILL ALIVE.

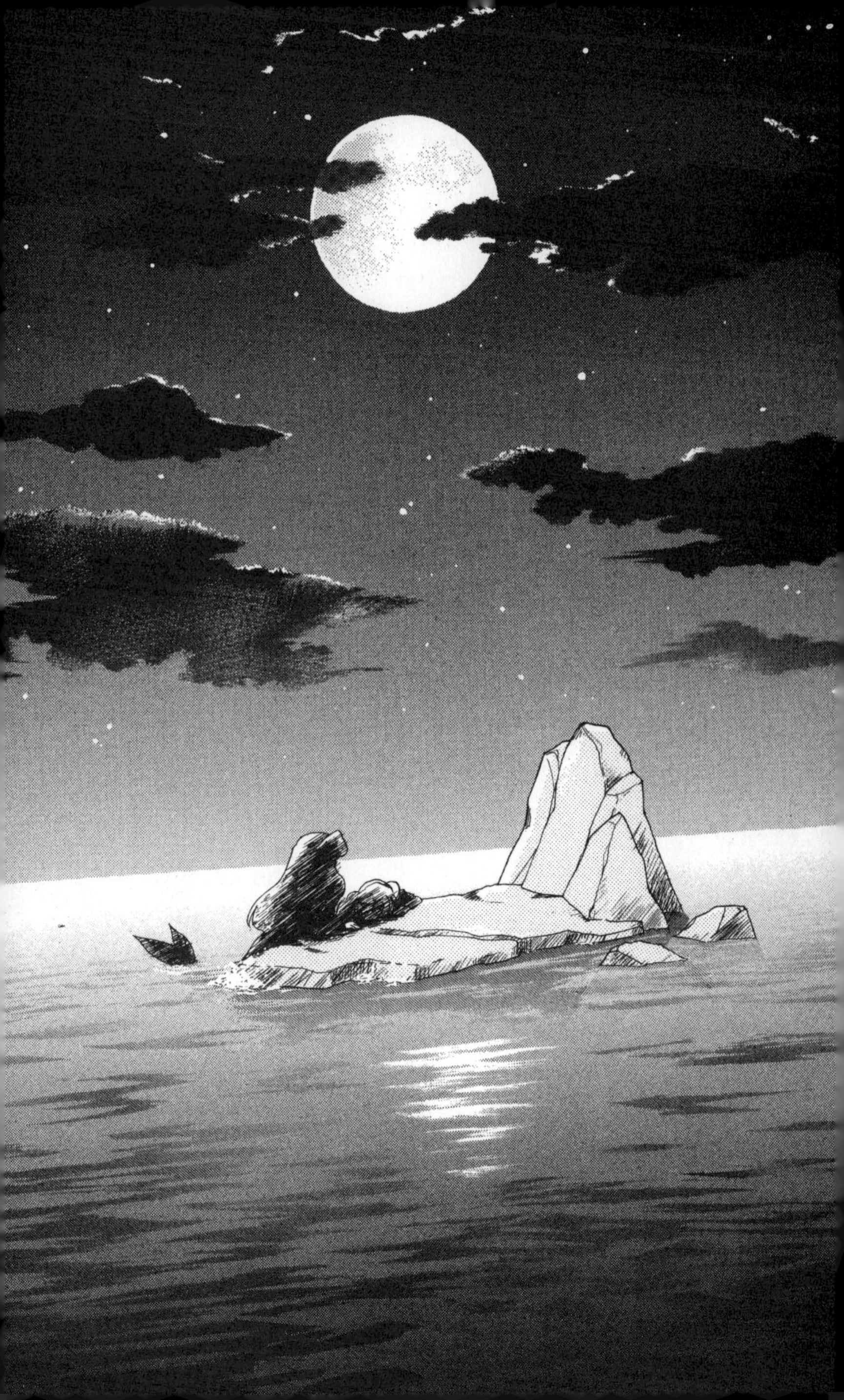

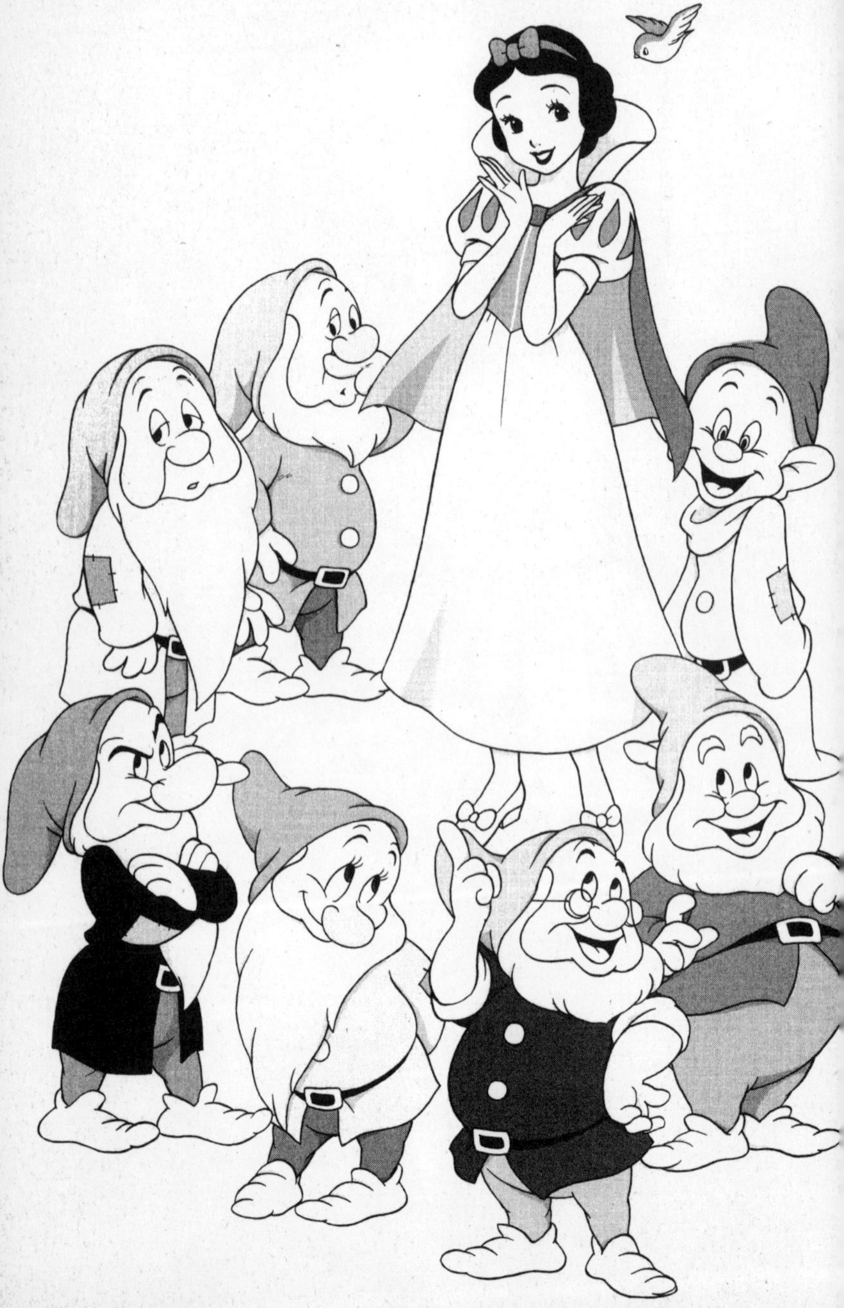

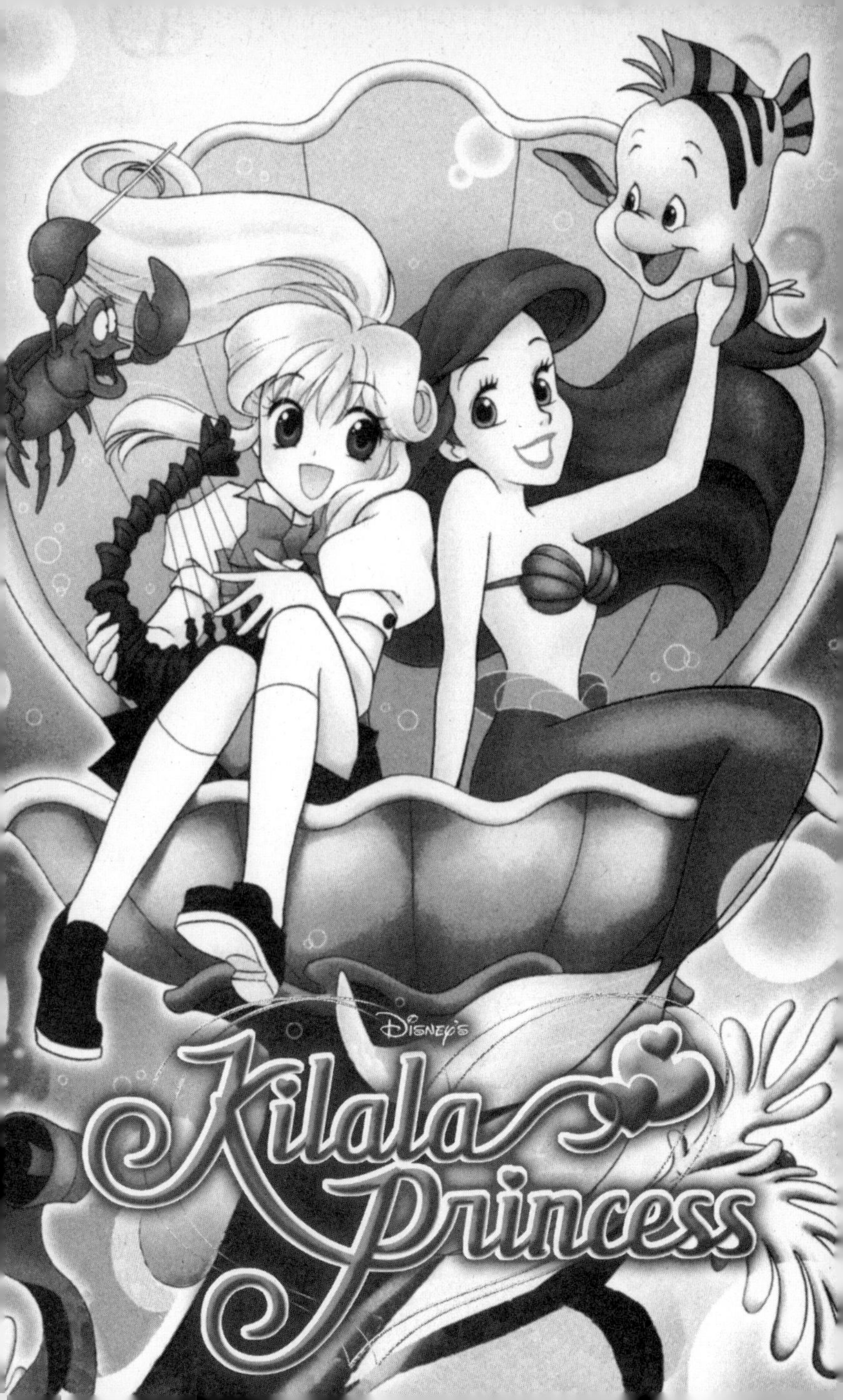
Disney's
Kilala Princess

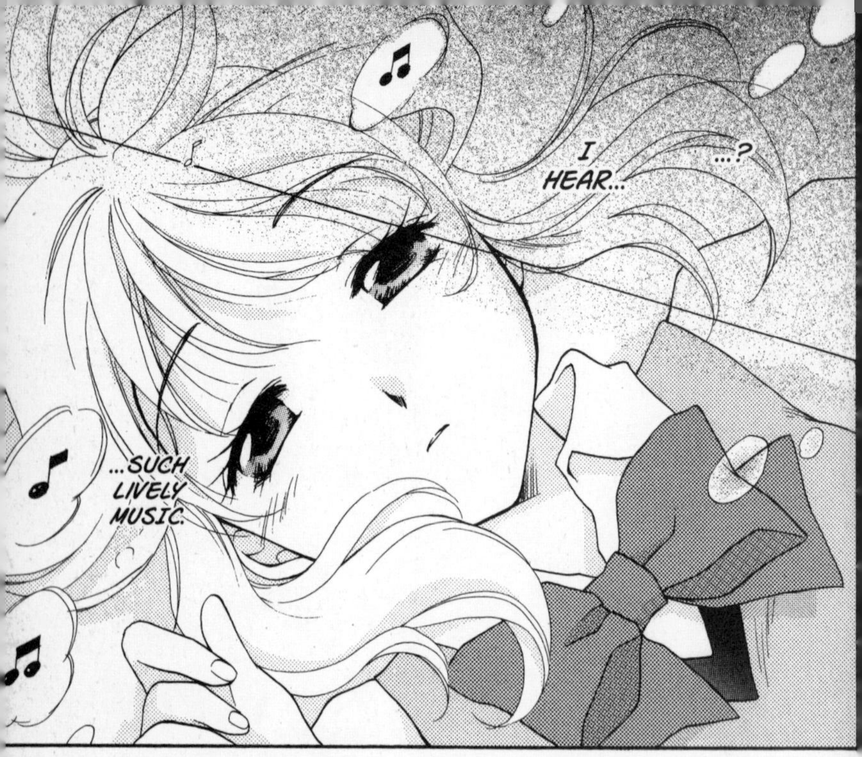
...?
I HEAR...
...SUCH LIVELY MUSIC.

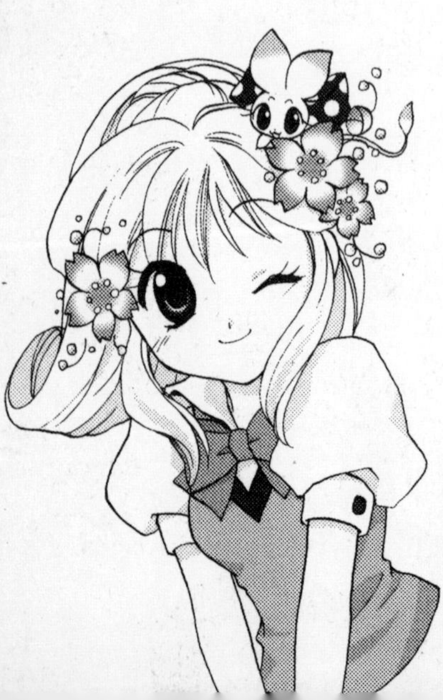

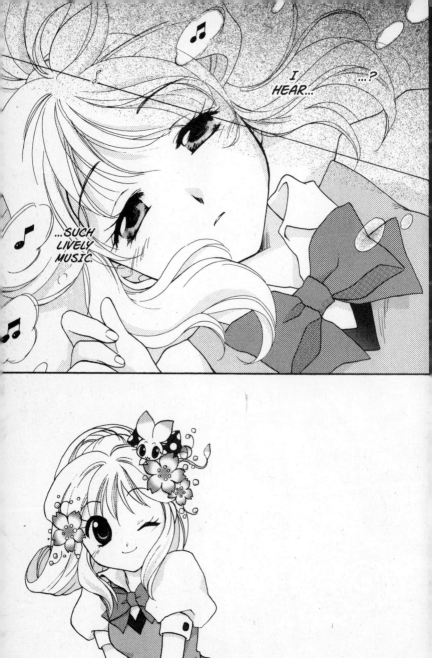

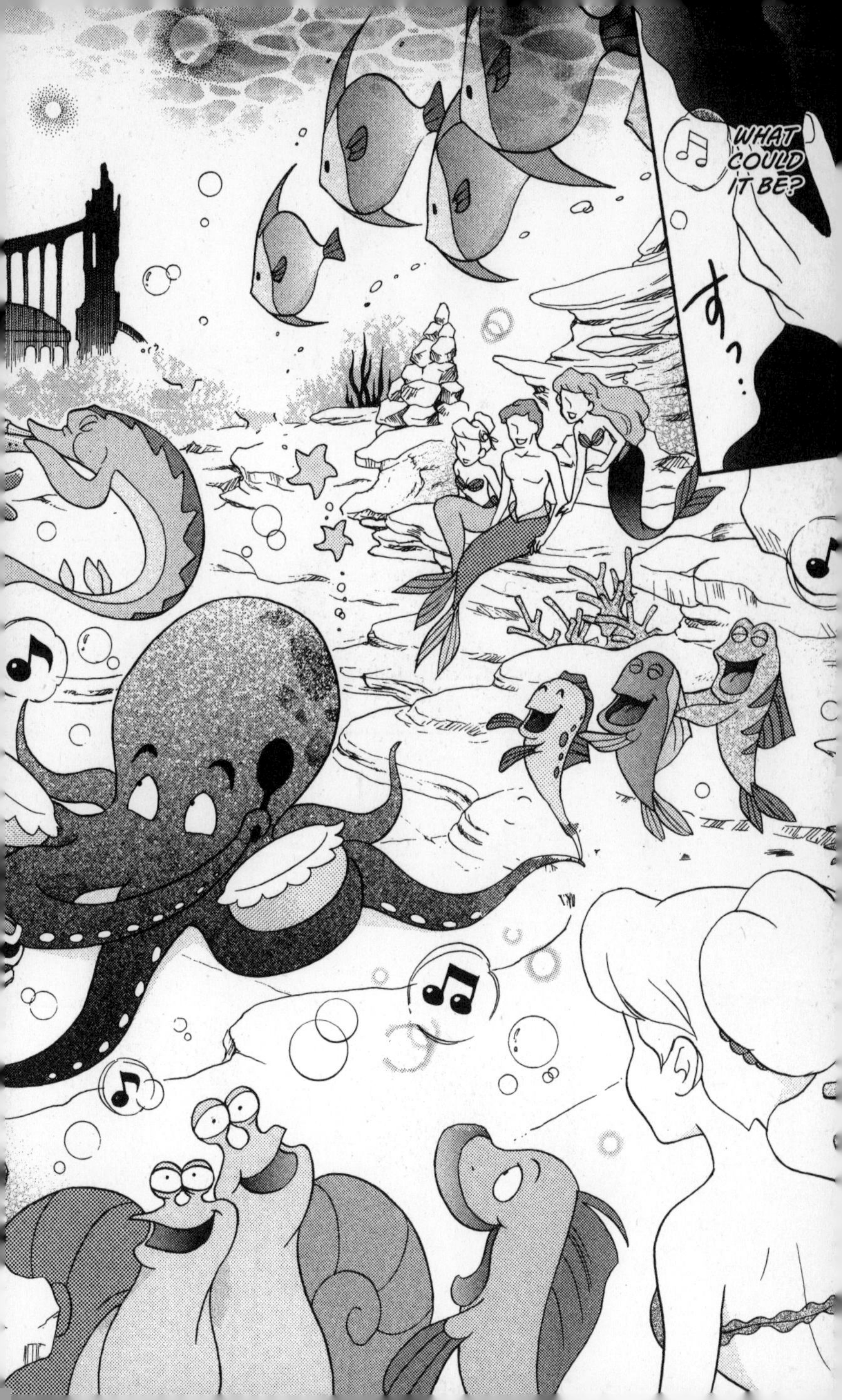
WHAT COULD IT BE?
すっ…

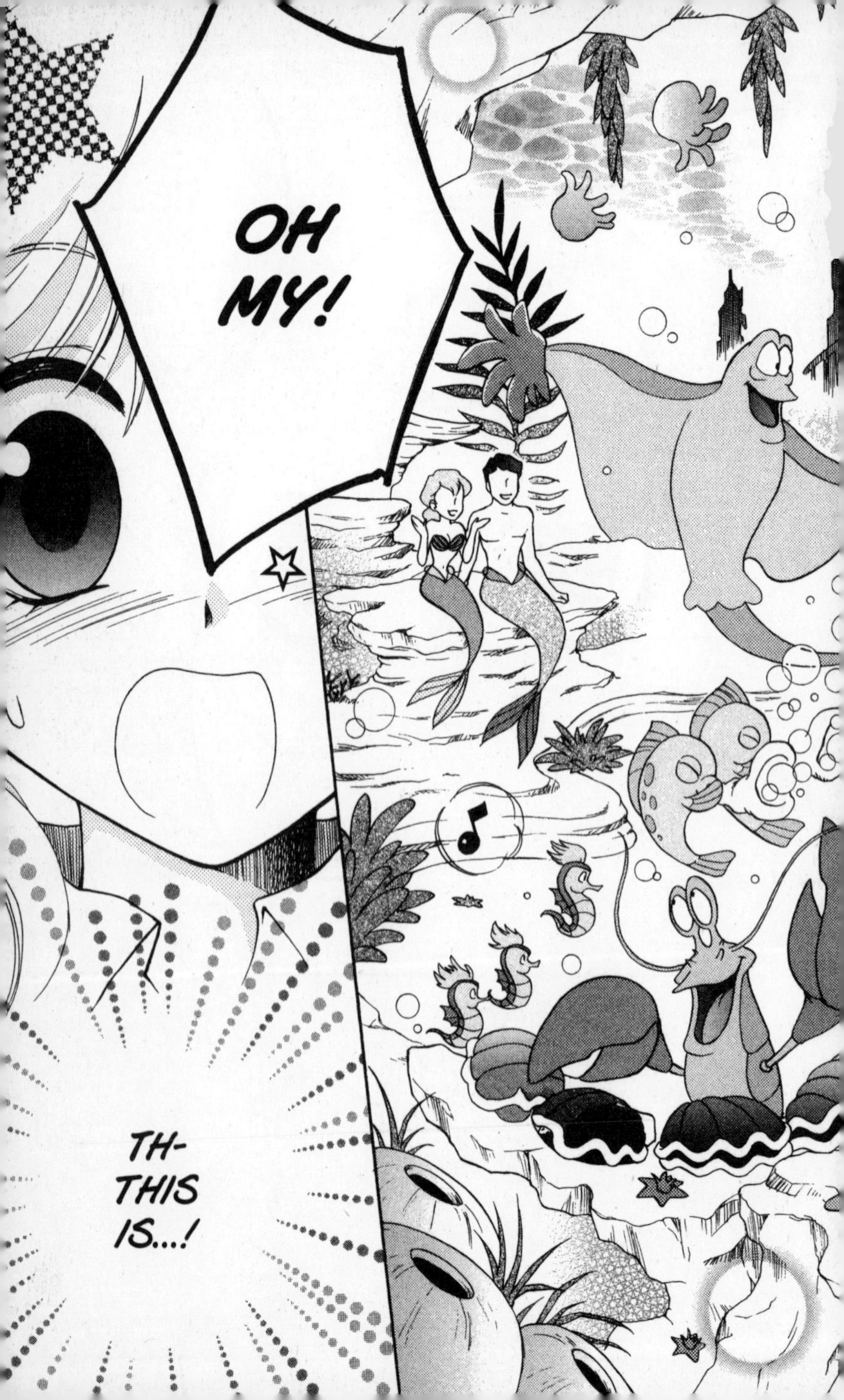
OH MY!
TH- THIS IS...!

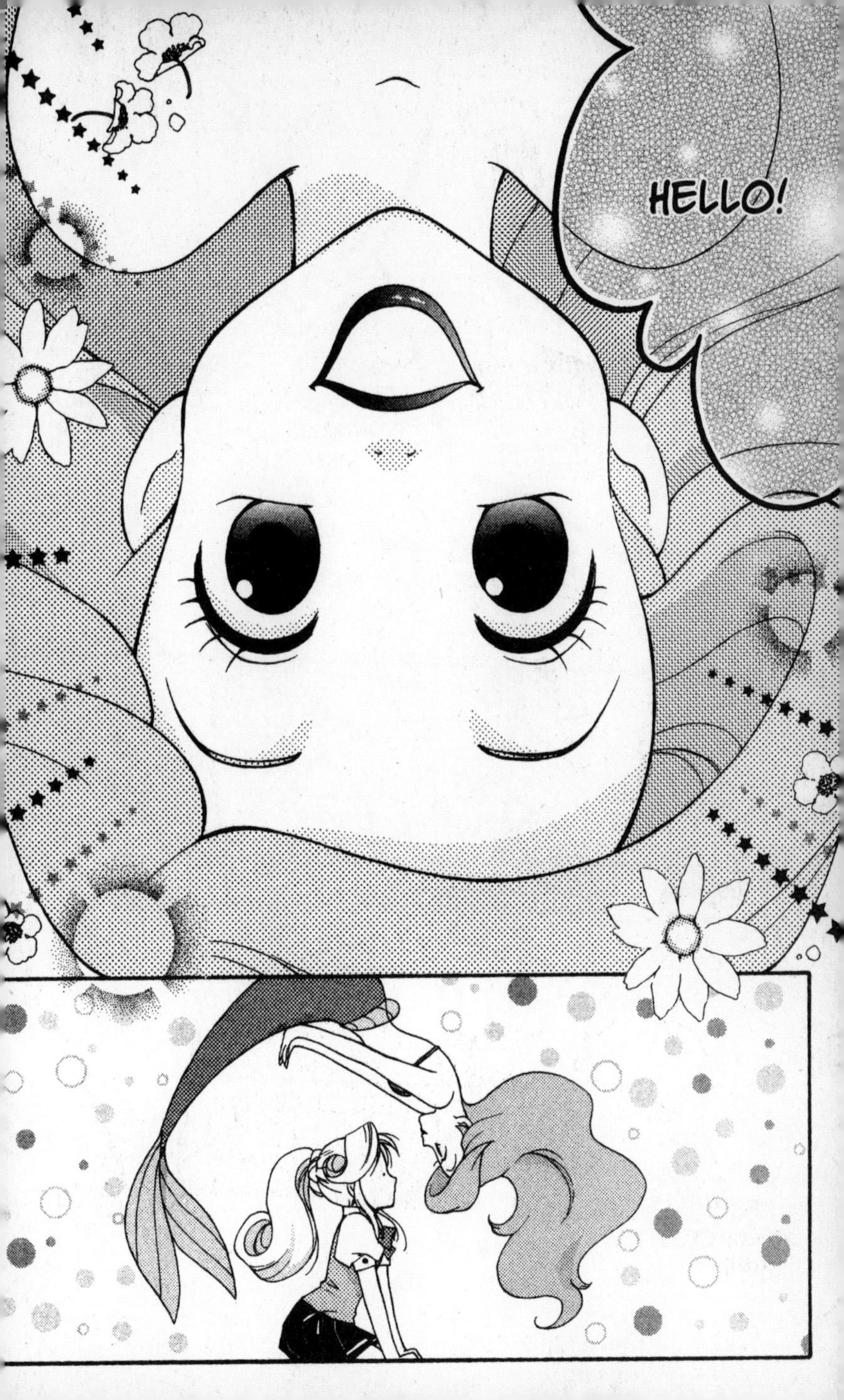
HELLO!

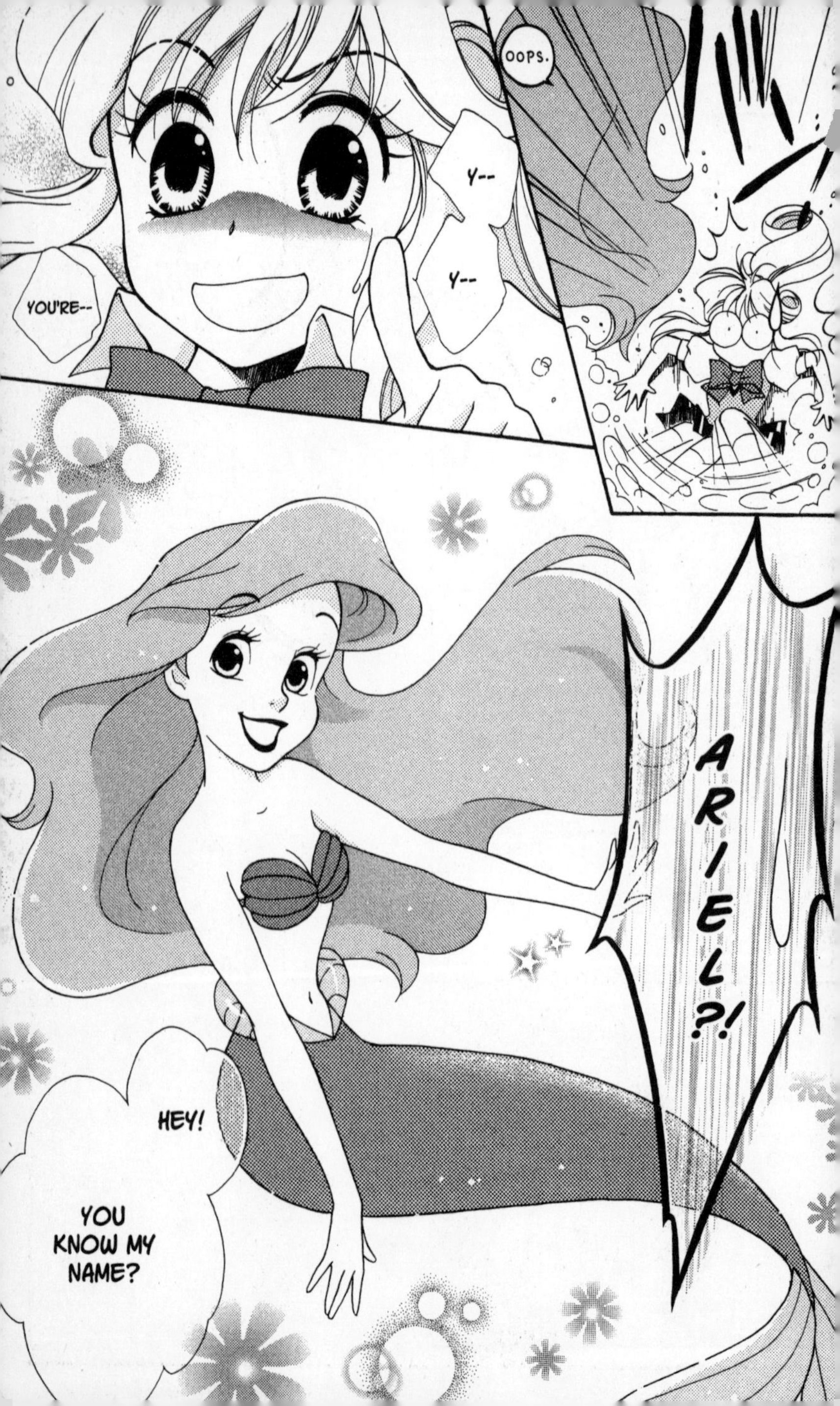
OOPS.
Y--
Y--
YOU'RE--
ARIEL?!
HEY!
YOU KNOW MY NAME?

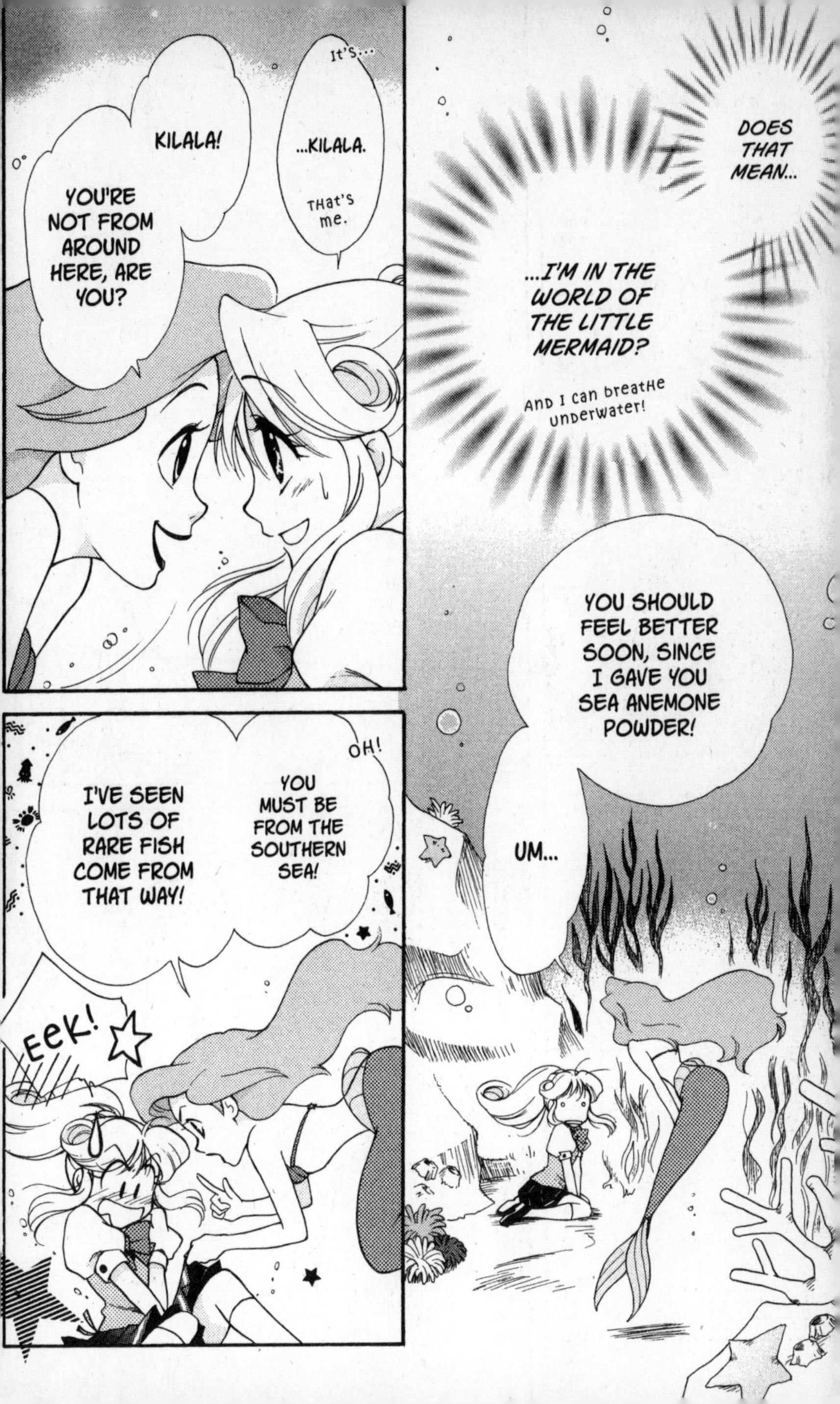
DOES THAT MEAN...
...I'M IN THE WORLD OF THE LITTLE MERMAID?
And I can breathe underwater!
YOU SHOULD FEEL BETTER SOON, SINCE I GAVE YOU SEA ANEMONE POWDER!
UM...
It's...
...KILALA.
That's me.
KILALA!
YOU'RE NOT FROM AROUND HERE, ARE YOU?
OH!
YOU MUST BE FROM THE SOUTHERN SEA!
I'VE SEEN LOTS OF RARE FISH COME FROM THAT WAY!
EEK!

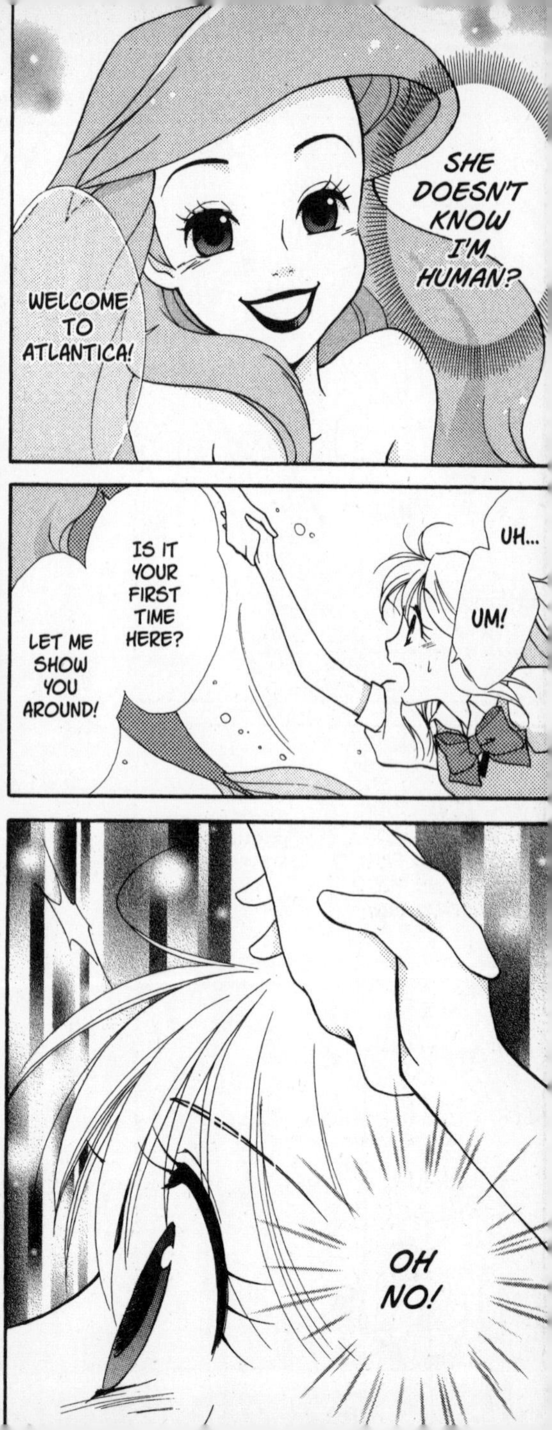
SHE DOESN'T KNOW I'M HUMAN?
WELCOME TO ATLANTICA!
UH...
UM!
IS IT YOUR FIRST TIME HERE?
LET ME SHOW YOU AROUND!
OH NO!

A WORD FROM TIPPE

1

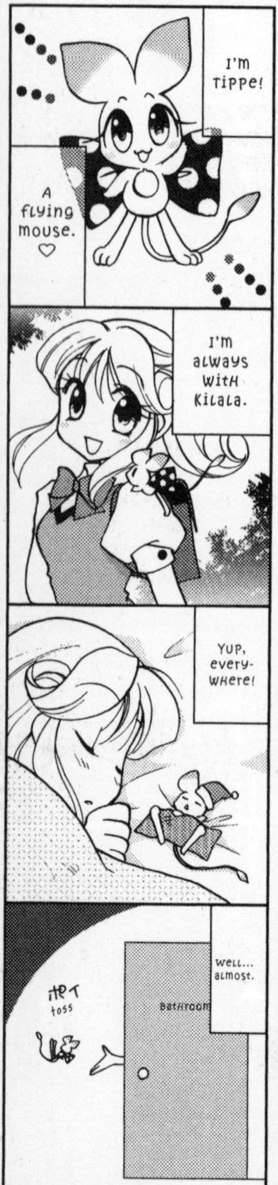
I'm Tippe!
A flying mouse. ♡
I'm always with Kilala.
Yup, every-where!
well... almost.
Bathroom
ポイ
toss

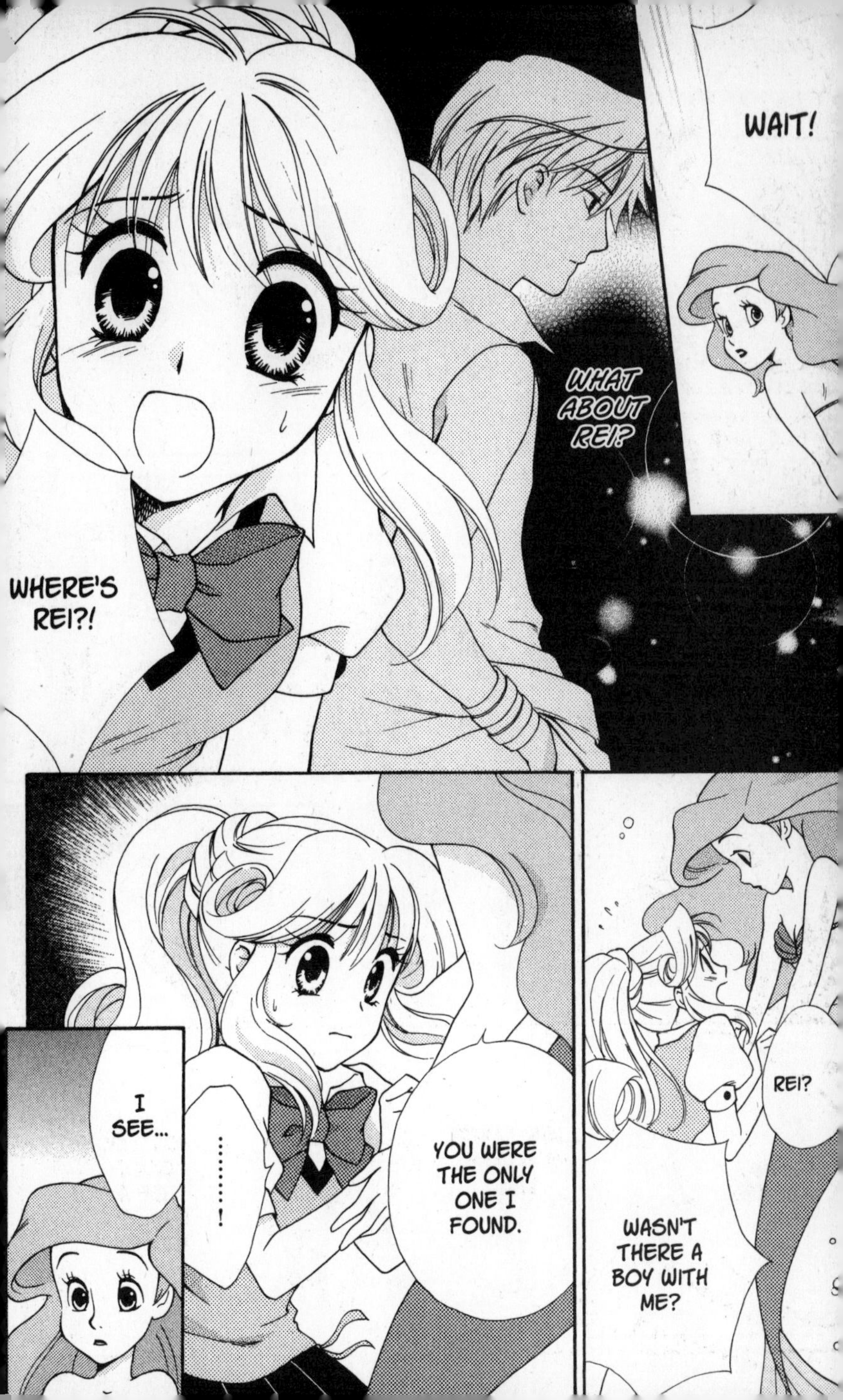
WAIT!
WHAT ABOUT REI?
WHERE'S REI?!
REI?
WASN'T THERE A BOY WITH ME?
YOU WERE THE ONLY ONE I FOUND.
……!
I SEE...

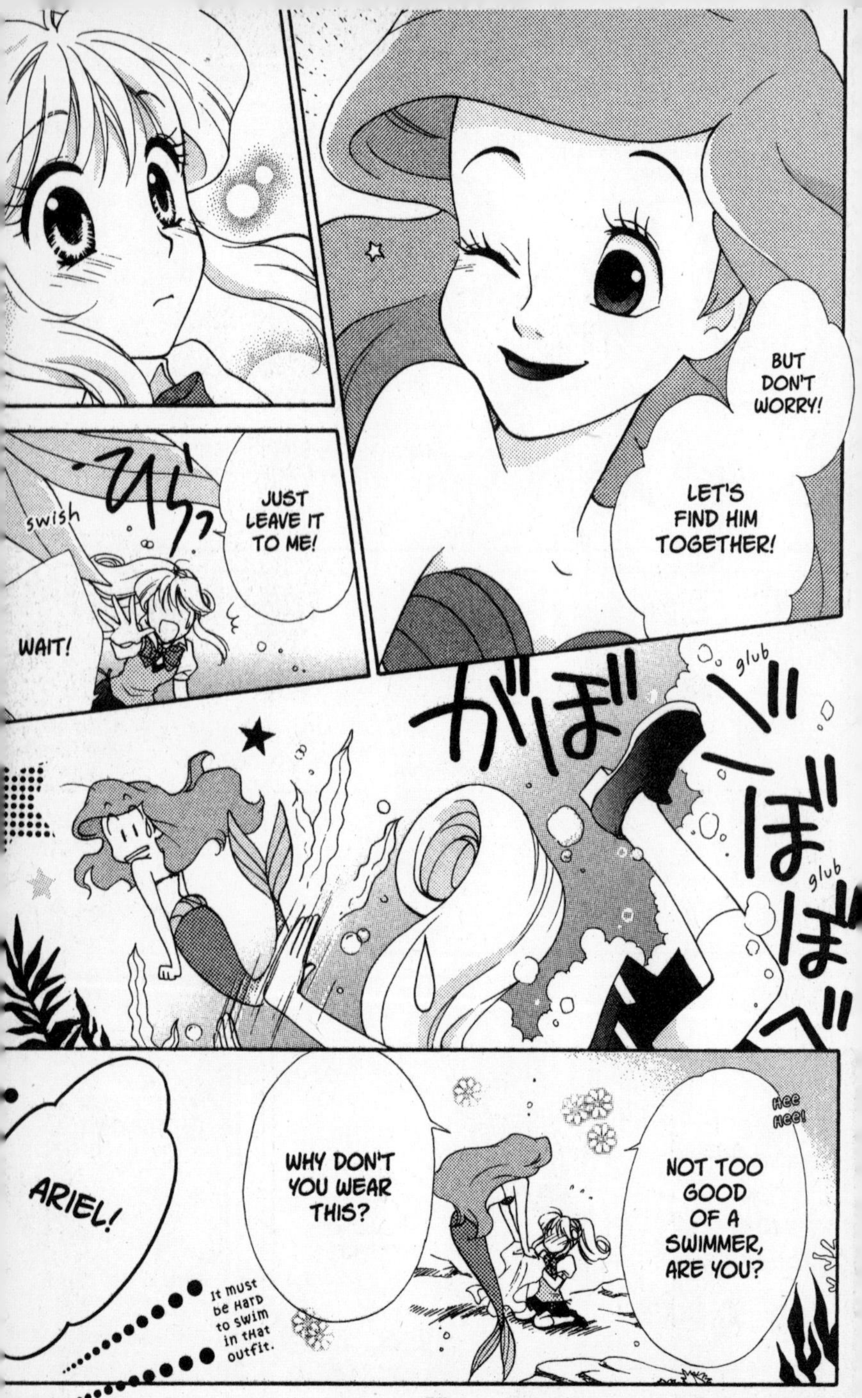

BUT DON'T WORRY!
LET'S FIND HIM TOGETHER!
ひらっ
swish
JUST LEAVE IT TO ME!
WAIT!
がぼ
glub
glub
Hee Hee!
NOT TOO GOOD OF A SWIMMER, ARE YOU?
WHY DON'T YOU WEAR THIS?
ARIEL!
It must be hard to swim in that outfit.

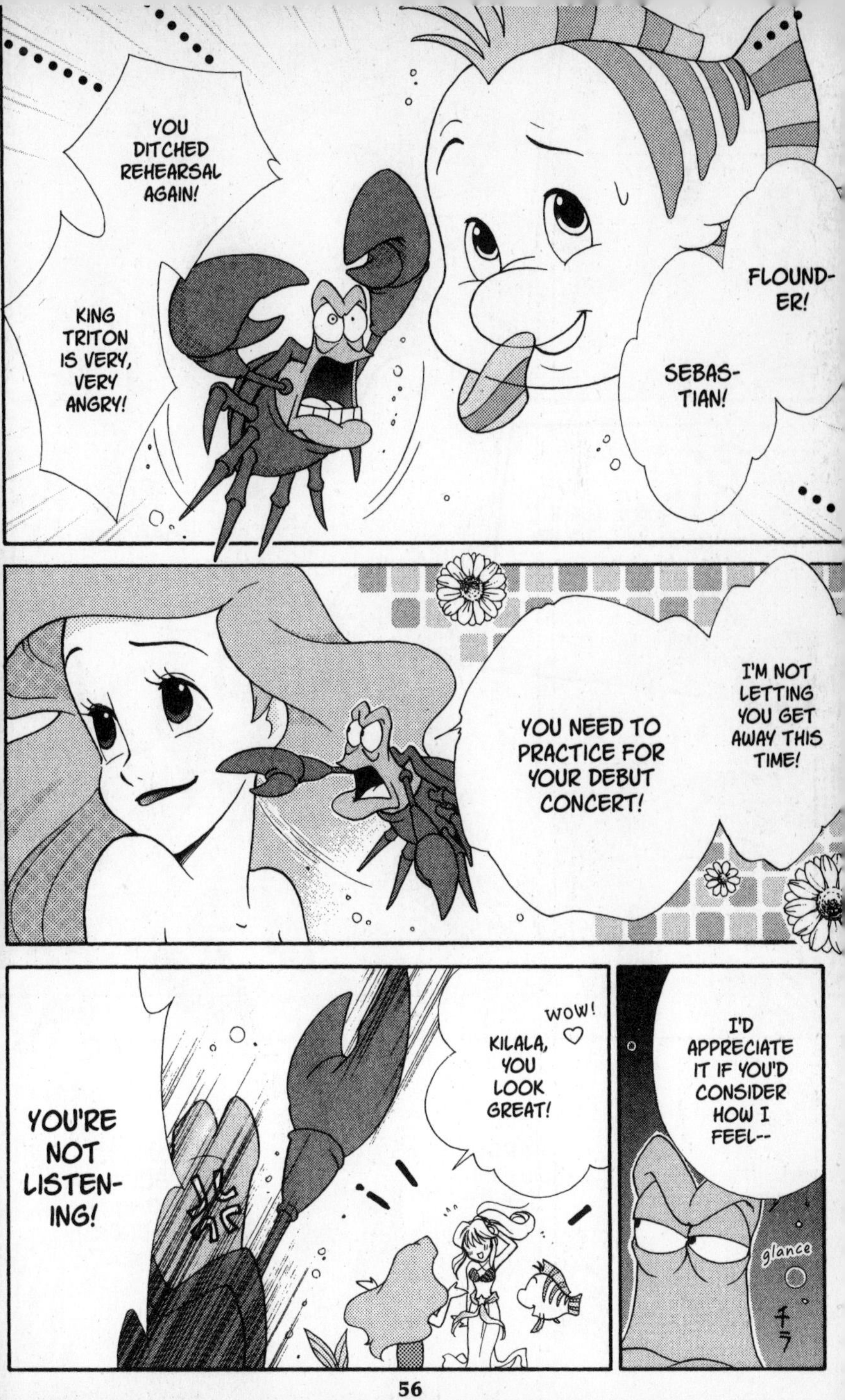
FLOUNDER!
SEBASTIAN!
YOU DITCHED REHEARSAL AGAIN!
KING TRITON IS VERY, VERY ANGRY!
I'M NOT LETTING YOU GET AWAY THIS TIME!
YOU NEED TO PRACTICE FOR YOUR DEBUT CONCERT!
I'D APPRECIATE IT IF YOU'D CONSIDER HOW I FEEL--
glance
チラ
WOW! ♡
KILALA, YOU LOOK GREAT!
YOU'RE NOT LISTENING!

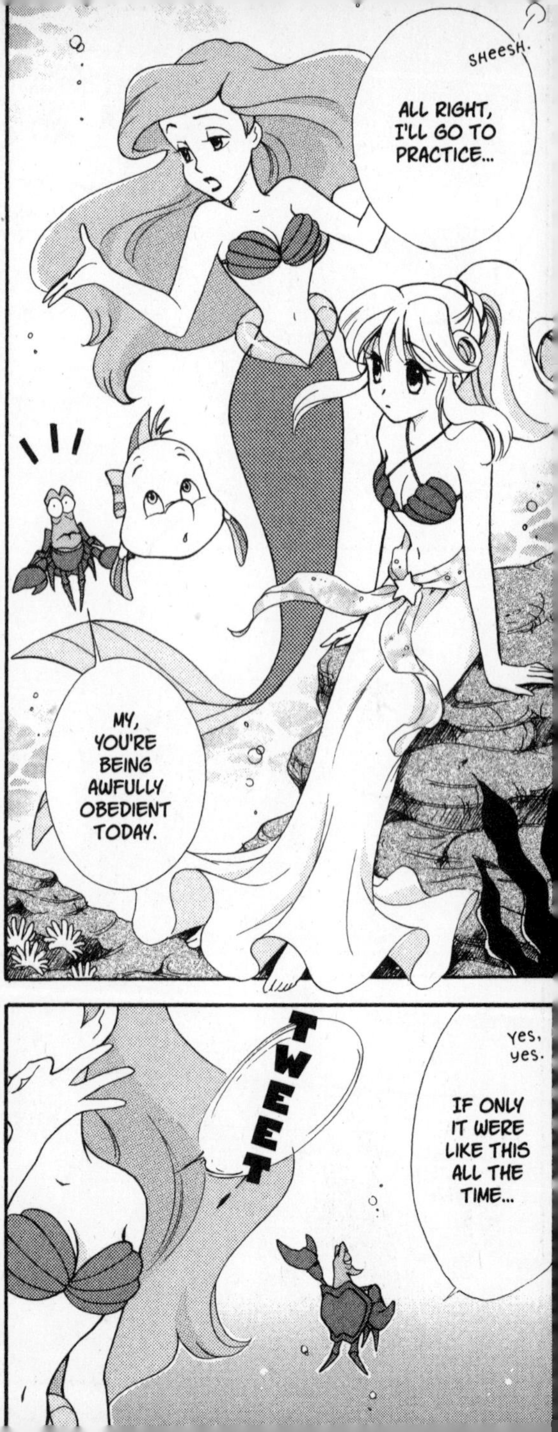
SHEESH.
ALL RIGHT, I'LL GO TO PRACTICE...
MY, YOU'RE BEING AWFULLY OBEDIENT TODAY.
Yes, yes.
IF ONLY IT WERE LIKE THIS ALL THE TIME...
TWEET

A WORD FROM TIPPE

2

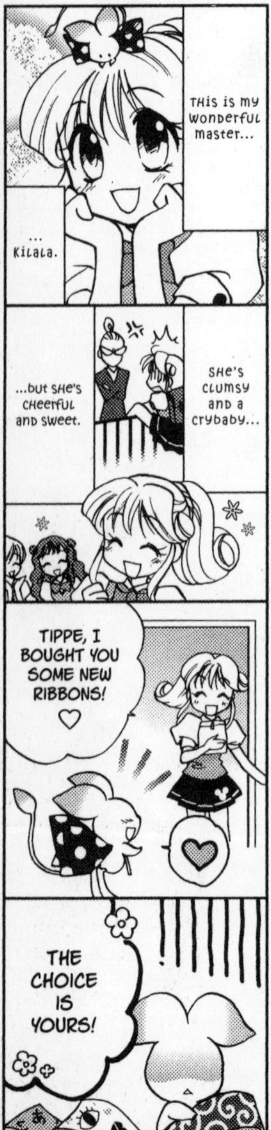
This is my wonderful master...
... Kilala.
She's clumsy and a crybaby...
...but she's cheerful and sweet.
TIPPE, I BOUGHT YOU SOME NEW RIBBONS! ♡
THE CHOICE IS YOURS!

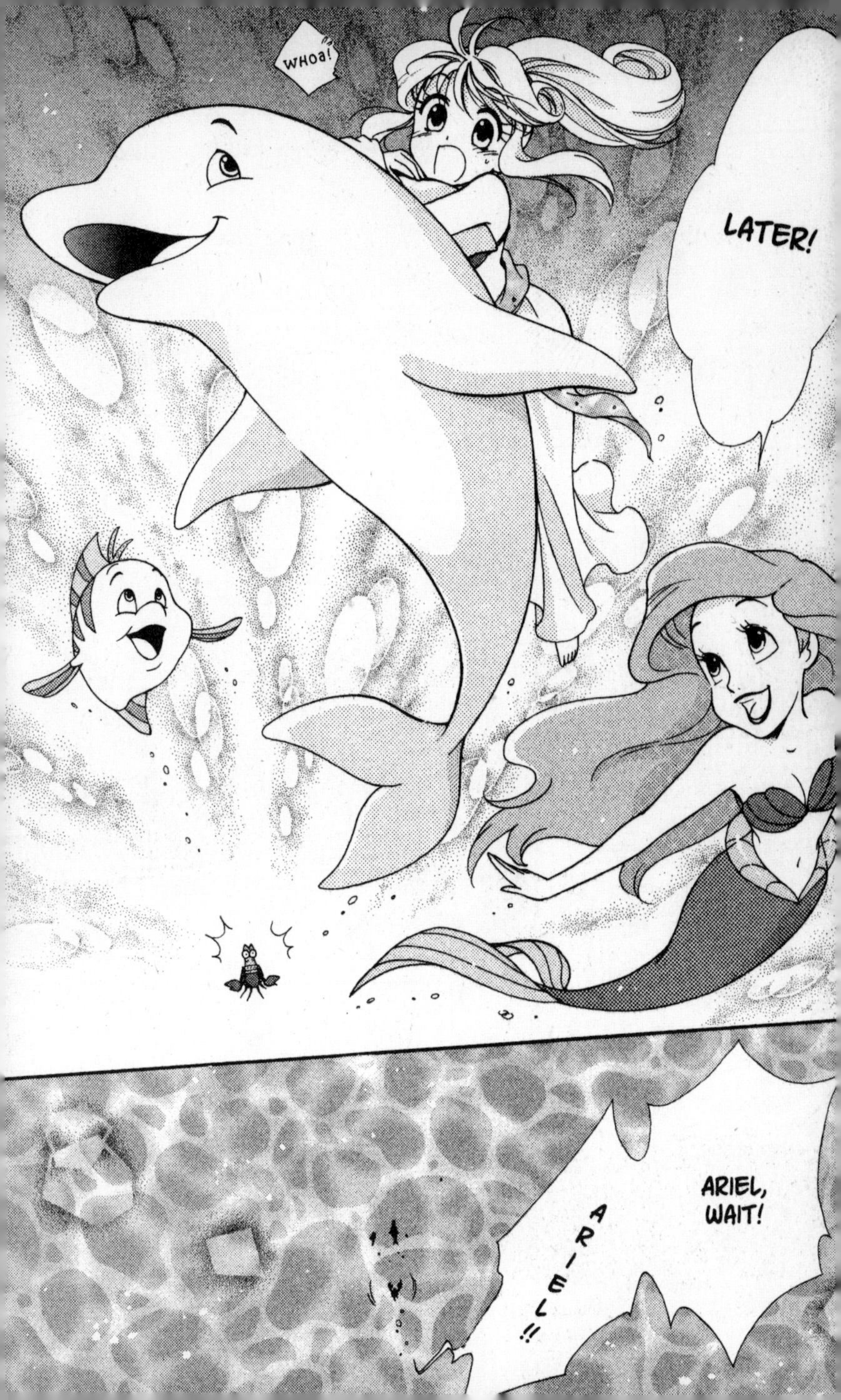
WHOA!
LATER!
ARIEL, WAIT!
ARIEL!!

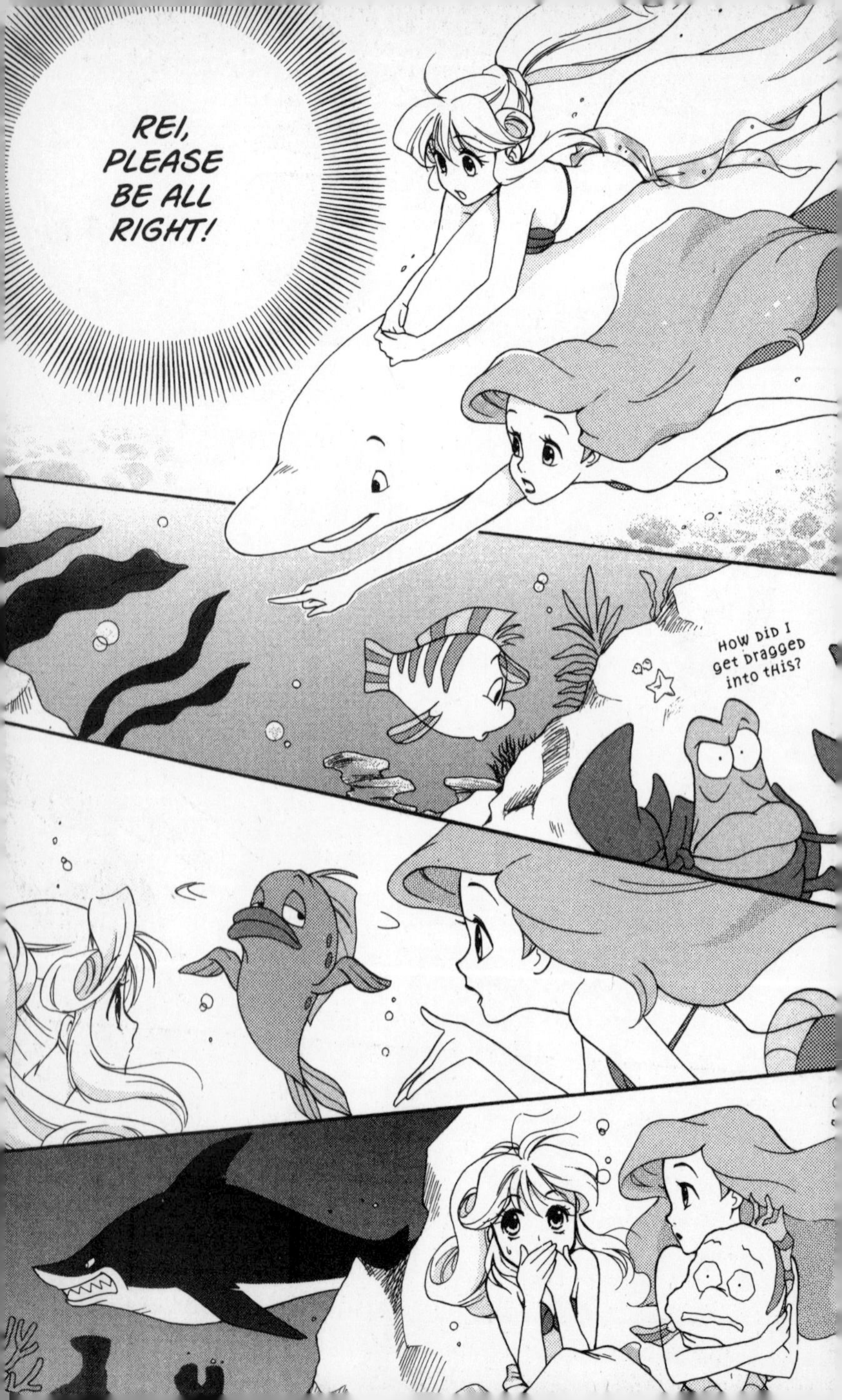
REI, PLEASE BE ALL RIGHT!
HOW DID I get Dragged into tHIS?

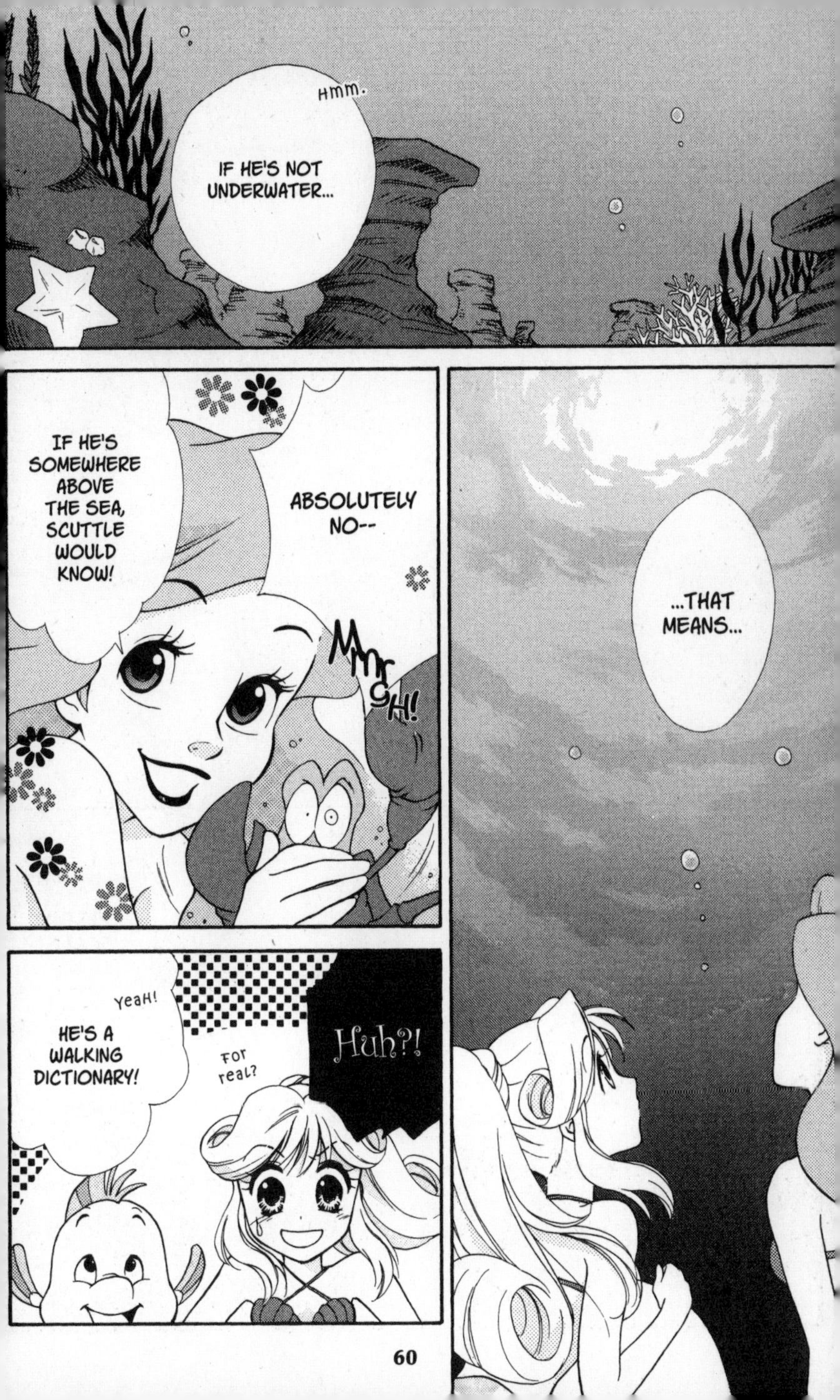
Hmm.
IF HE'S NOT UNDERWATER...
...THAT MEANS...
IF HE'S SOMEWHERE ABOVE THE SEA, SCUTTLE WOULD KNOW!
ABSOLUTELY NO--
MMRGH!
Huh?!
For real?
Yeah!
HE'S A WALKING DICTIONARY!

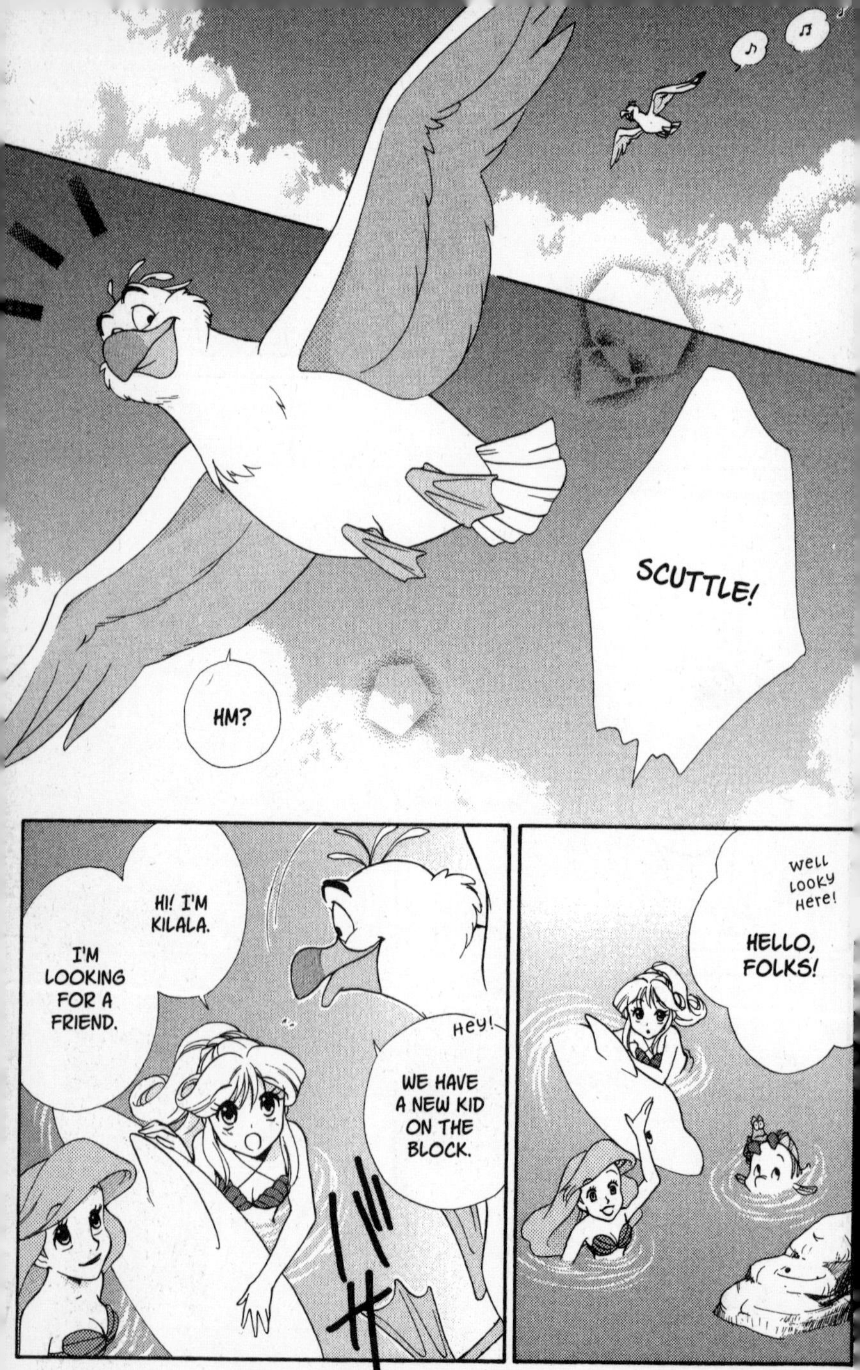
SCUTTLE!
HM?
Well looky Here!
HELLO, FOLKS!
Hey!
WE HAVE A NEW KID ON THE BLOCK.
HI! I'M KILALA.
I'M LOOKING FOR A FRIEND.

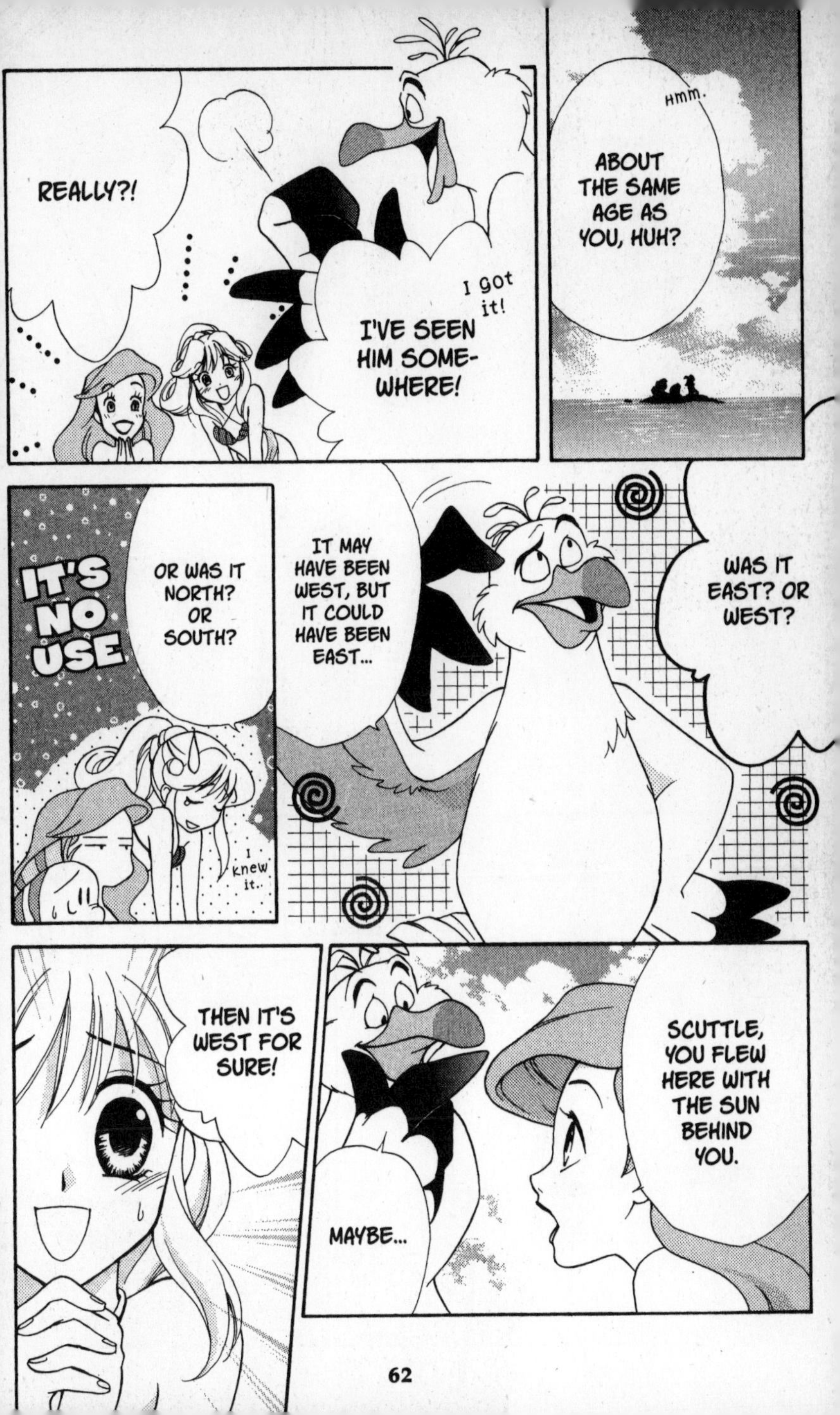
Hmm.
ABOUT THE SAME AGE AS YOU, HUH?
I got it!
I'VE SEEN HIM SOME-WHERE!
REALLY?!
WAS IT EAST? OR WEST?
IT MAY HAVE BEEN WEST, BUT IT COULD HAVE BEEN EAST...
OR WAS IT NORTH? OR SOUTH?
IT'S NO USE
I knew it..
SCUTTLE, YOU FLEW HERE WITH THE SUN BEHIND YOU.
MAYBE...
THEN IT'S WEST FOR SURE!

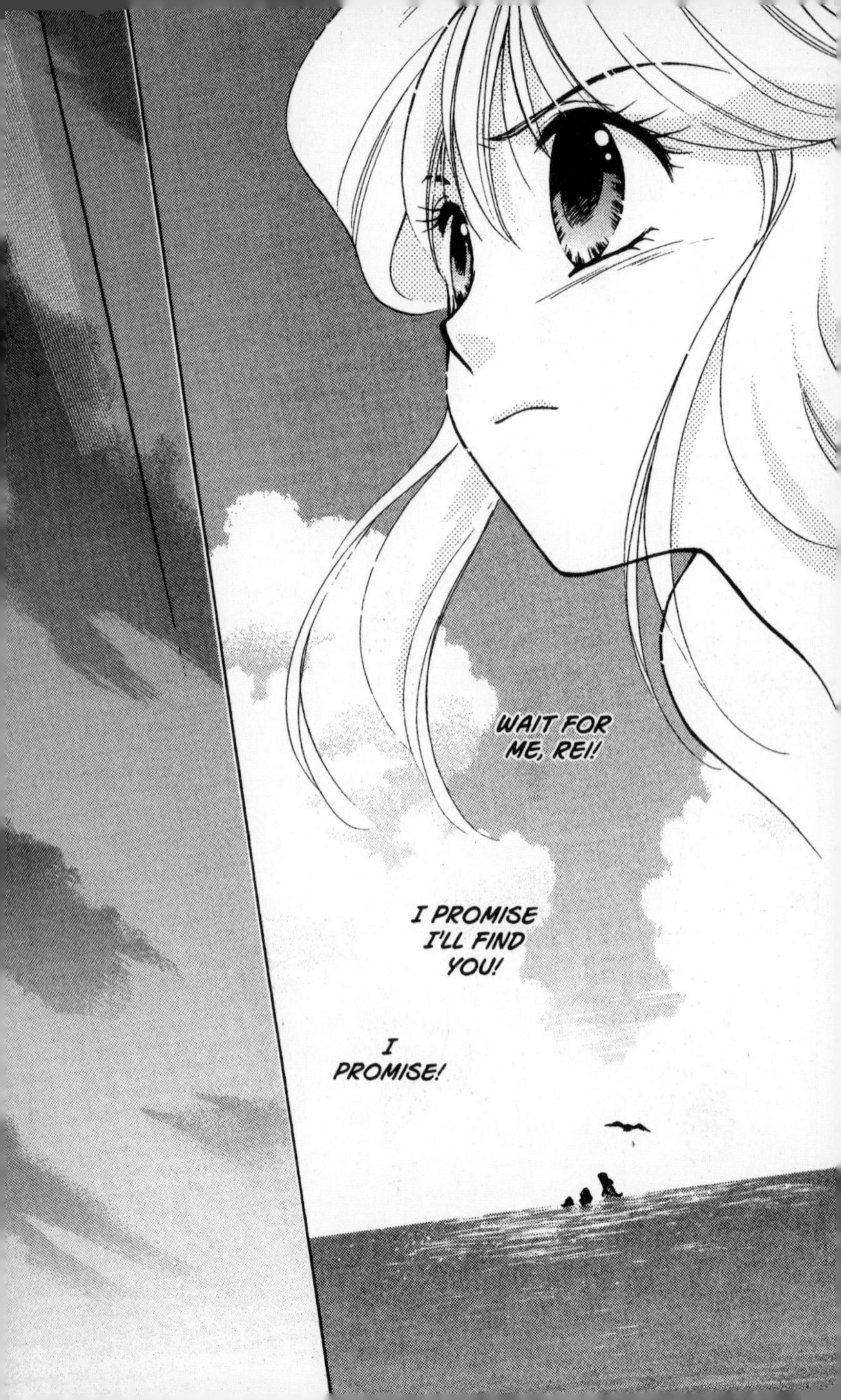
WAIT FOR ME, REI!
I PROMISE I'LL FIND YOU!
I PROMISE!

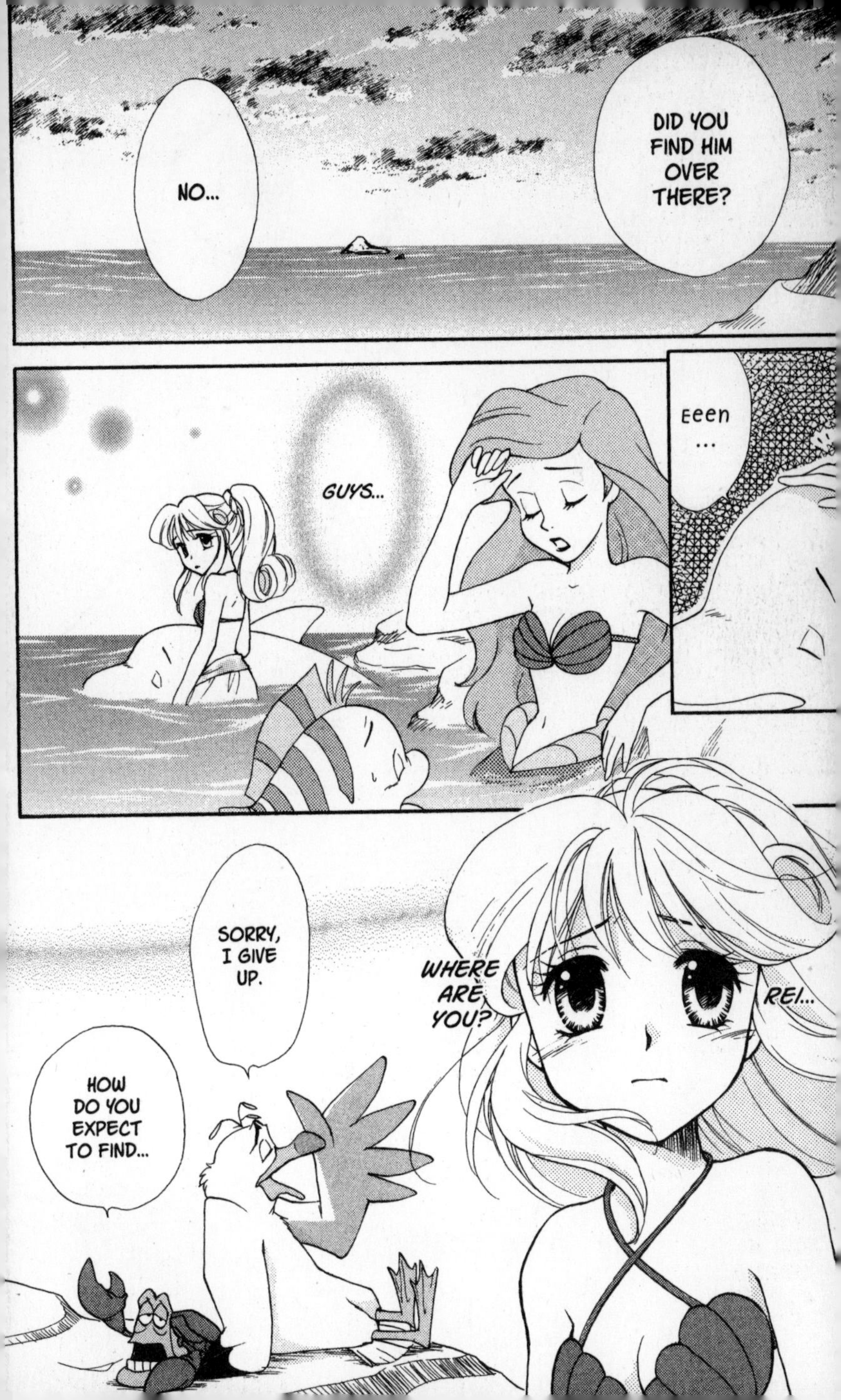
DID YOU FIND HIM OVER THERE?
NO...
Eeen ...
GUYS...
REI...
WHERE ARE YOU?
SORRY, I GIVE UP.
HOW DO YOU EXPECT TO FIND...

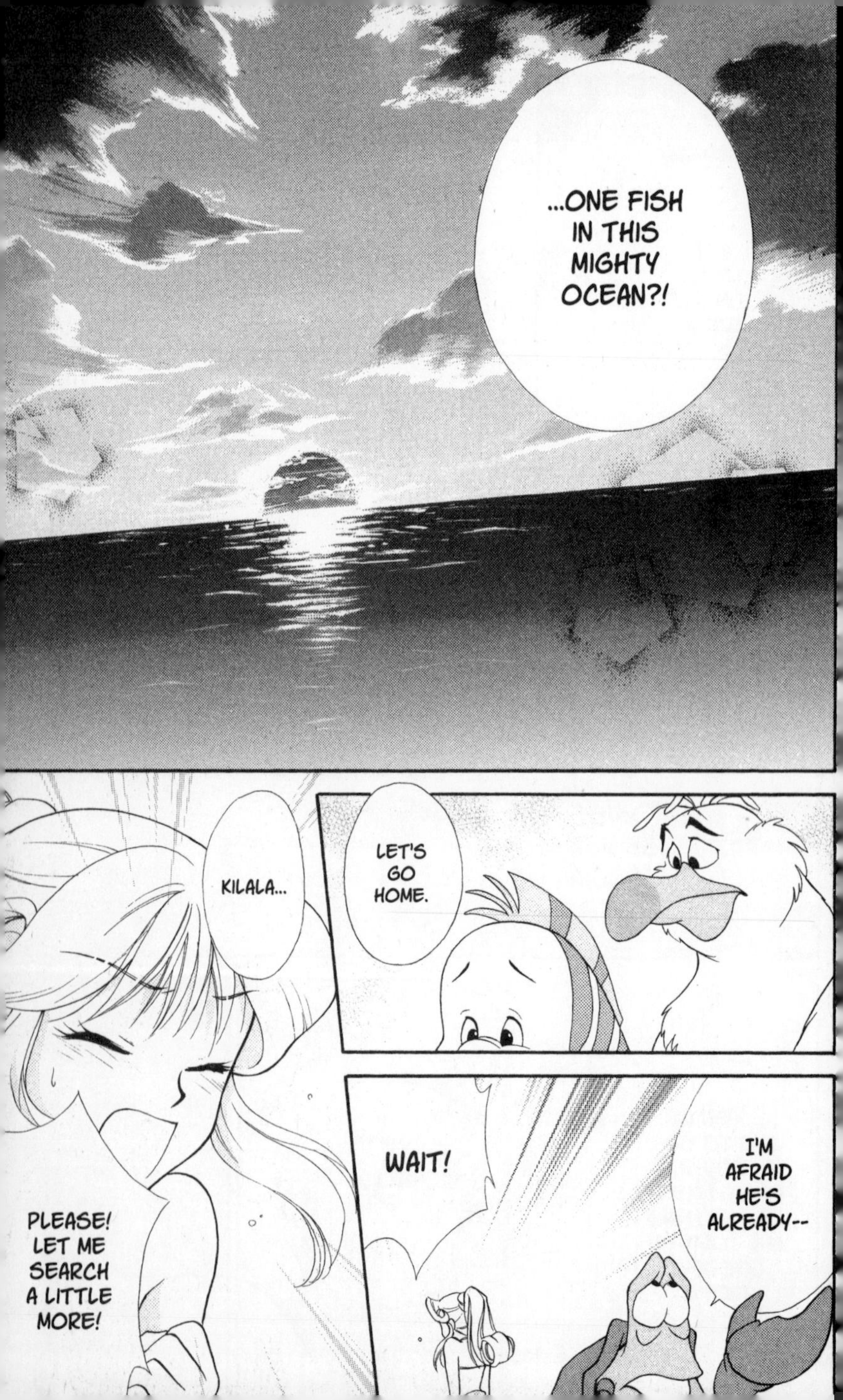
...ONE FISH IN THIS MIGHTY OCEAN?!
LET'S GO HOME.
I'M AFRAID HE'S ALREADY--
WAIT!
KILALA...
PLEASE! LET ME SEARCH A LITTLE MORE!

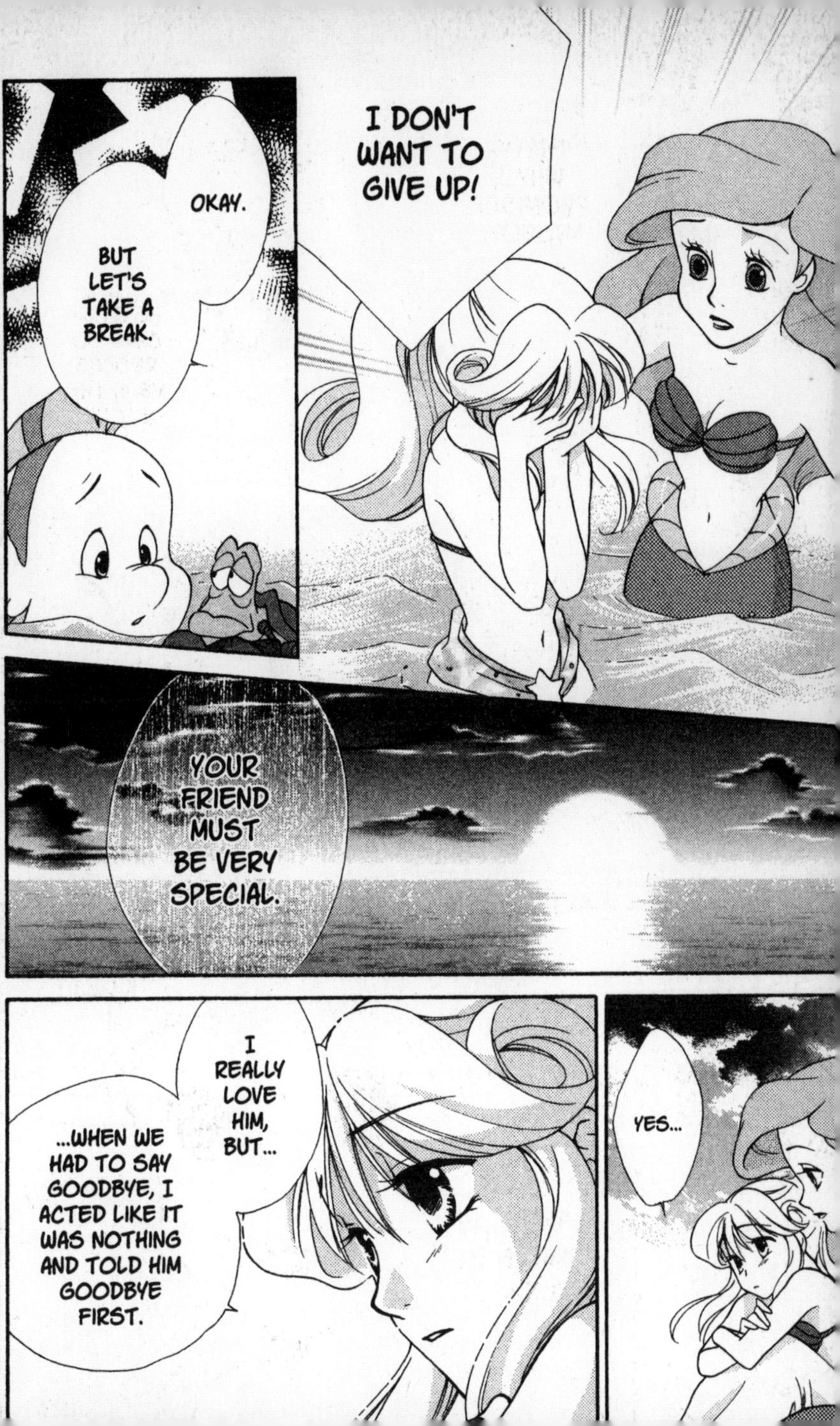
I DON'T WANT TO GIVE UP!
OKAY.
BUT LET'S TAKE A BREAK.
YOUR FRIEND MUST BE VERY SPECIAL.
YES...
I REALLY LOVE HIM, BUT...
...WHEN WE HAD TO SAY GOODBYE, I ACTED LIKE IT WAS NOTHING AND TOLD HIM GOODBYE FIRST.

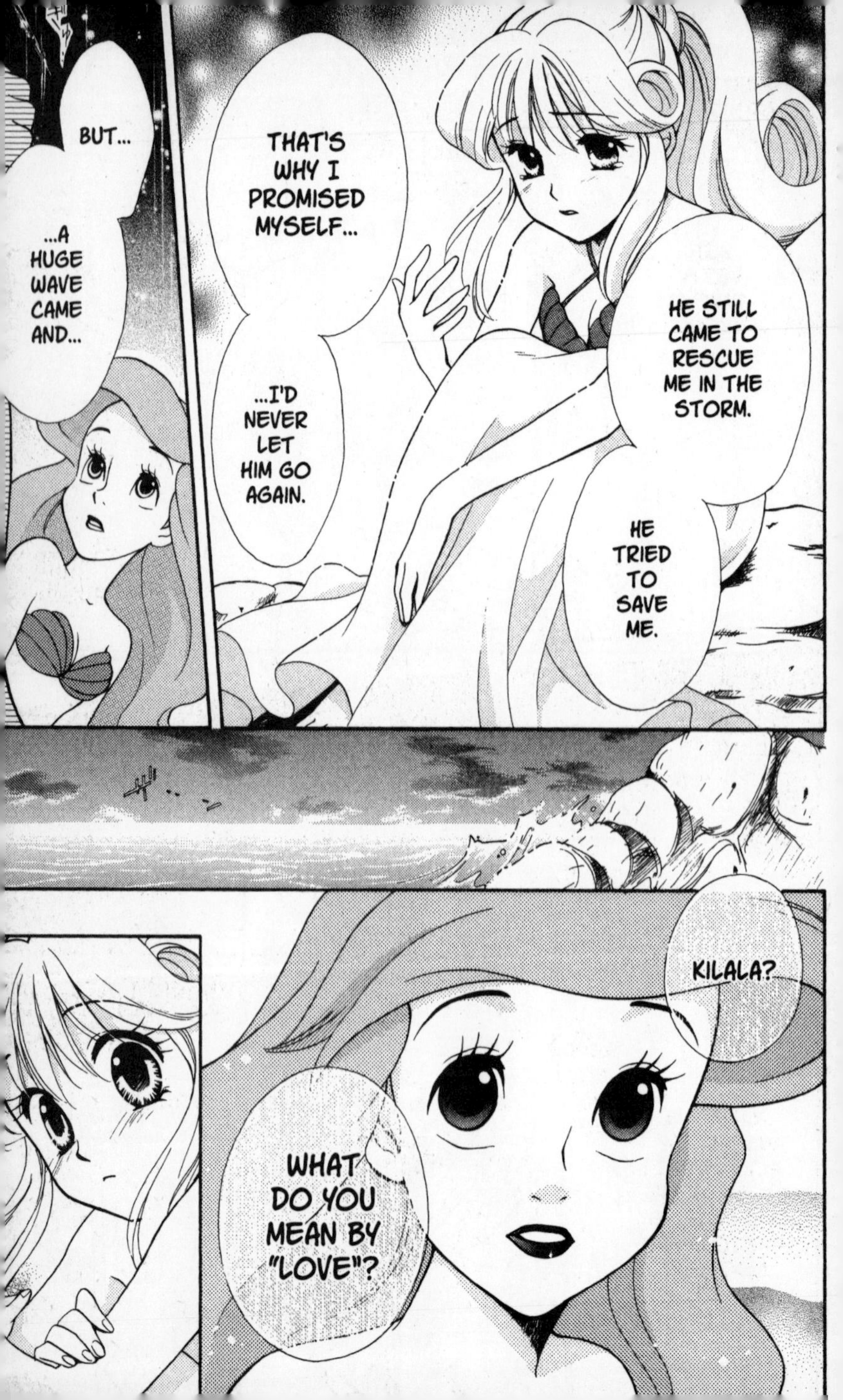
HE STILL CAME TO RESCUE ME IN THE STORM.
HE TRIED TO SAVE ME.
THAT'S WHY I PROMISED MYSELF...
...I'D NEVER LET HIM GO AGAIN.
BUT...
...A HUGE WAVE CAME AND...
KILALA?
WHAT DO YOU MEAN BY "LOVE"?

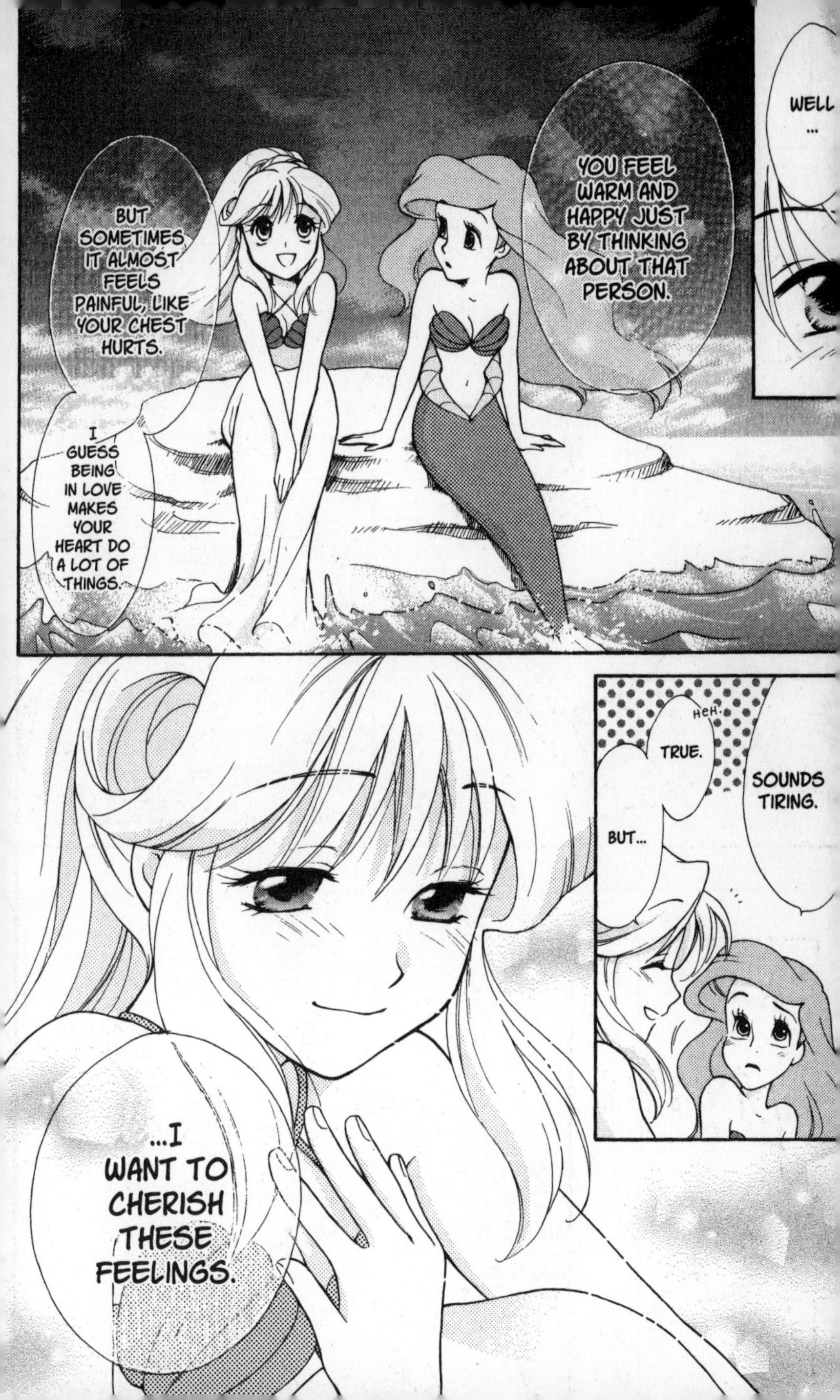
WELL ...
YOU FEEL WARM AND HAPPY JUST BY THINKING ABOUT THAT PERSON.
BUT SOMETIMES IT ALMOST FEELS PAINFUL, LIKE YOUR CHEST HURTS.
I GUESS BEING IN LOVE MAKES YOUR HEART DO A LOT OF THINGS.
SOUNDS TIRING.
HEH.
TRUE.
BUT...
...I WANT TO CHERISH THESE FEELINGS.

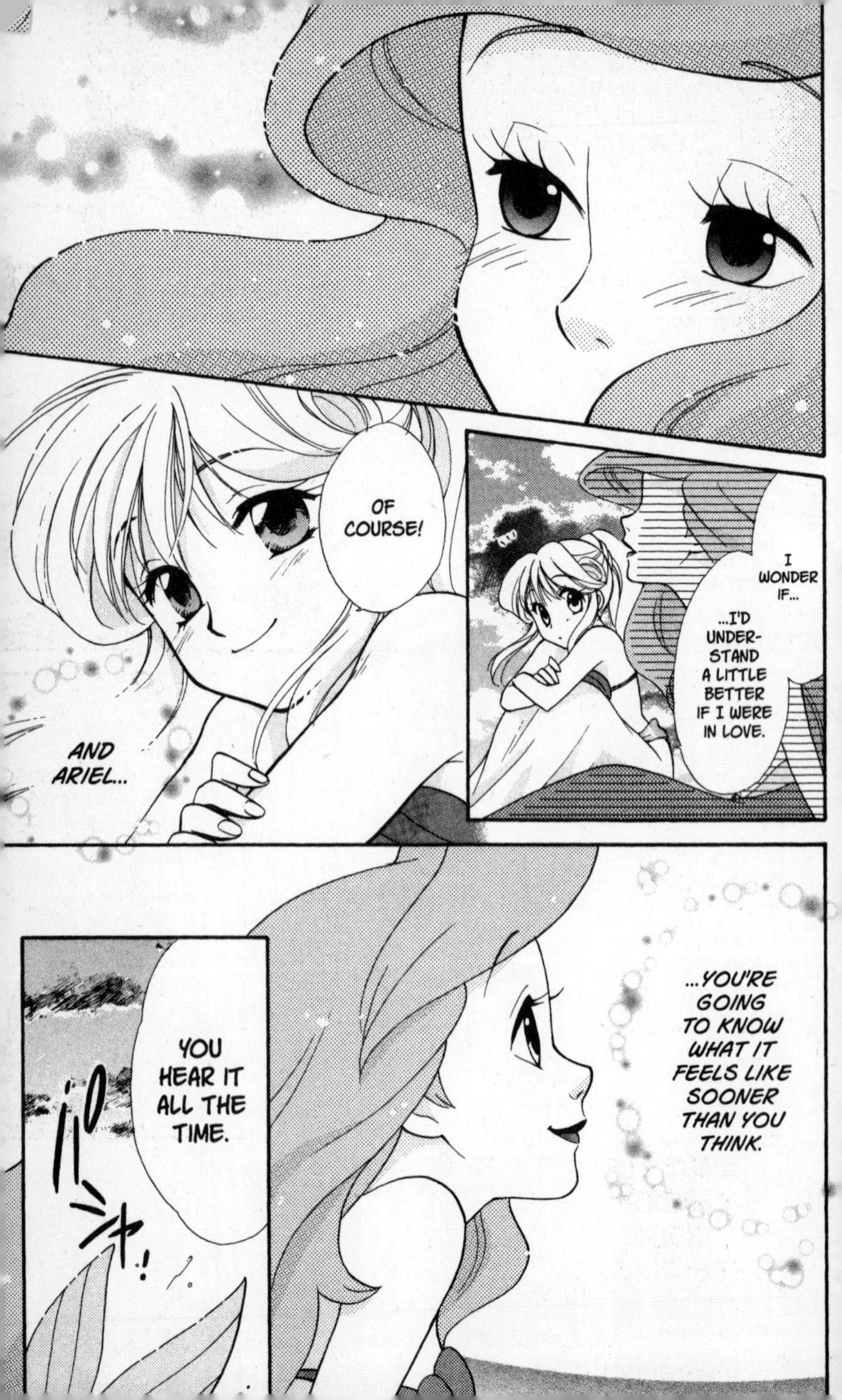
I WONDER IF...
...I'D UNDER-STAND A LITTLE BETTER IF I WERE IN LOVE.
OF COURSE!
AND ARIEL...
...YOU'RE GOING TO KNOW WHAT IT FEELS LIKE SOONER THAN YOU THINK.
YOU HEAR IT ALL THE TIME.
パシャ!

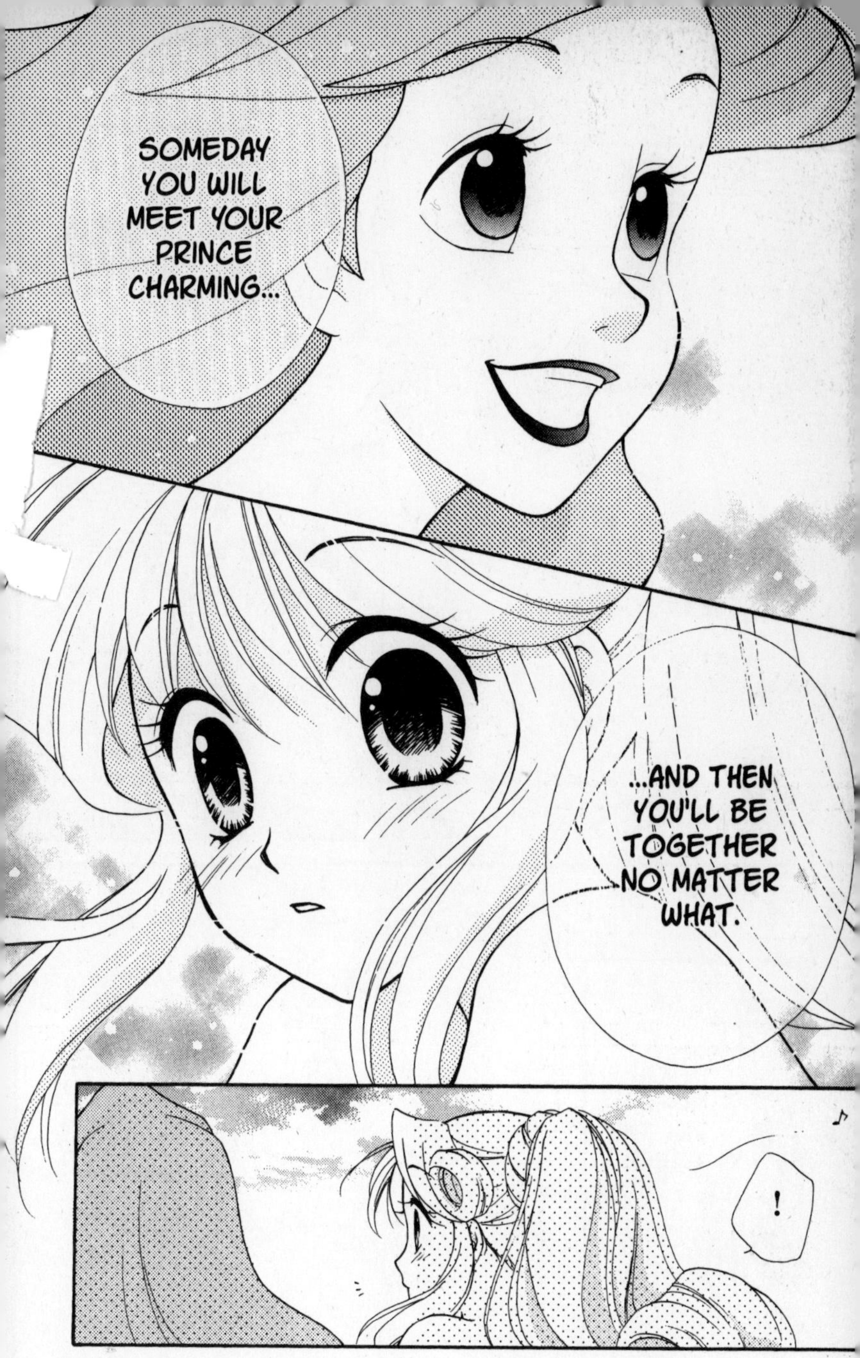
SOMEDAY YOU WILL MEET YOUR PRINCE CHARMING...
...AND THEN YOU'LL BE TOGETHER NO MATTER WHAT.
!

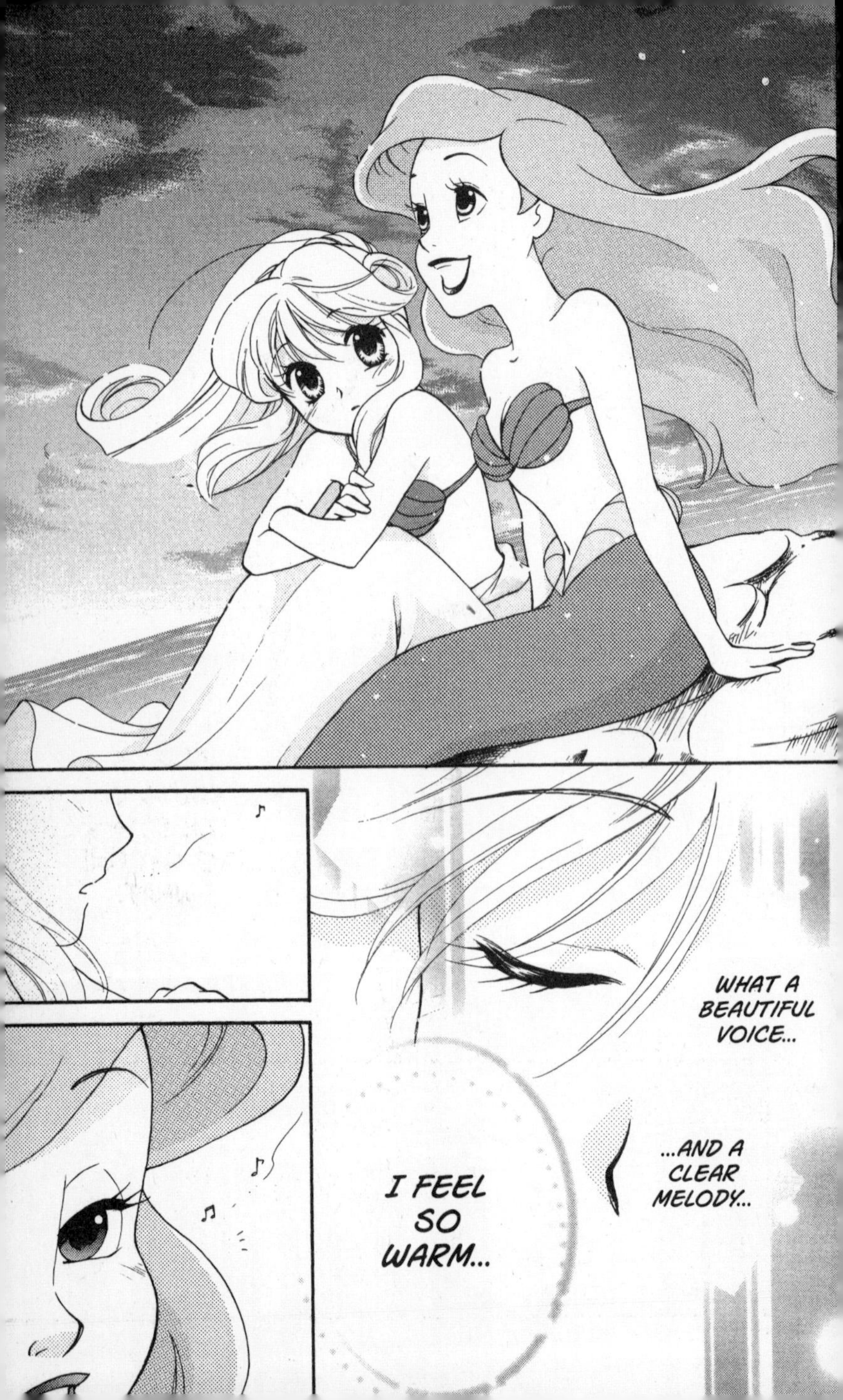
WHAT A BEAUTIFUL VOICE...
...AND A CLEAR MELODY...
I FEEL SO WARM...

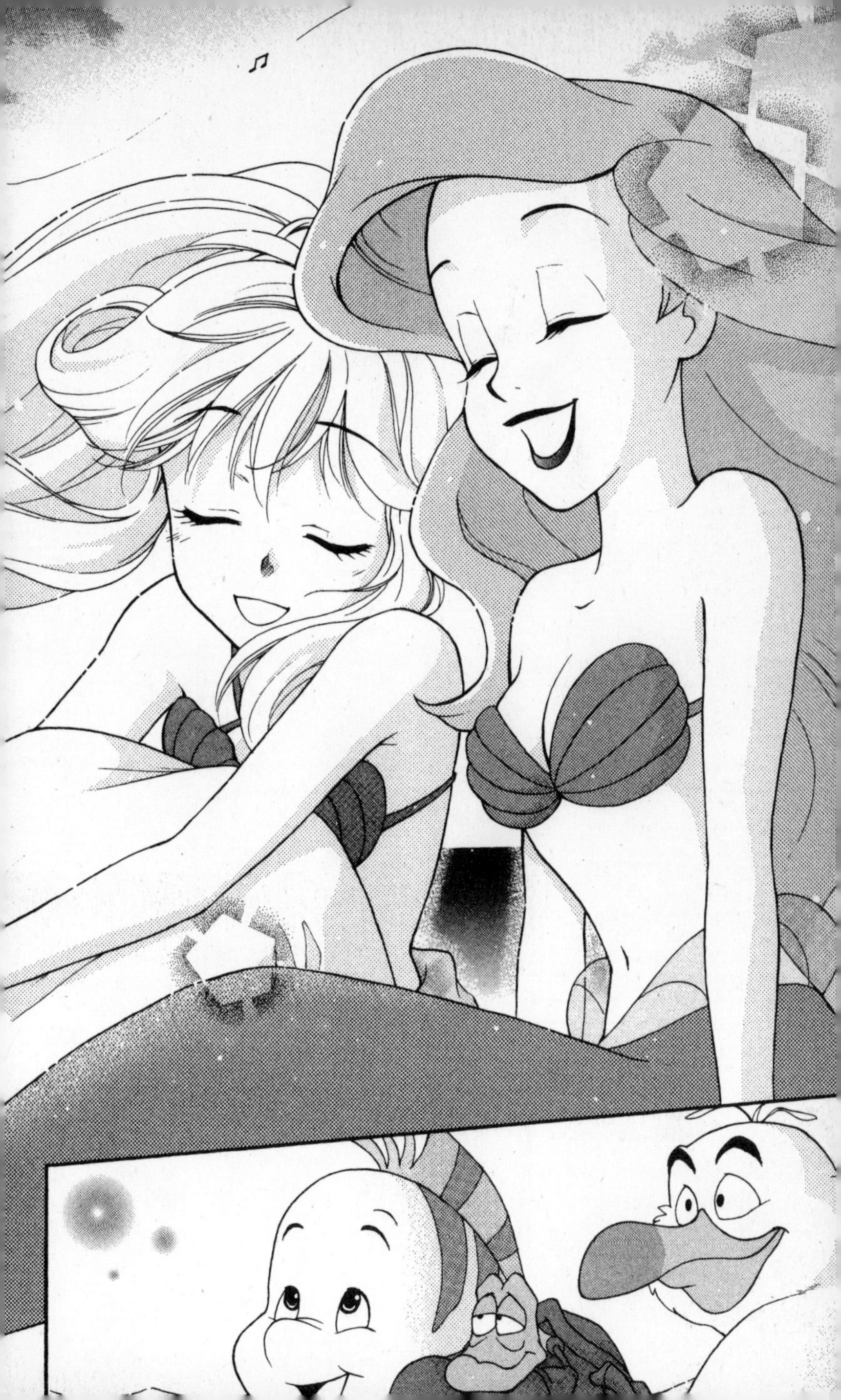

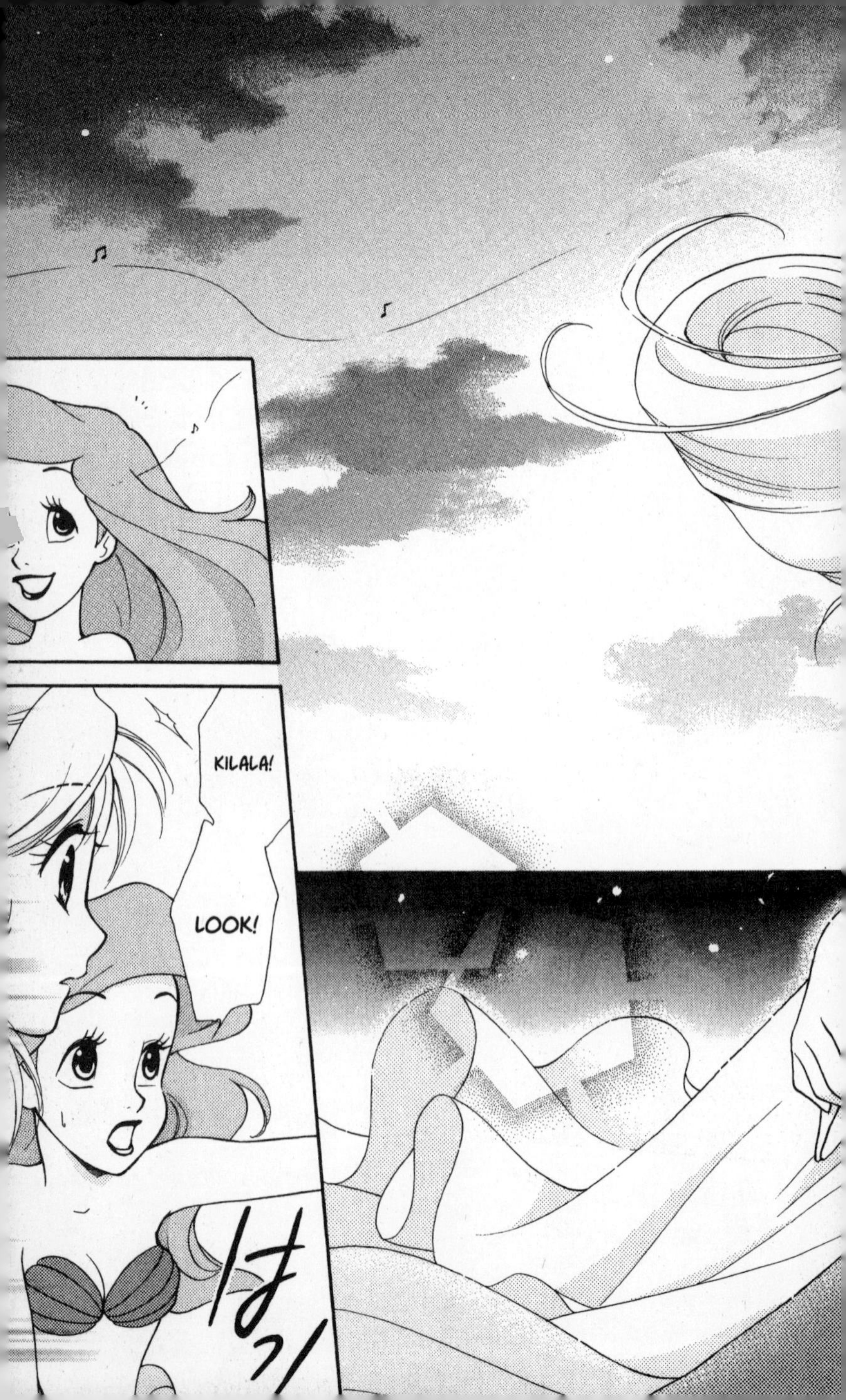
KILALA!
LOOK!
はっ

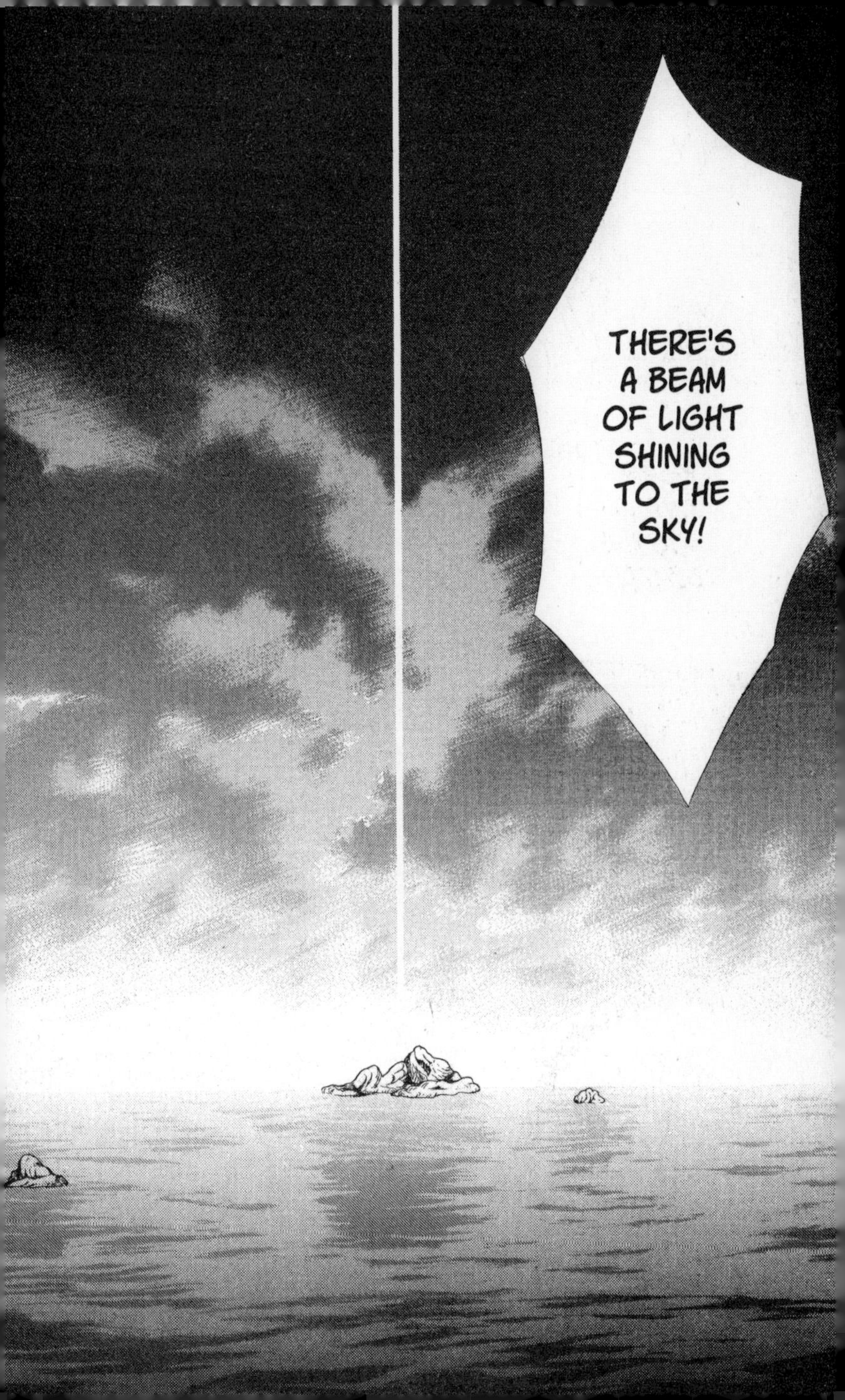
THERE'S A BEAM OF LIGHT SHINING TO THE SKY!

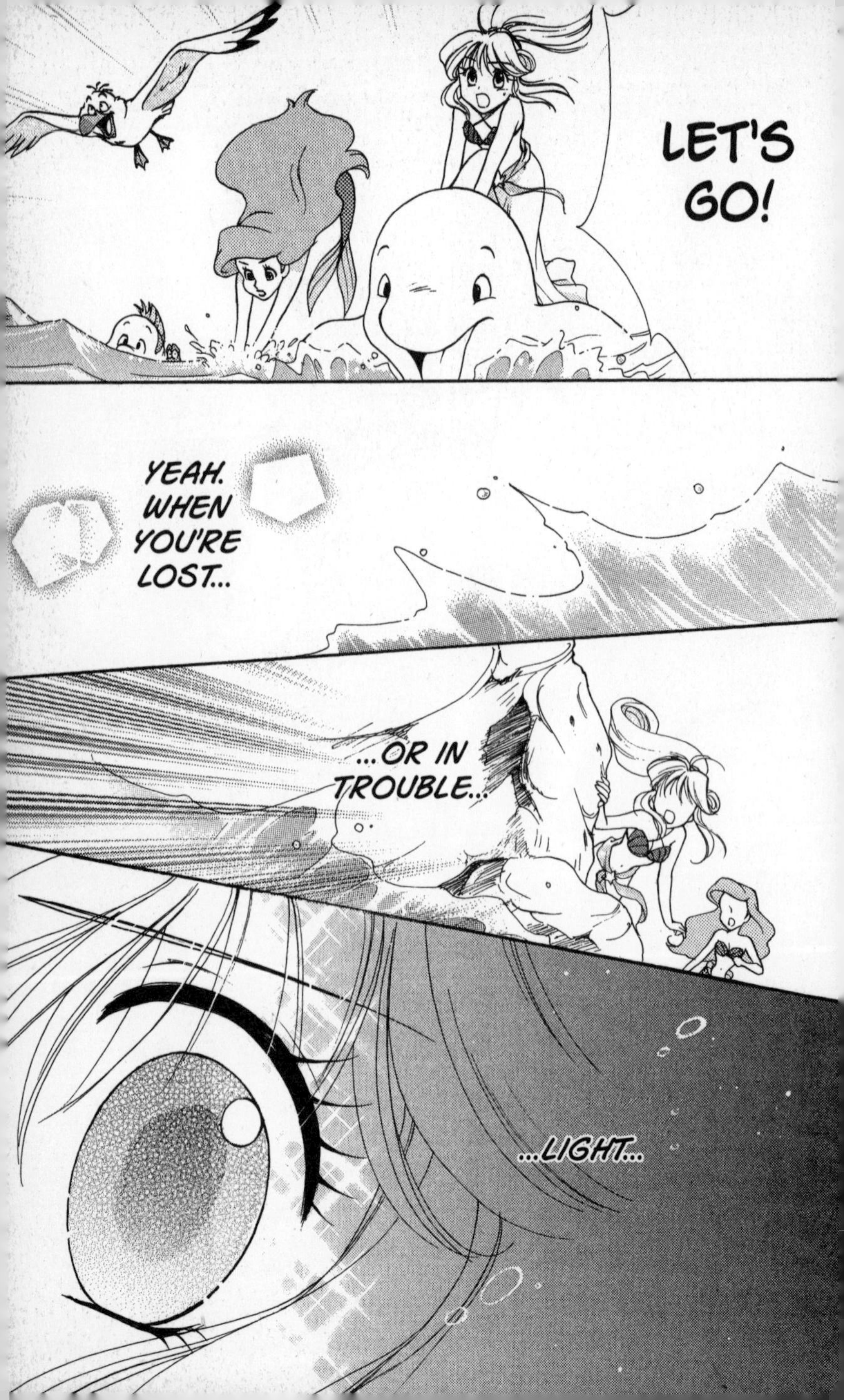
LET'S GO!
YEAH. WHEN YOU'RE LOST...
...OR IN TROUBLE...
...LIGHT...

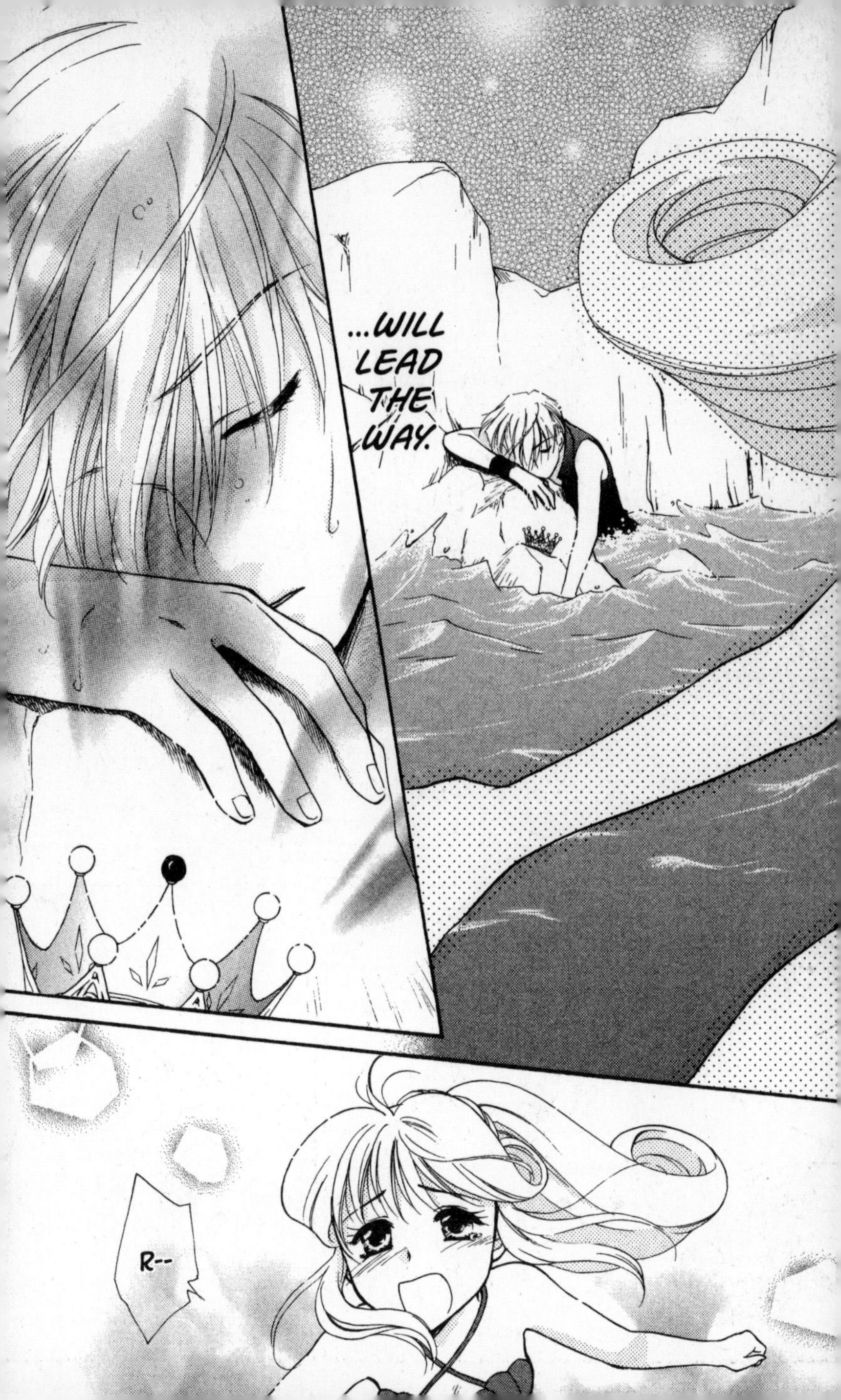
...WILL LEAD THE WAY.
R--

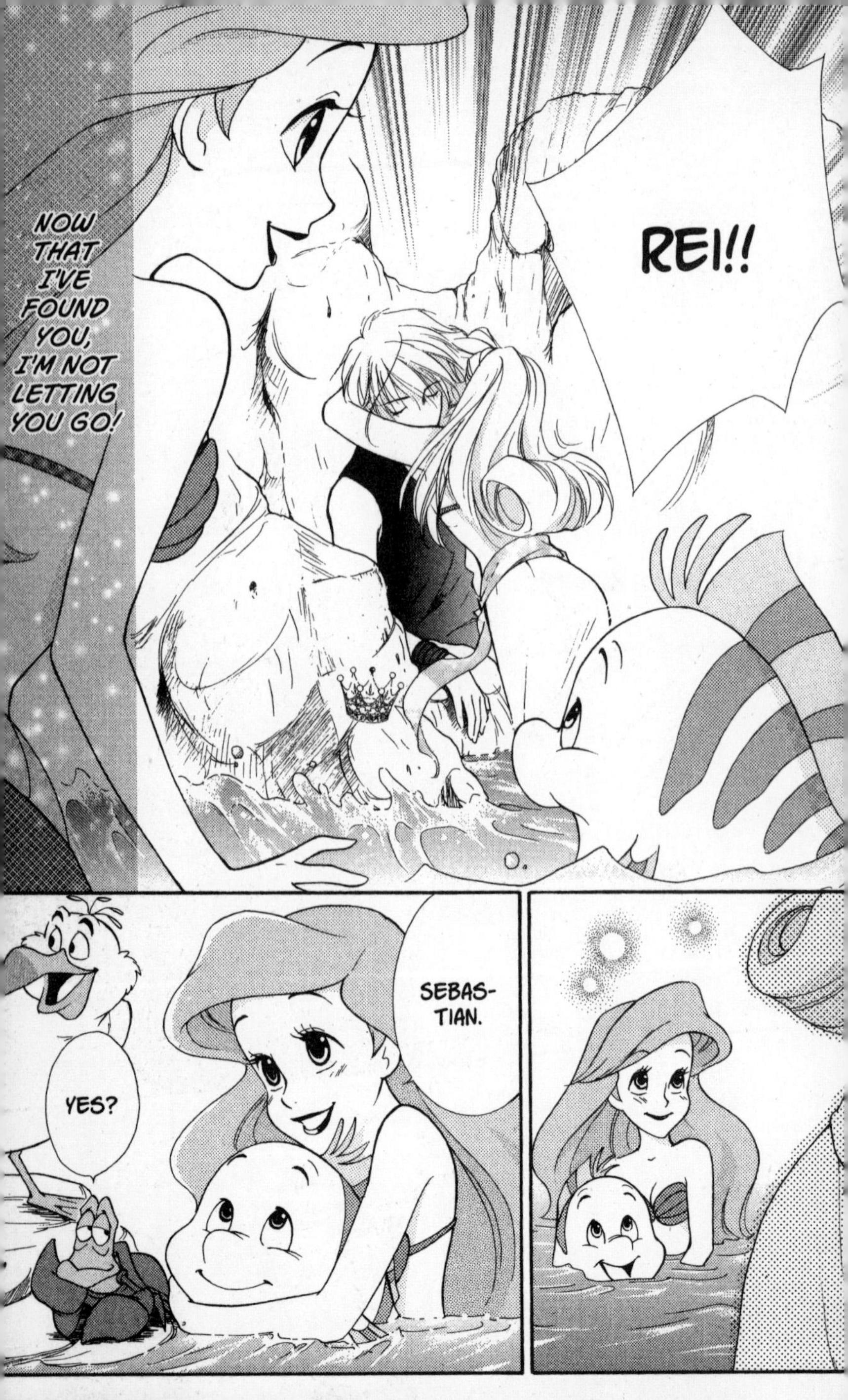
REI!!
NOW THAT I'VE FOUND YOU, I'M NOT LETTING YOU GO!
SEBAS-TIAN.
YES?

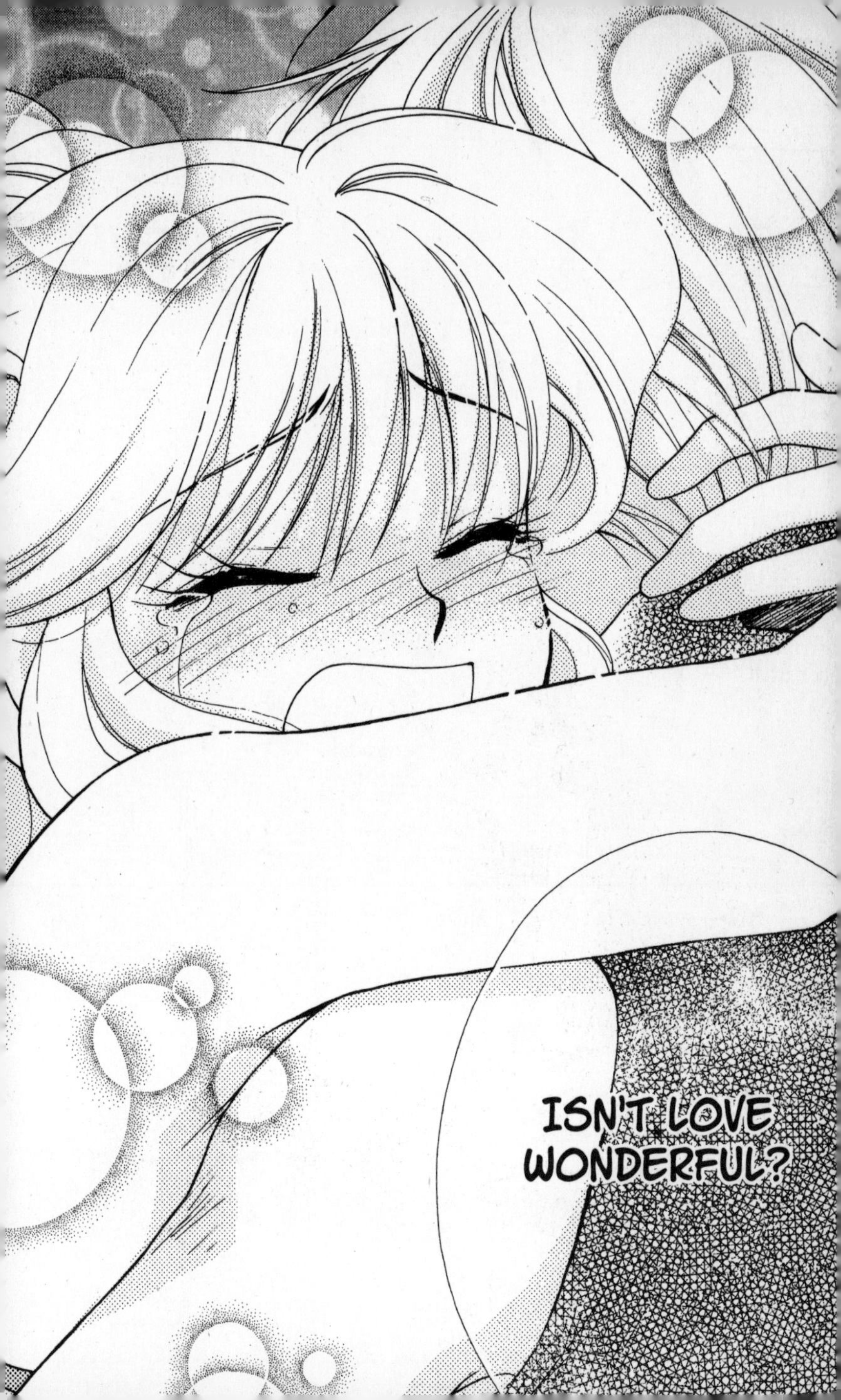
ISN'T LOVE
WONDERFUL?

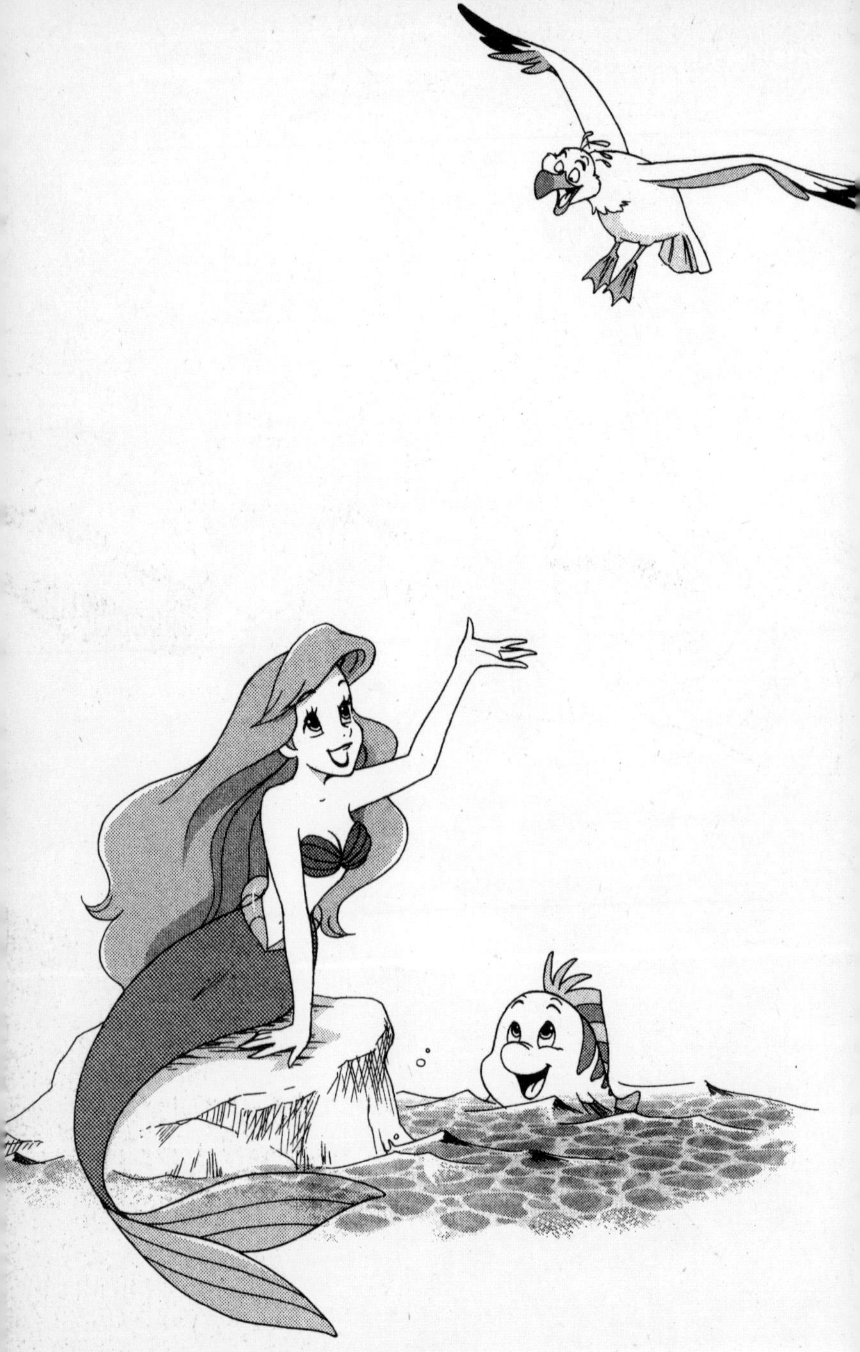

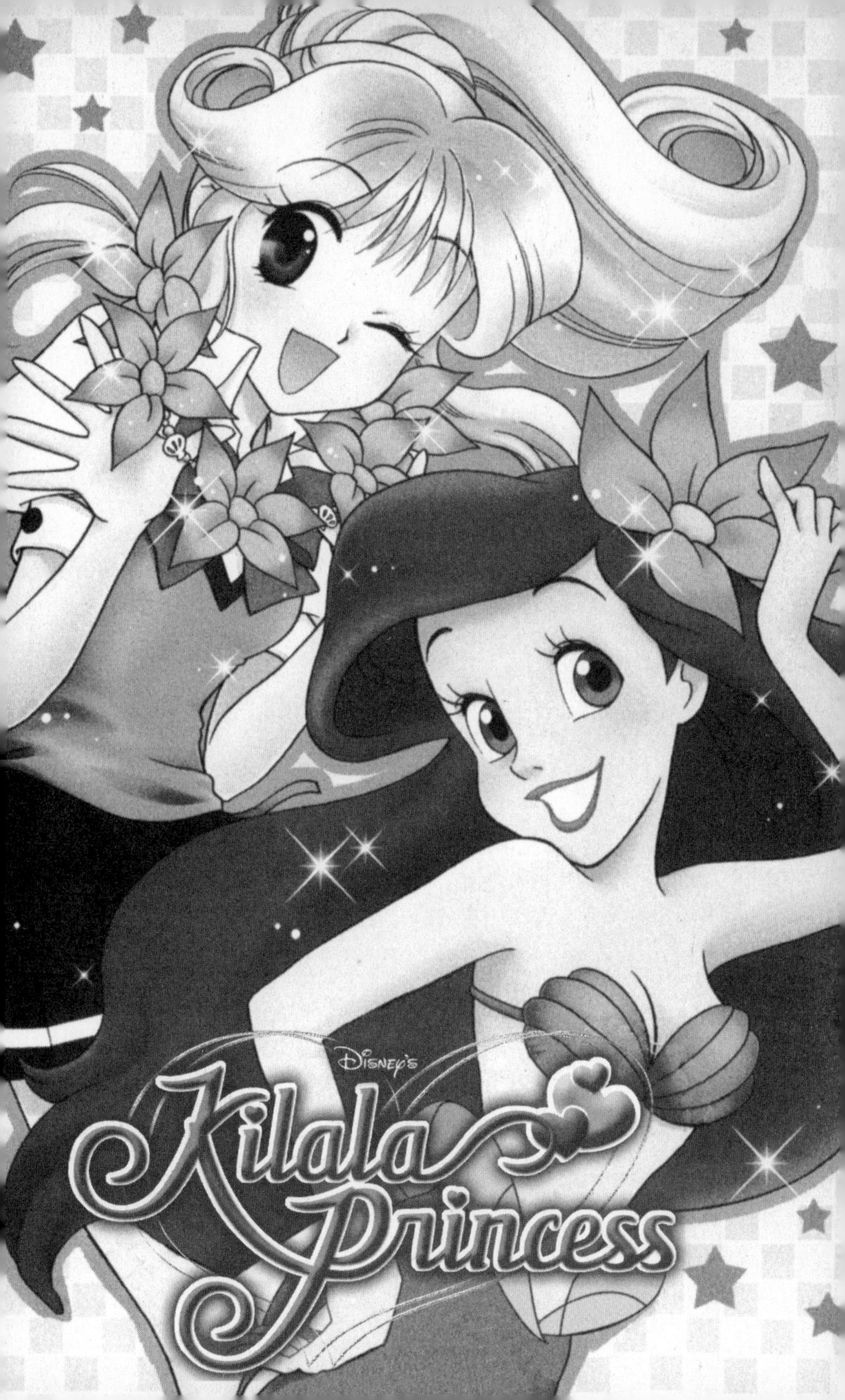
Disney's
Kilala Princess

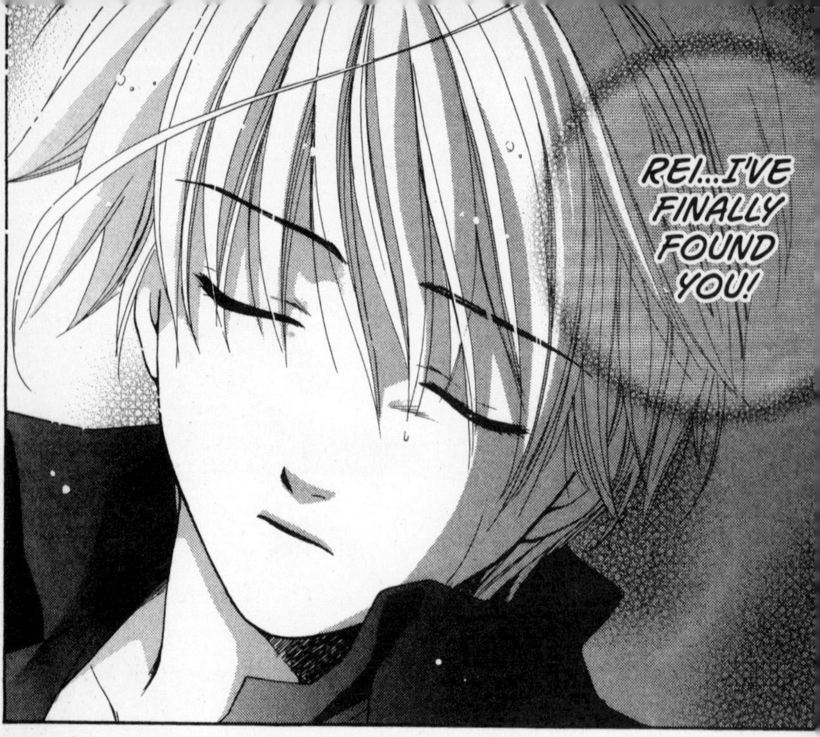
REI...I'VE FINALLY FOUND YOU!

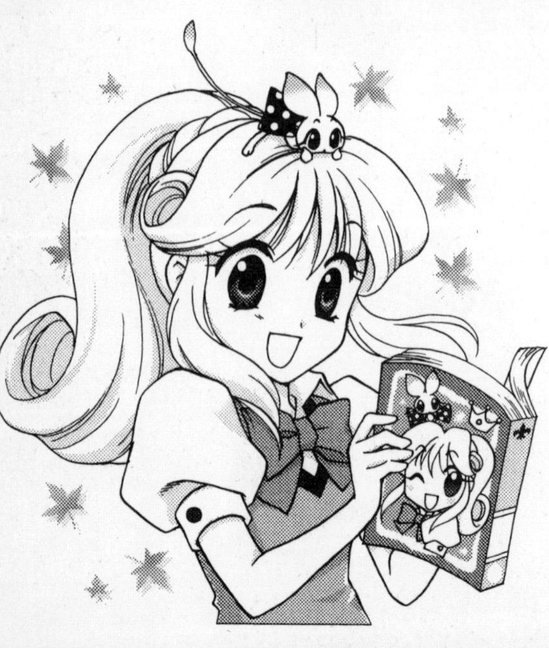

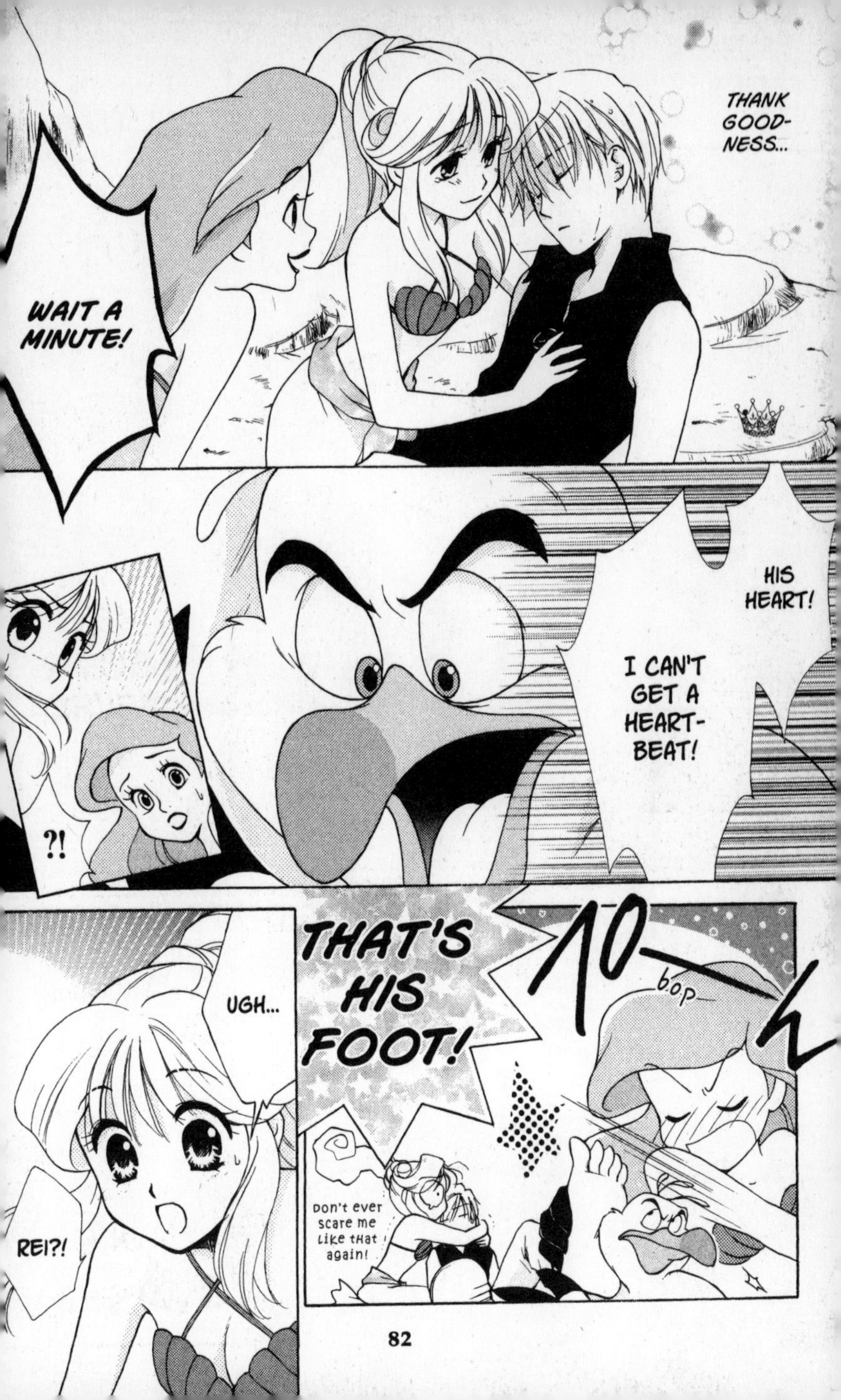
THANK GOODNESS...
WAIT A MINUTE!
HIS HEART!
I CAN'T GET A HEARTBEAT!
?!
THAT'S HIS FOOT!
bop
Don't ever scare me like that again!
UGH...
REI?!

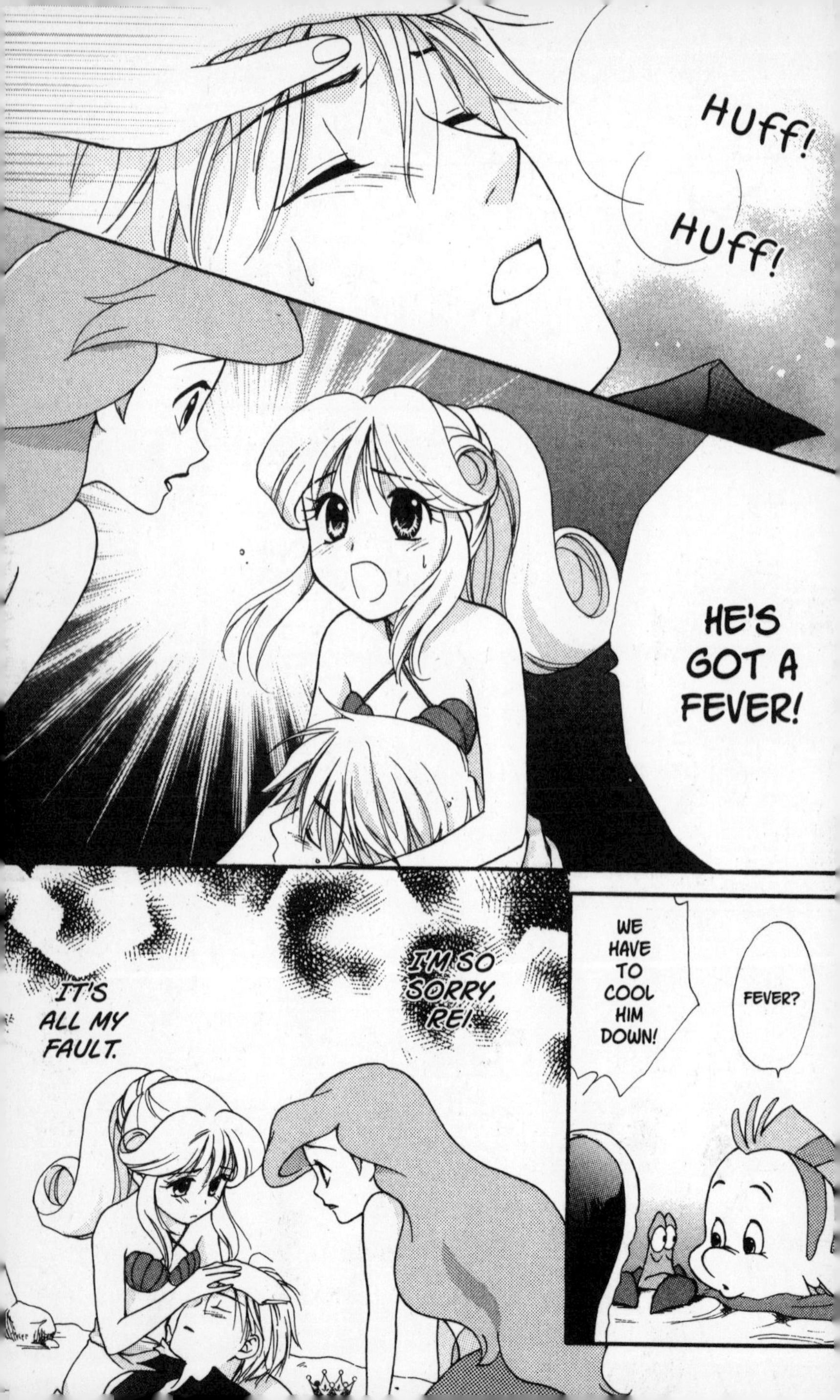
HUFF!
HUFF!
HE'S GOT A FEVER!
FEVER?
WE HAVE TO COOL HIM DOWN!
I'M SO SORRY, REI.
IT'S ALL MY FAULT.

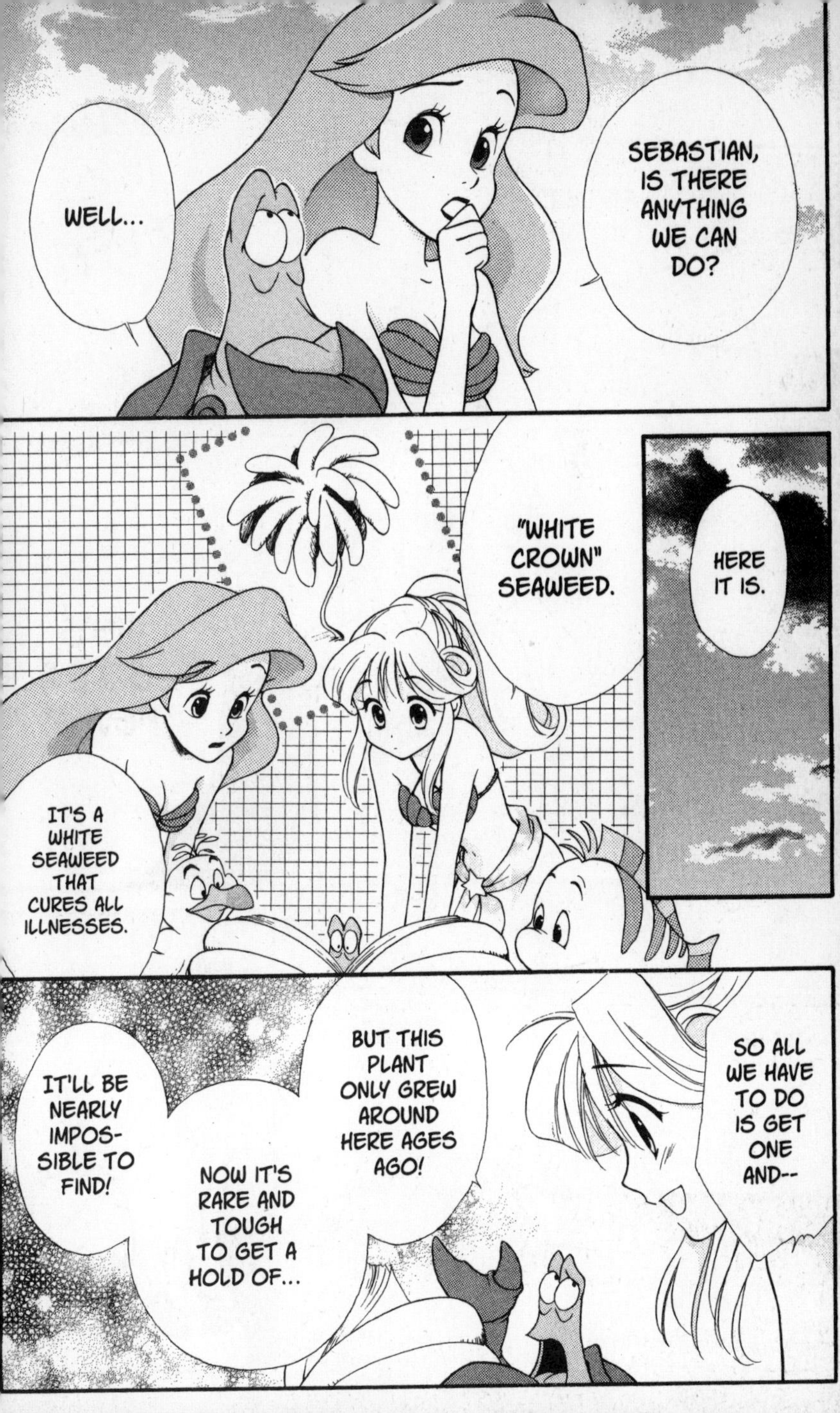
SEBASTIAN, IS THERE ANYTHING WE CAN DO?
WELL...
HERE IT IS.
"WHITE CROWN" SEAWEED.
IT'S A WHITE SEAWEED THAT CURES ALL ILLNESSES.
SO ALL WE HAVE TO DO IS GET ONE AND--
BUT THIS PLANT ONLY GREW AROUND HERE AGES AGO!
NOW IT'S RARE AND TOUGH TO GET A HOLD OF...
IT'LL BE NEARLY IMPOS-SIBLE TO FIND!

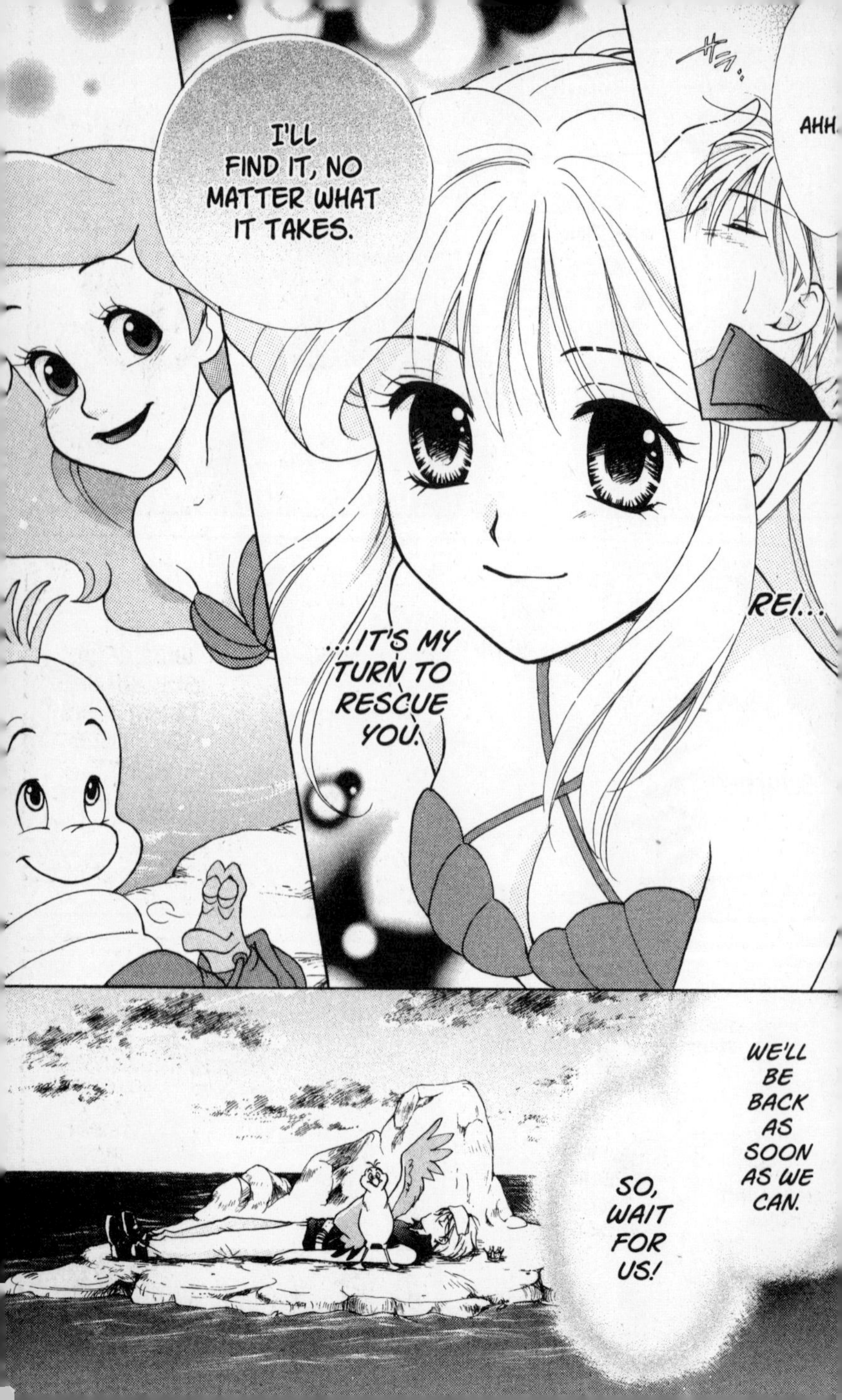
AHH...
REI...
I'LL FIND IT, NO MATTER WHAT IT TAKES.
...IT'S MY TURN TO RESCUE YOU.
WE'LL BE BACK AS SOON AS WE CAN.
SO, WAIT FOR US!

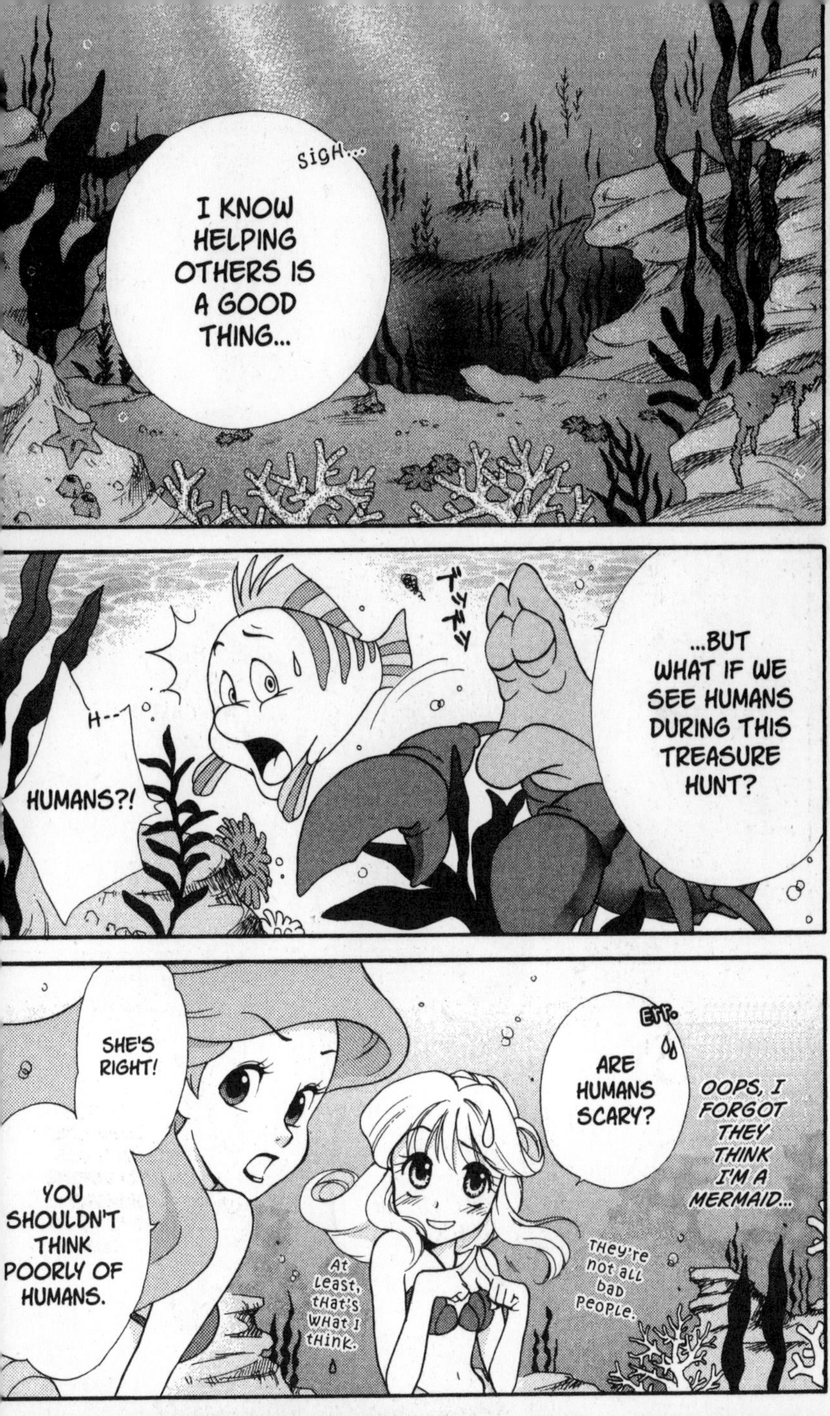
SIGH...
I KNOW HELPING OTHERS IS A GOOD THING...
...BUT WHAT IF WE SEE HUMANS DURING THIS TREASURE HUNT?
H--
HUMANS?!
OOPS, I FORGOT THEY THINK I'M A MERMAID...
Err.
ARE HUMANS SCARY?
They're not all bad people.
At least, that's what I think.
SHE'S RIGHT!
YOU SHOULDN'T THINK POORLY OF HUMANS.

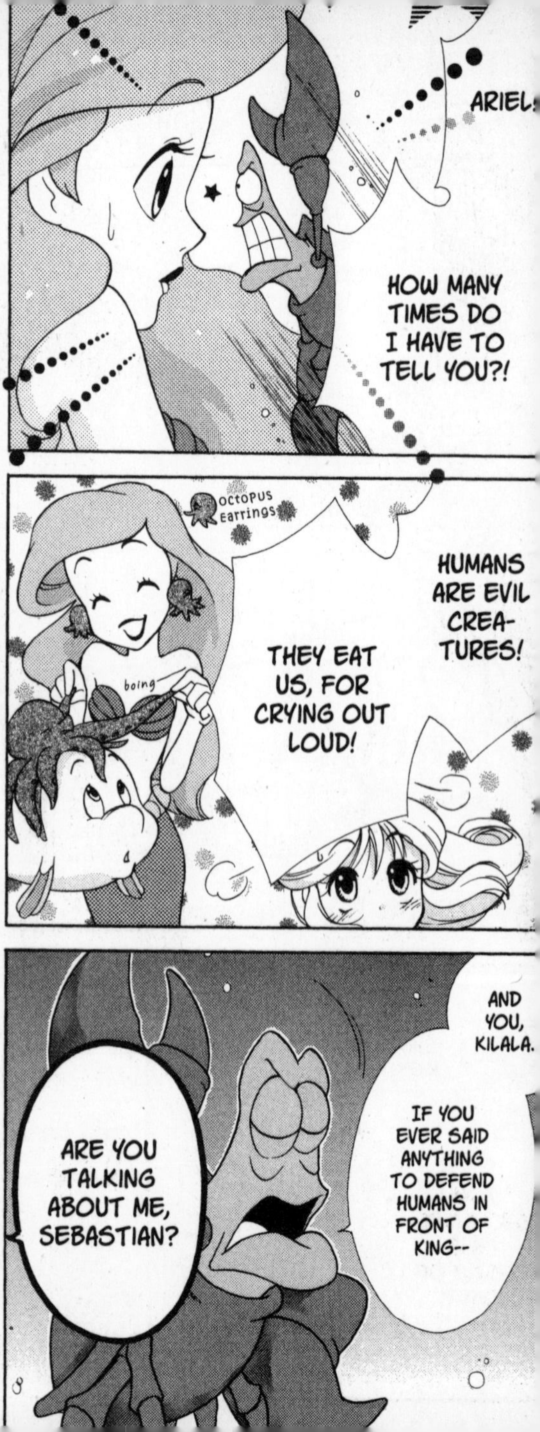
ARIEL!
HOW MANY TIMES DO I HAVE TO TELL YOU?!
HUMANS ARE EVIL CREA- TURES!
THEY EAT US, FOR CRYING OUT LOUD!
Octopus Earrings
boing
AND YOU, KILALA.
IF YOU EVER SAID ANYTHING TO DEFEND HUMANS IN FRONT OF KING--
ARE YOU TALKING ABOUT ME, SEBASTIAN?

A WORD FROM TIPPE

3

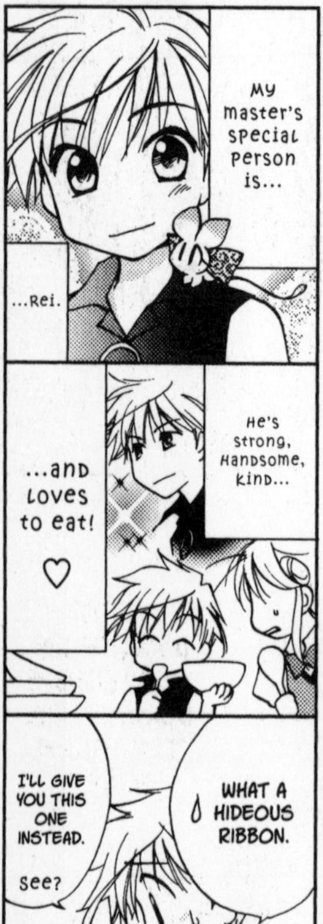
My master's special person is...
...Rei.
He's strong, handsome, kind...
...and loves to eat! ♡
WHAT A HIDEOUS RIBBON.
I'LL GIVE YOU THIS ONE INSTEAD.
see?
...♡
um.
HOW DO YOU TIE A BOW AGAIN?
!!!

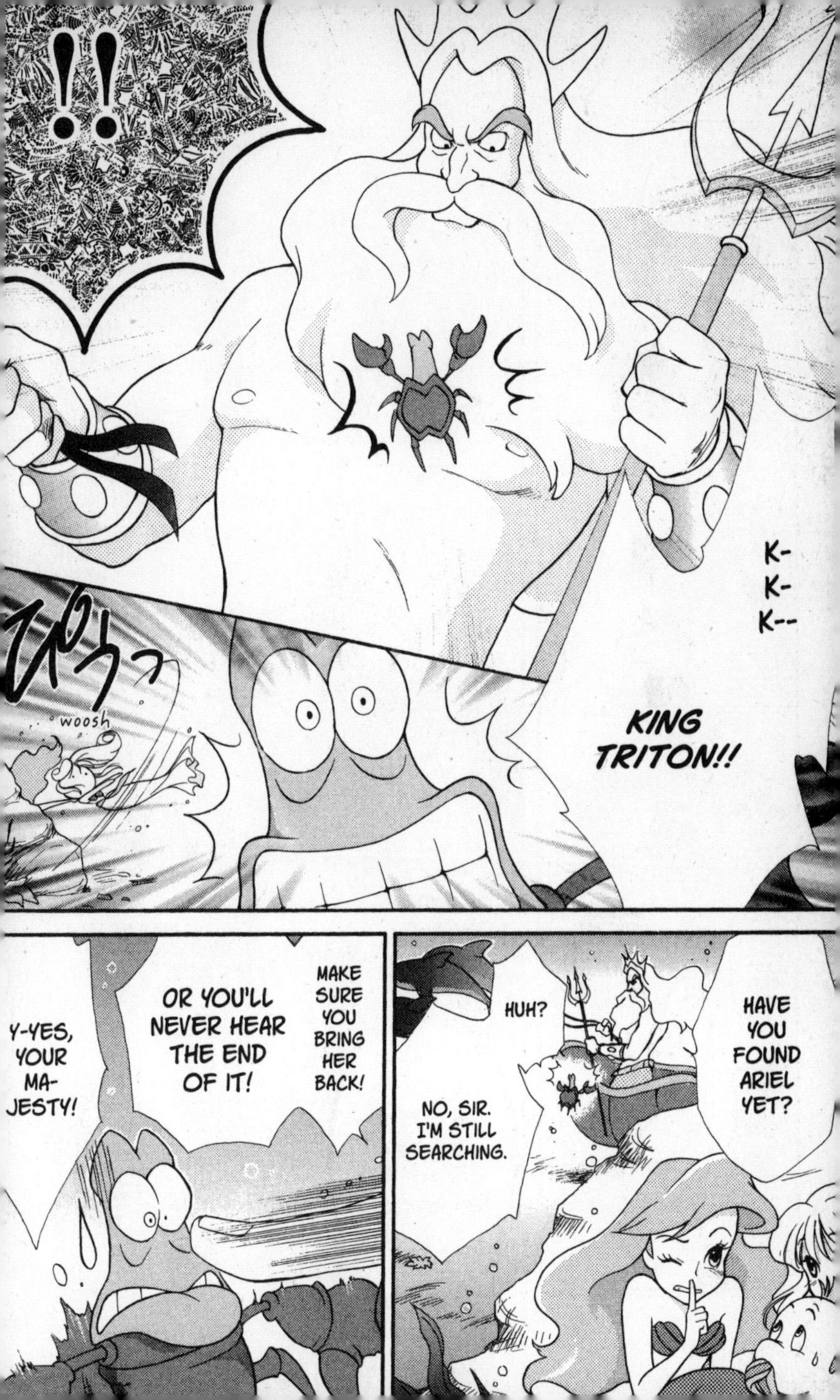
!!
K-
K-
K--
KING TRITON!!
woosh
HAVE YOU FOUND ARIEL YET?
HUH?
NO, SIR. I'M STILL SEARCHING.
MAKE SURE YOU BRING HER BACK!
OR YOU'LL NEVER HEAR THE END OF IT!
Y-YES, YOUR MA-JESTY!

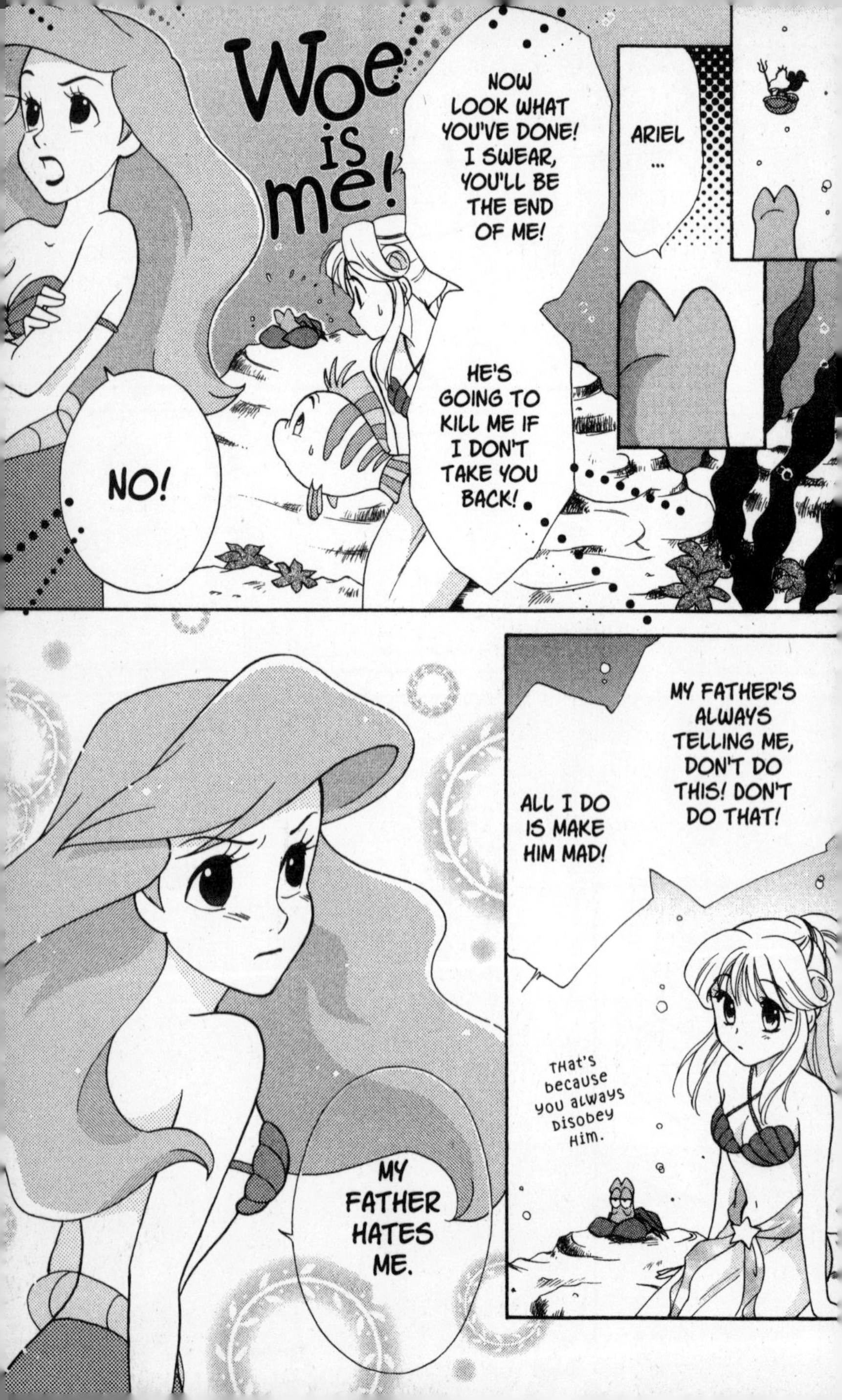
ARIEL ...
NOW LOOK WHAT YOU'VE DONE! I SWEAR, YOU'LL BE THE END OF ME!
Woe is me!
HE'S GOING TO KILL ME IF I DON'T TAKE YOU BACK!
NO!
MY FATHER'S ALWAYS TELLING ME, DON'T DO THIS! DON'T DO THAT!
ALL I DO IS MAKE HIM MAD!
That's because you always Disobey Him.
MY FATHER HATES ME.

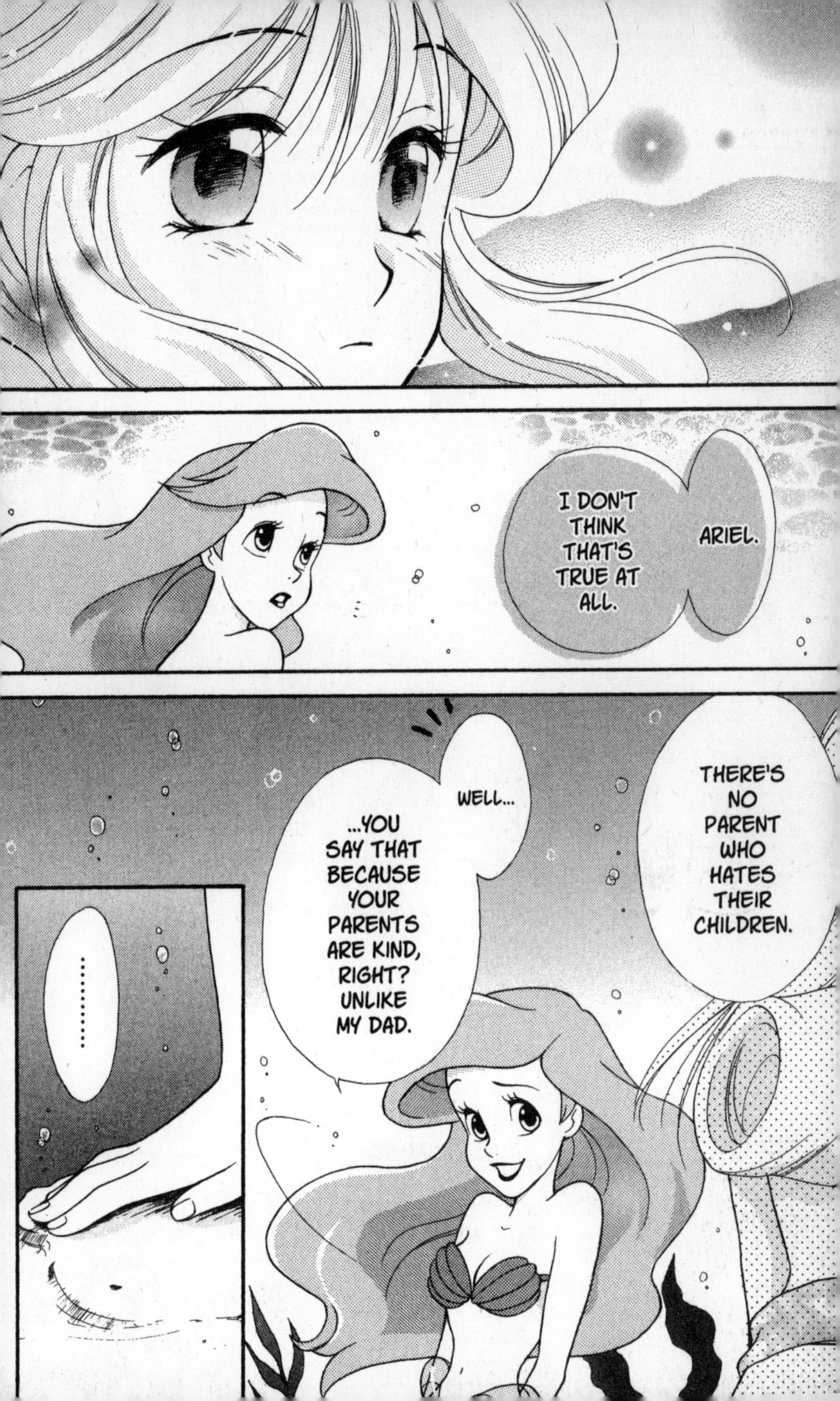
ARIEL.
I DON'T THINK THAT'S TRUE AT ALL.
THERE'S NO PARENT WHO HATES THEIR CHILDREN.
WELL...
...YOU SAY THAT BECAUSE YOUR PARENTS ARE KIND, RIGHT? UNLIKE MY DAD.
....

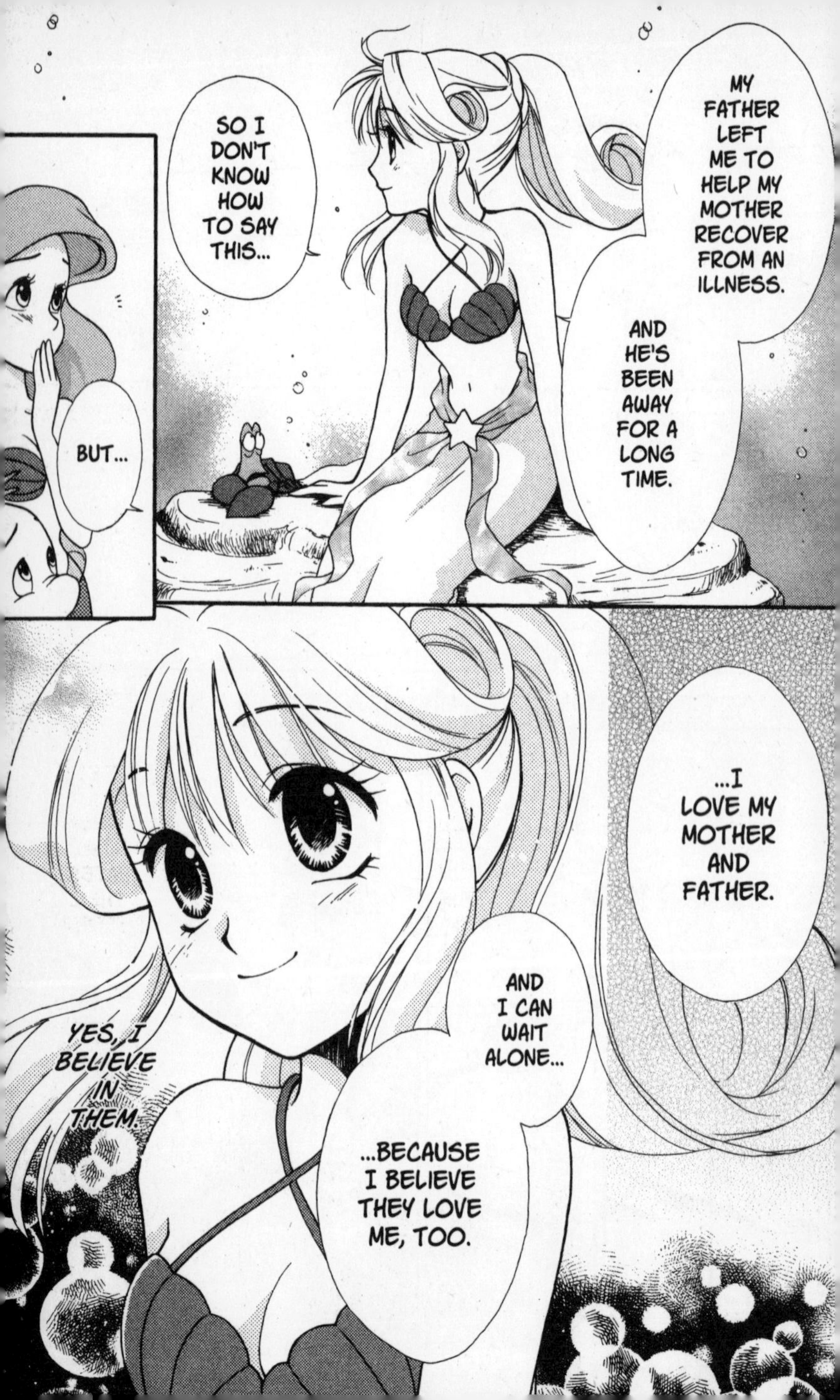
MY FATHER LEFT ME TO HELP MY MOTHER RECOVER FROM AN ILLNESS.
AND HE'S BEEN AWAY FOR A LONG TIME.
SO I DON'T KNOW HOW TO SAY THIS...
BUT...
...I LOVE MY MOTHER AND FATHER.
AND I CAN WAIT ALONE...
...BECAUSE I BELIEVE THEY LOVE ME, TOO.
YES, I BELIEVE IN THEM.

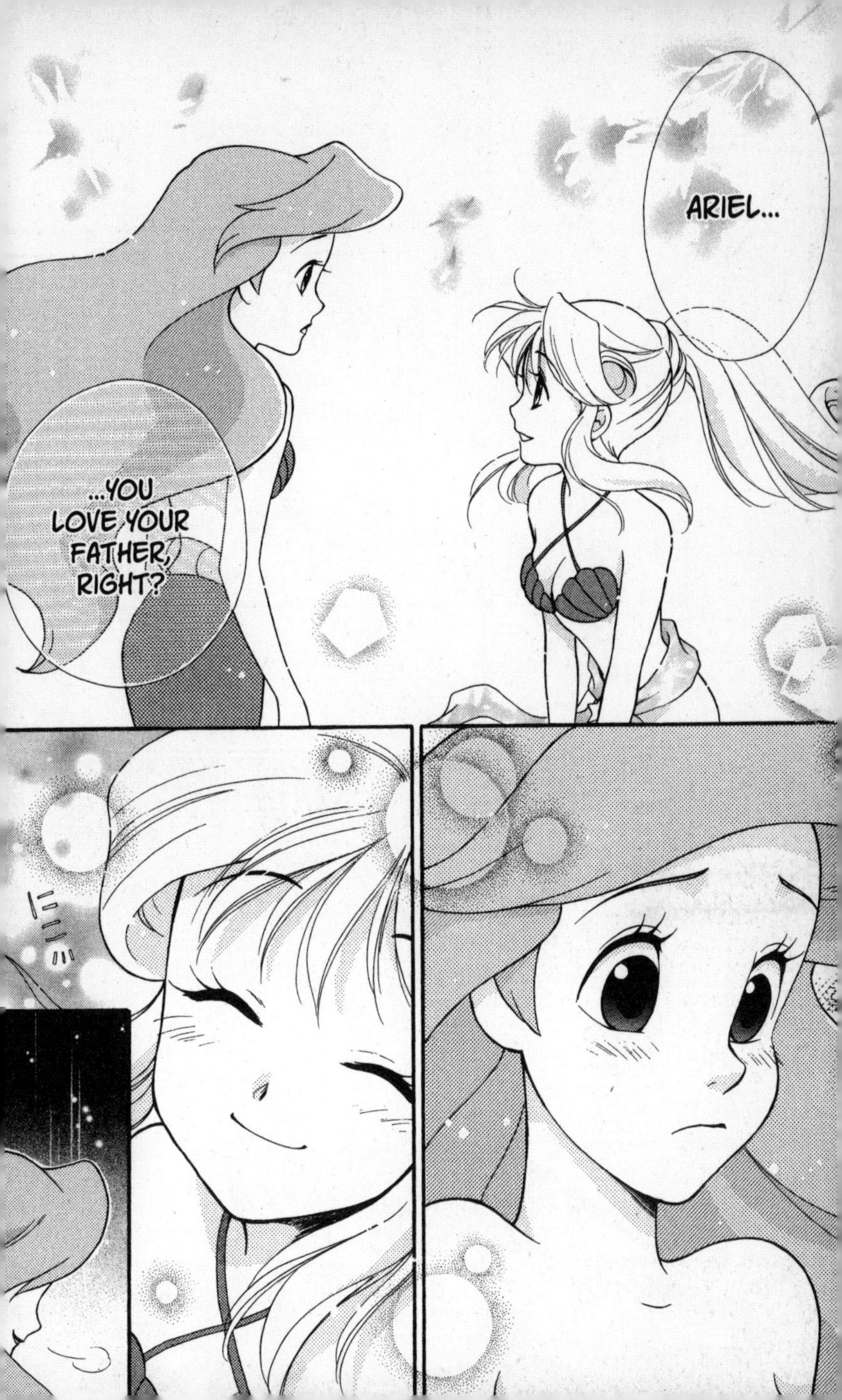
ARIEL...
...YOU LOVE YOUR FATHER, RIGHT?

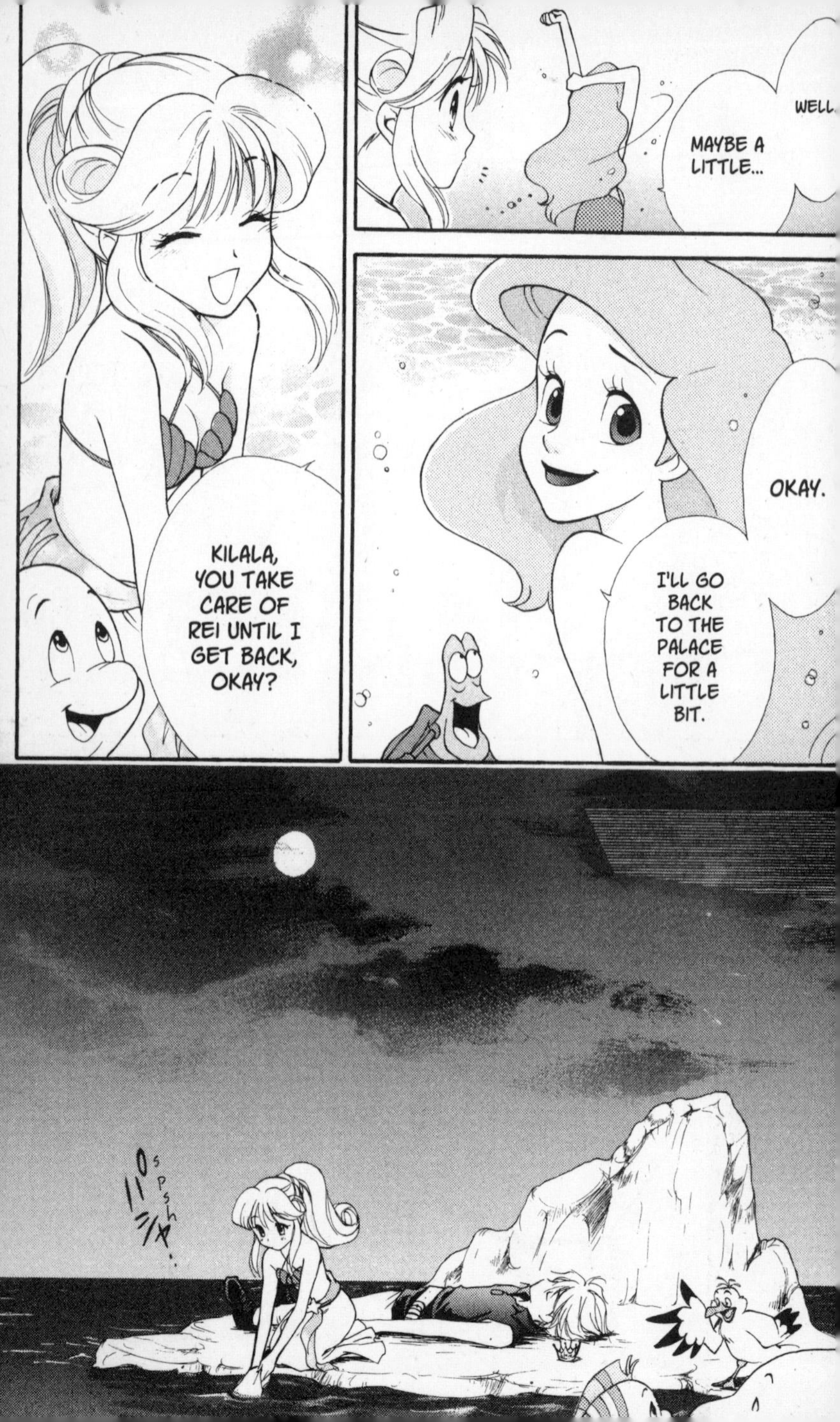
WELL...
MAYBE A LITTLE...
OKAY.
I'LL GO BACK TO THE PALACE FOR A LITTLE BIT.
KILALA, YOU TAKE CARE OF REI UNTIL I GET BACK, OKAY?
SPSH

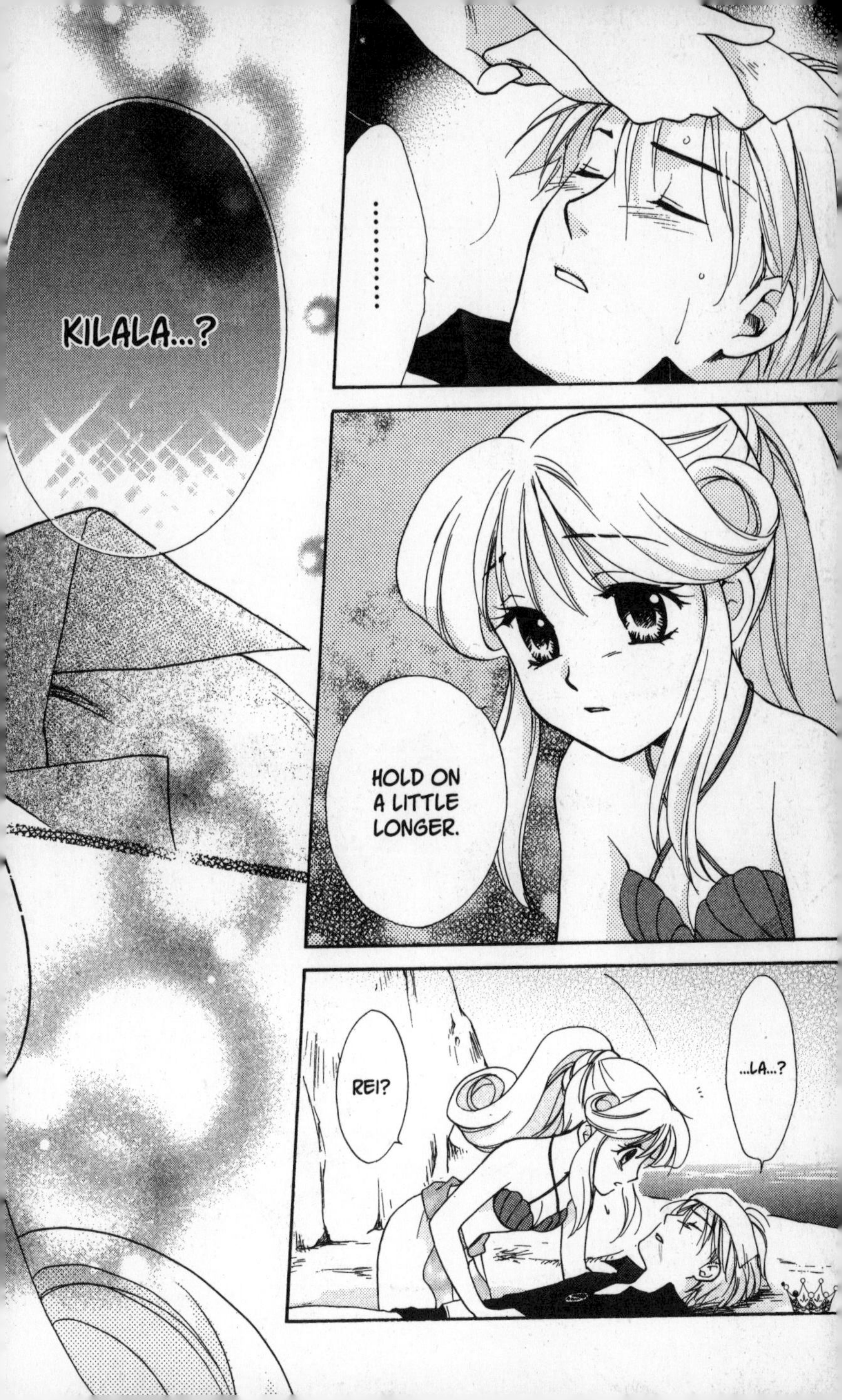
......
HOLD ON A LITTLE LONGER.
...LA...?
REI?
KILALA...?

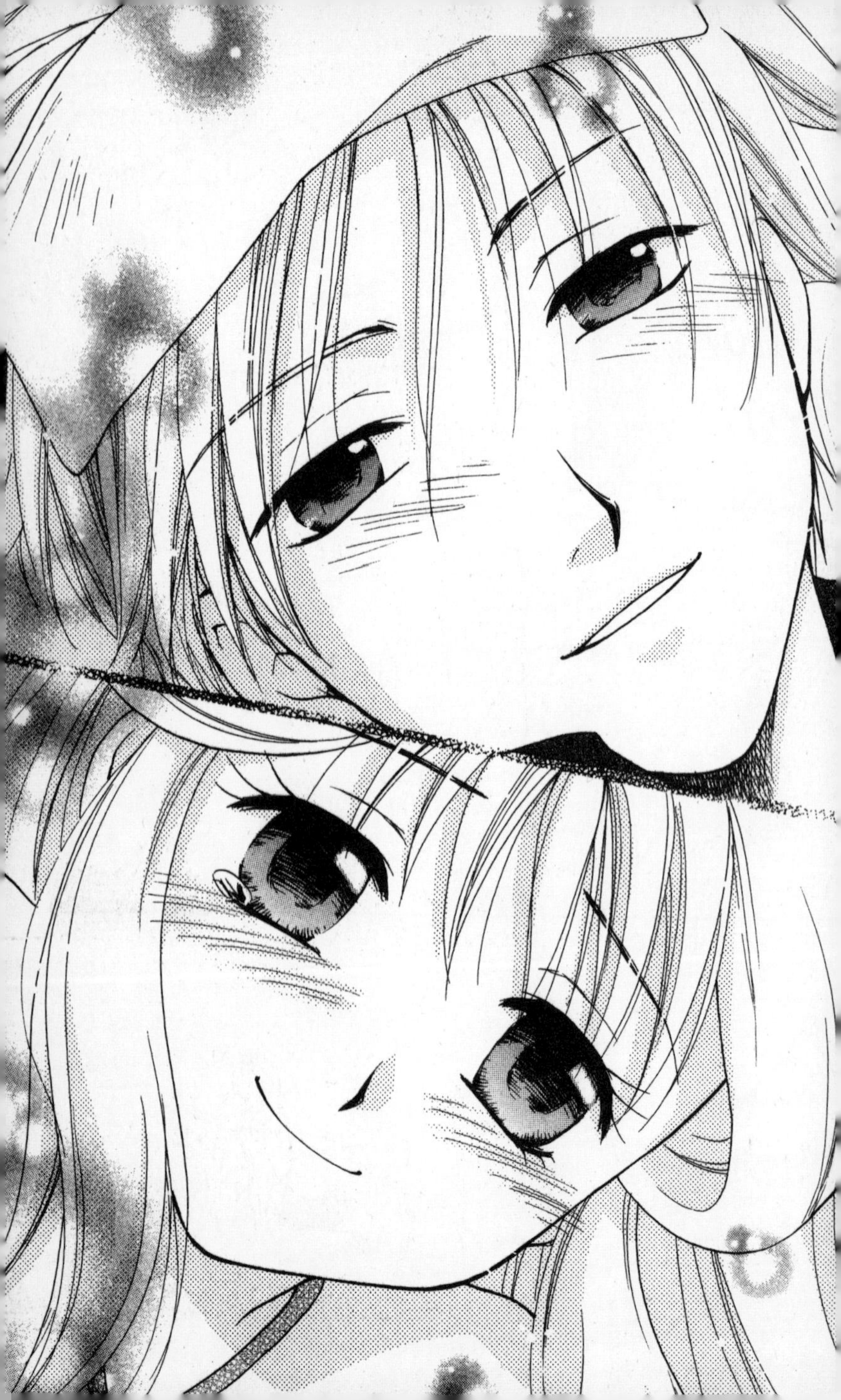

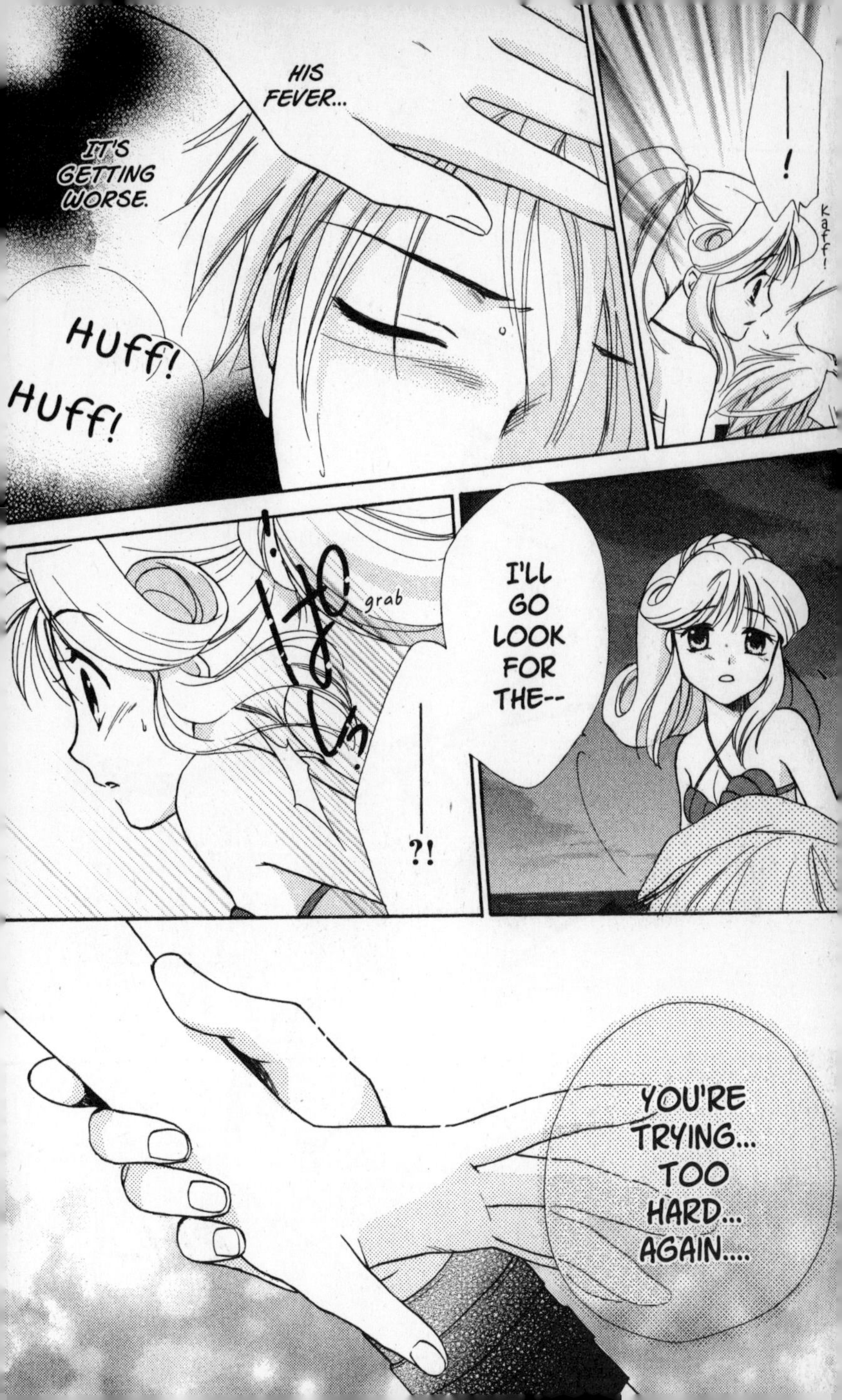
!
kaff!
HIS FEVER...
IT'S GETTING WORSE.
HUFF! HUFF!
I'LL GO LOOK FOR THE--
grab
?!
YOU'RE TRYING... TOO HARD... AGAIN....

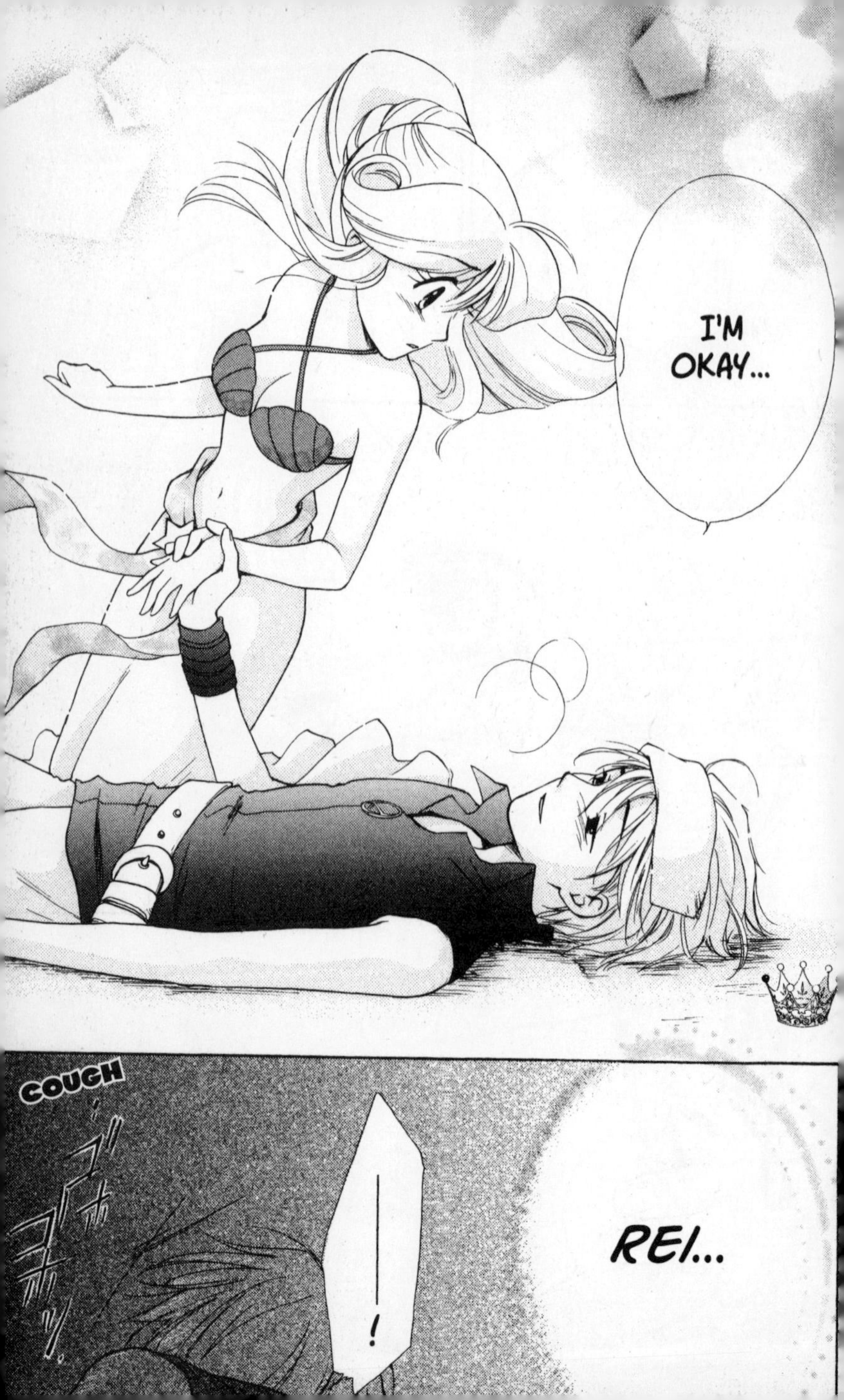
I'M OKAY...
REI...
!
COUGH

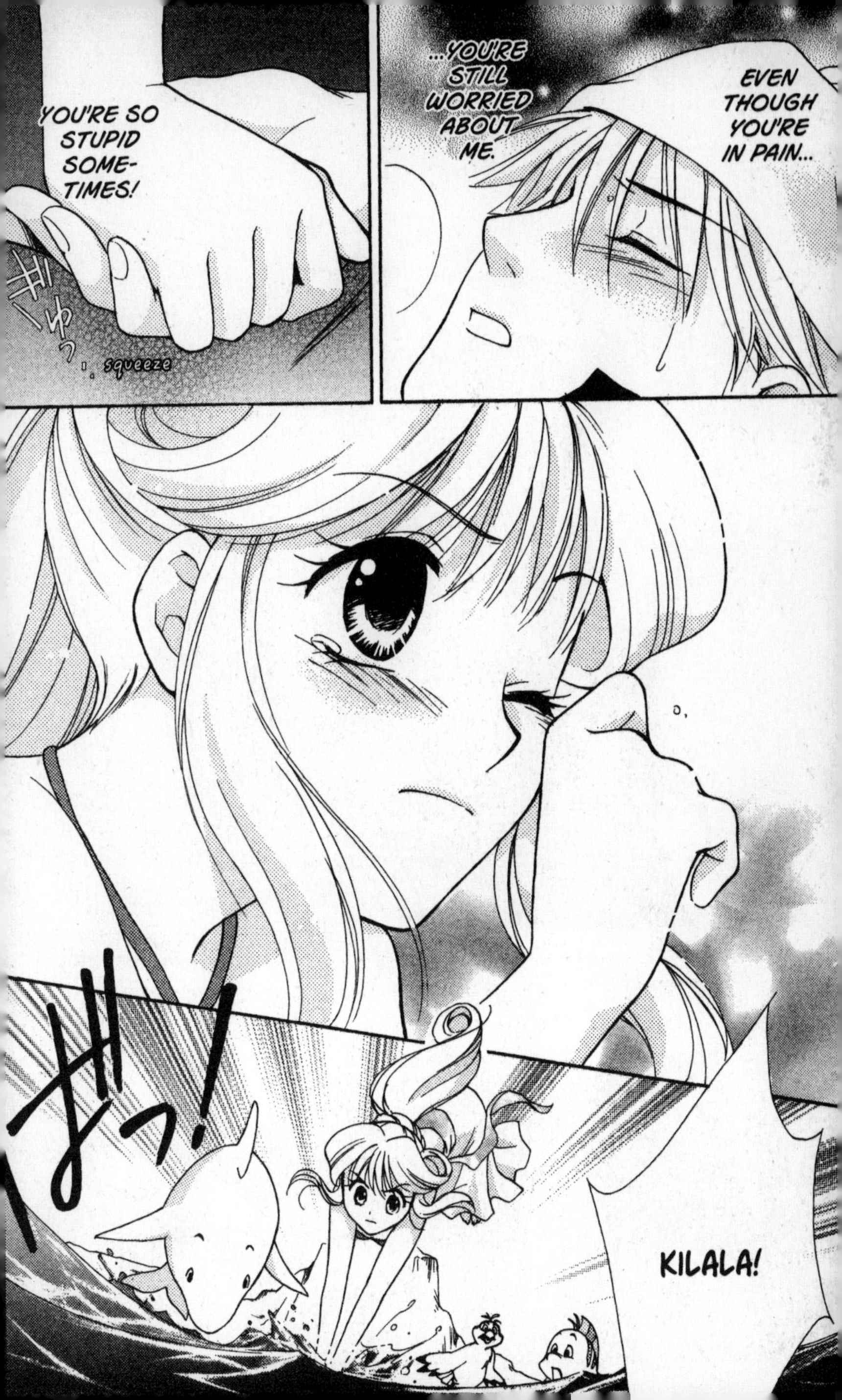
EVEN THOUGH YOU'RE IN PAIN...
...YOU'RE STILL WORRIED ABOUT ME.
YOU'RE SO STUPID SOME-TIMES!
squeeze
KILALA!

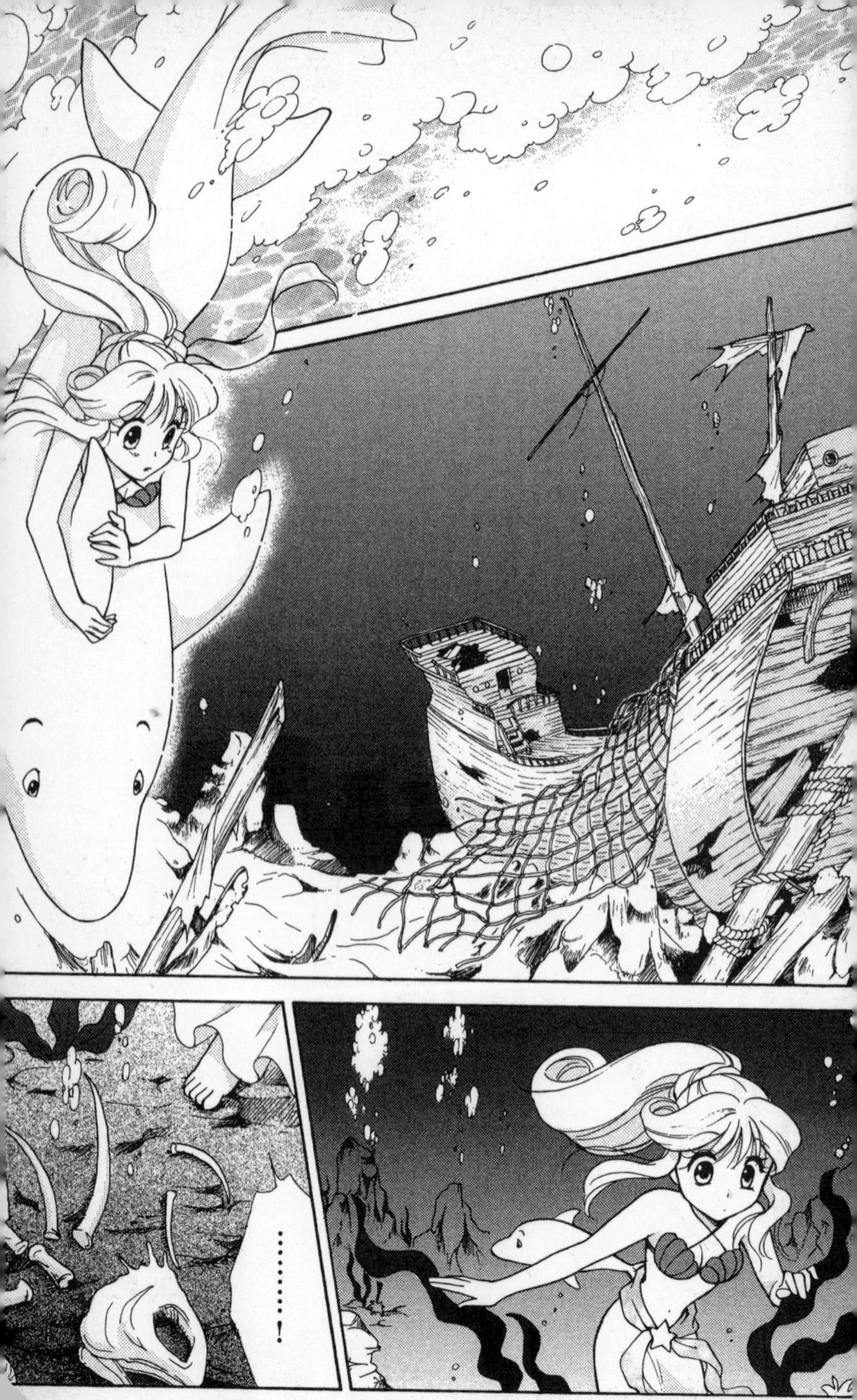

……!

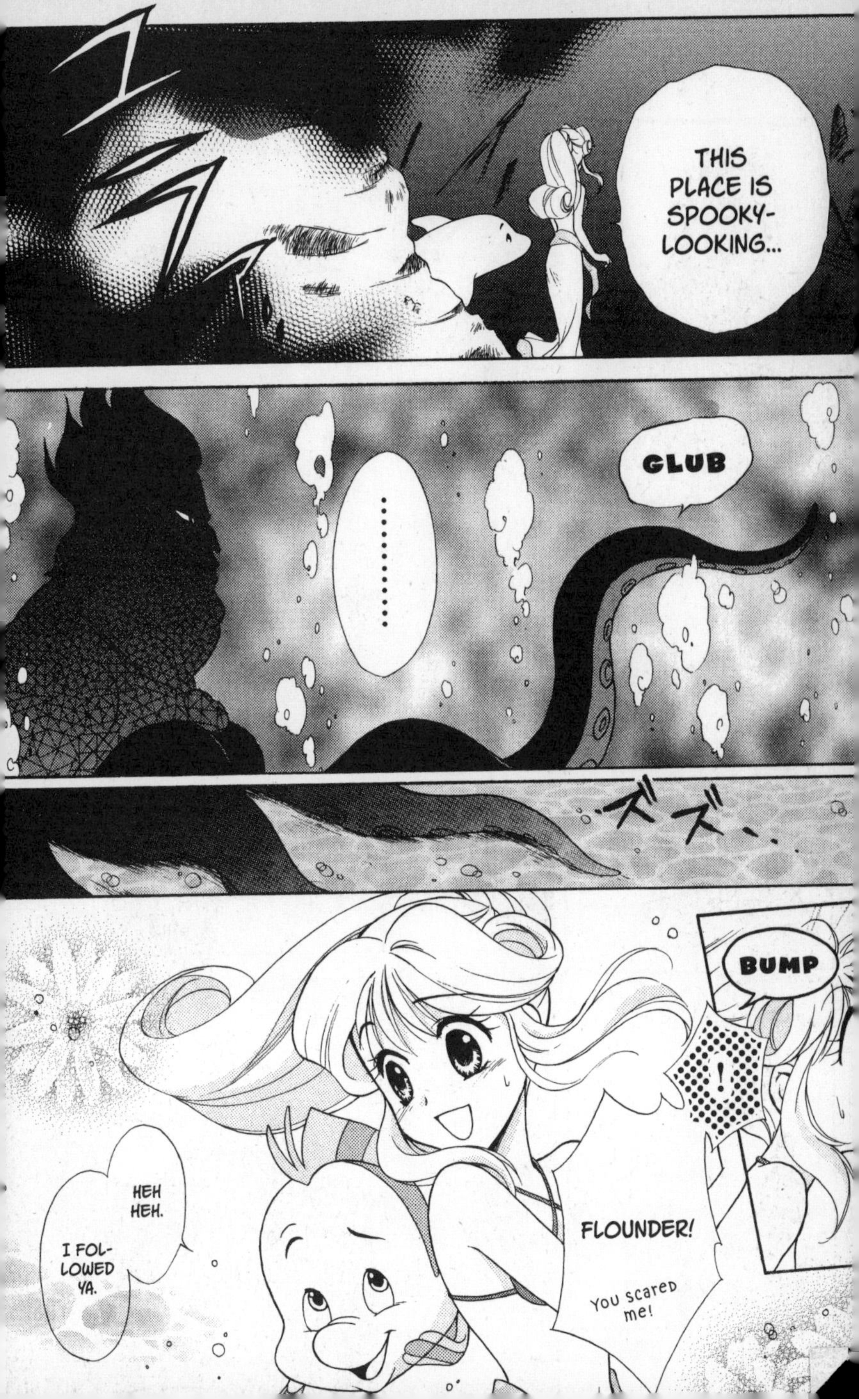
THIS PLACE IS SPOOKY-LOOKING...
GLUB
......
ズズ...
BUMP
!
FLOUNDER!
You scared me!
HEH HEH.
I FOL-LOWED YA.

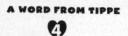

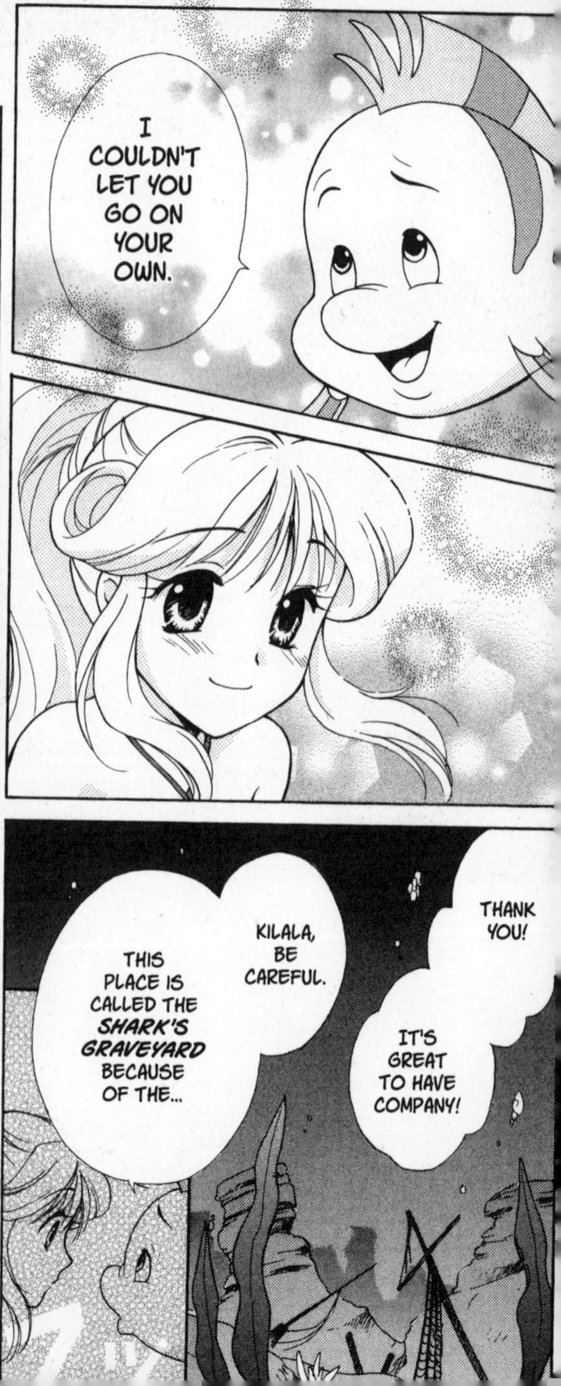
I COULDN'T LET YOU GO ON YOUR OWN.
THANK YOU!
IT'S GREAT TO HAVE COMPANY!
KILALA, BE CAREFUL.
THIS PLACE IS CALLED THE *SHARK'S GRAVEYARD* BECAUSE OF THE...

A WORD FROM TIPPE

4

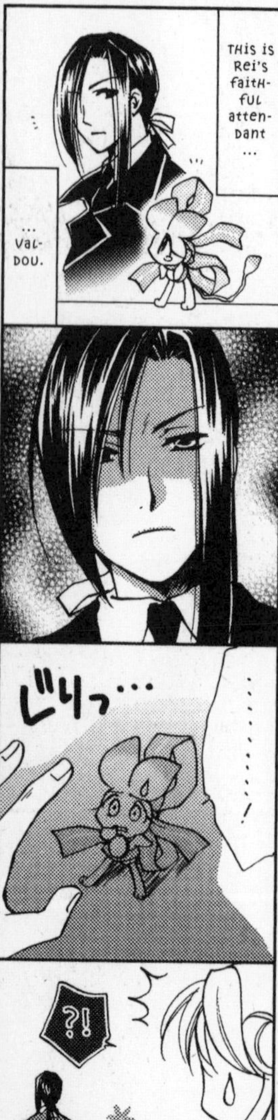
THIS IS Rei's faithful attendant ...
... Valdou.
じりっ…
……!
?!

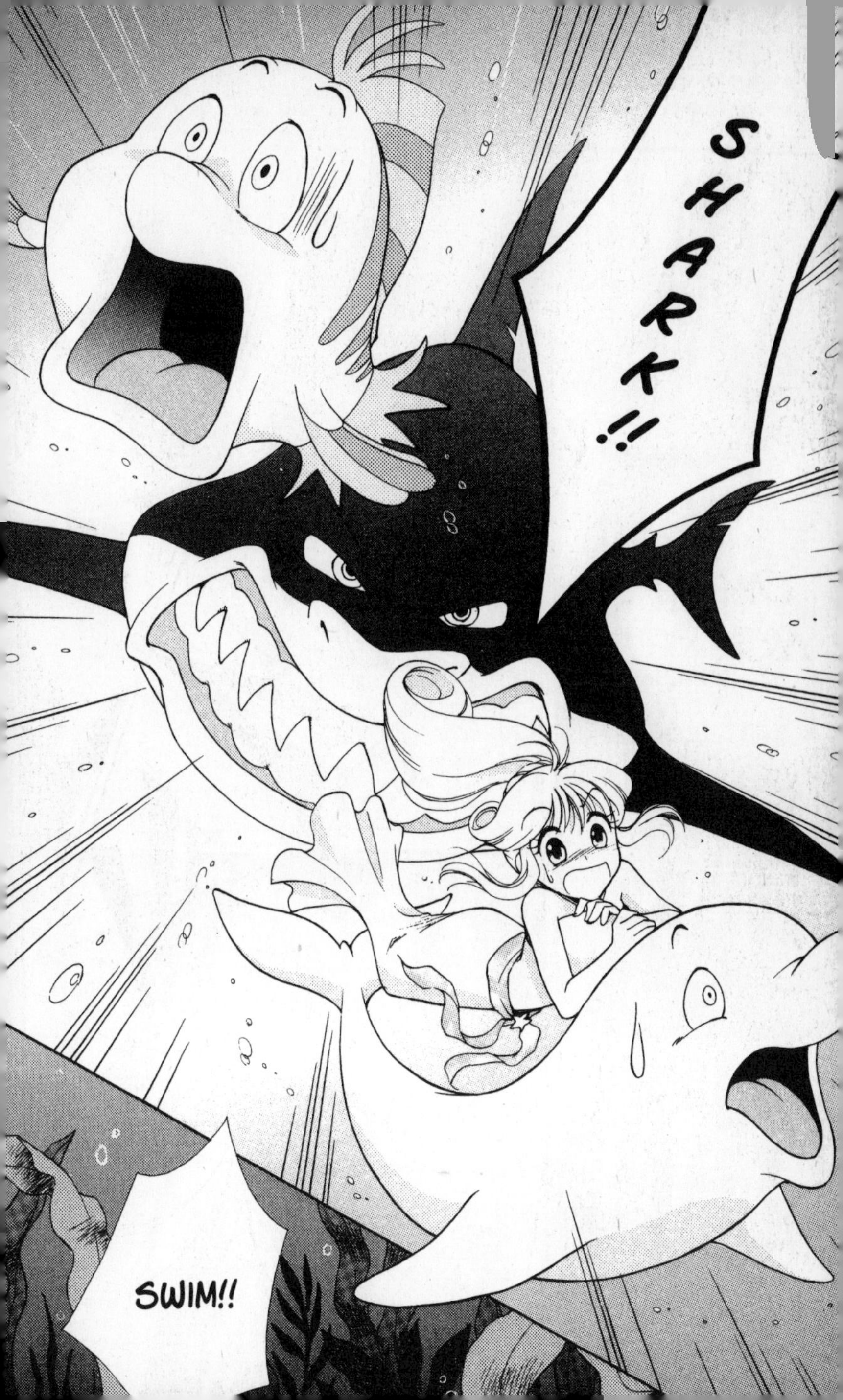
SHARK!!
SWIM!!

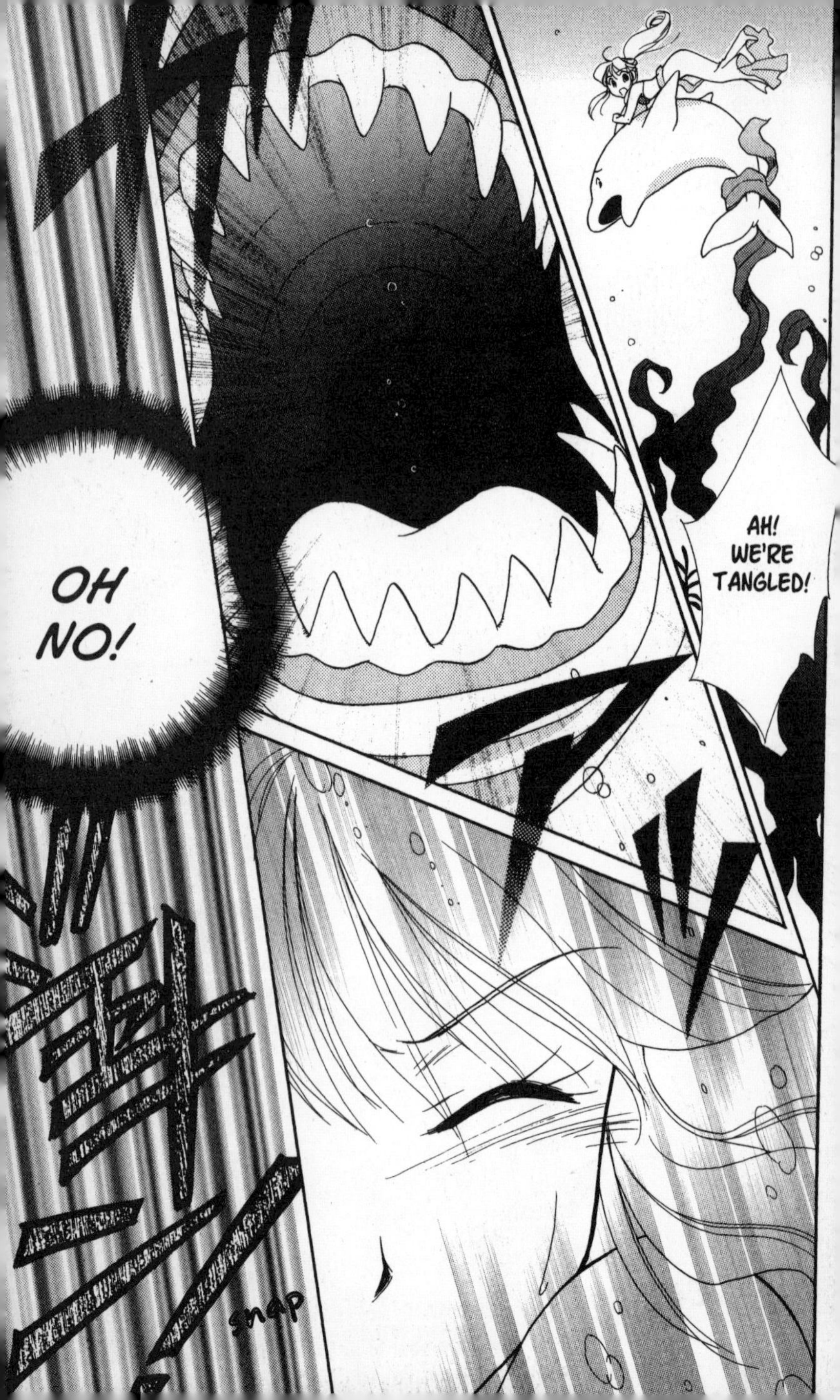
AH! WE'RE TANGLED!
OH NO!
snap

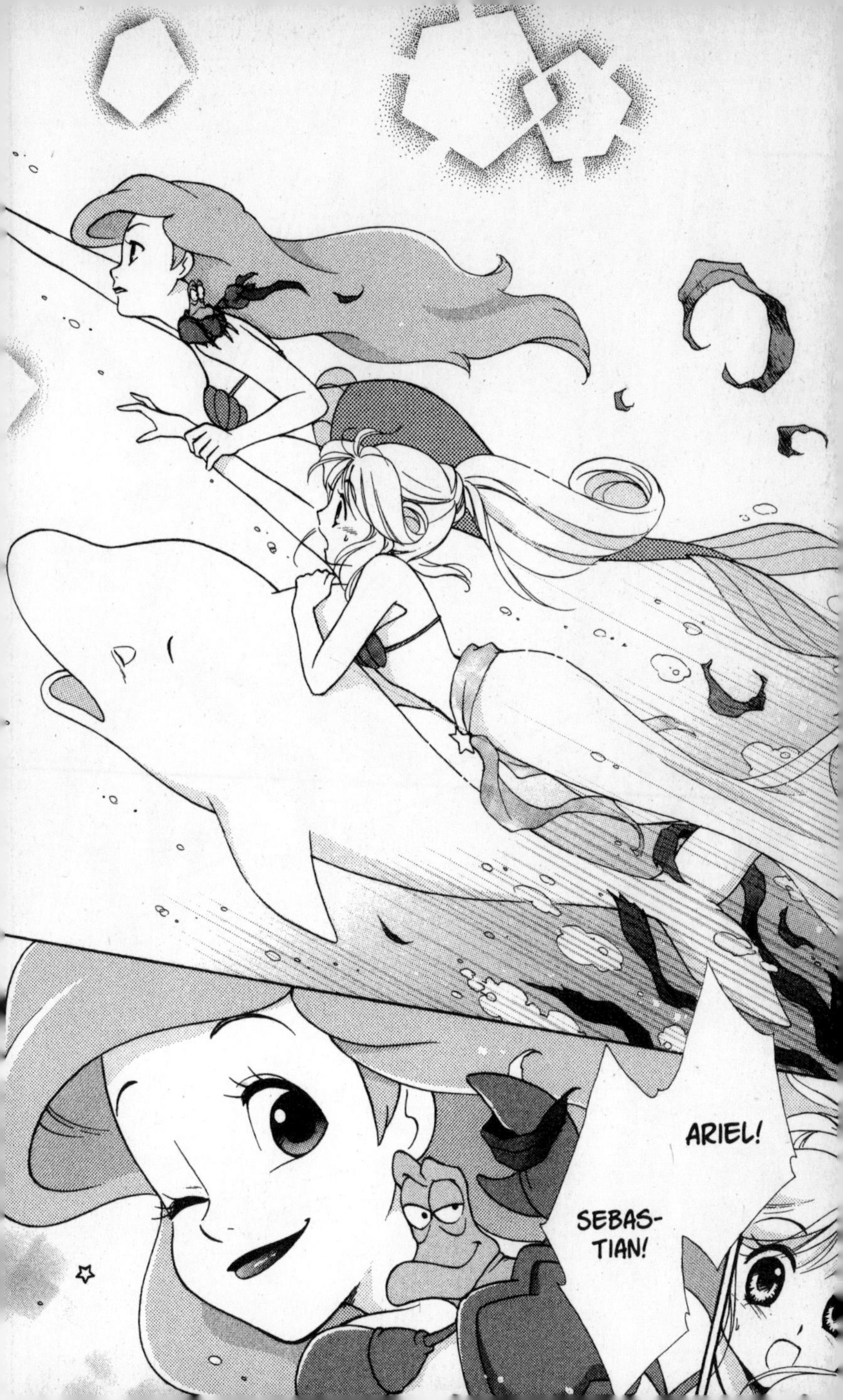
ARIEL!
SEBAS-
TIAN!

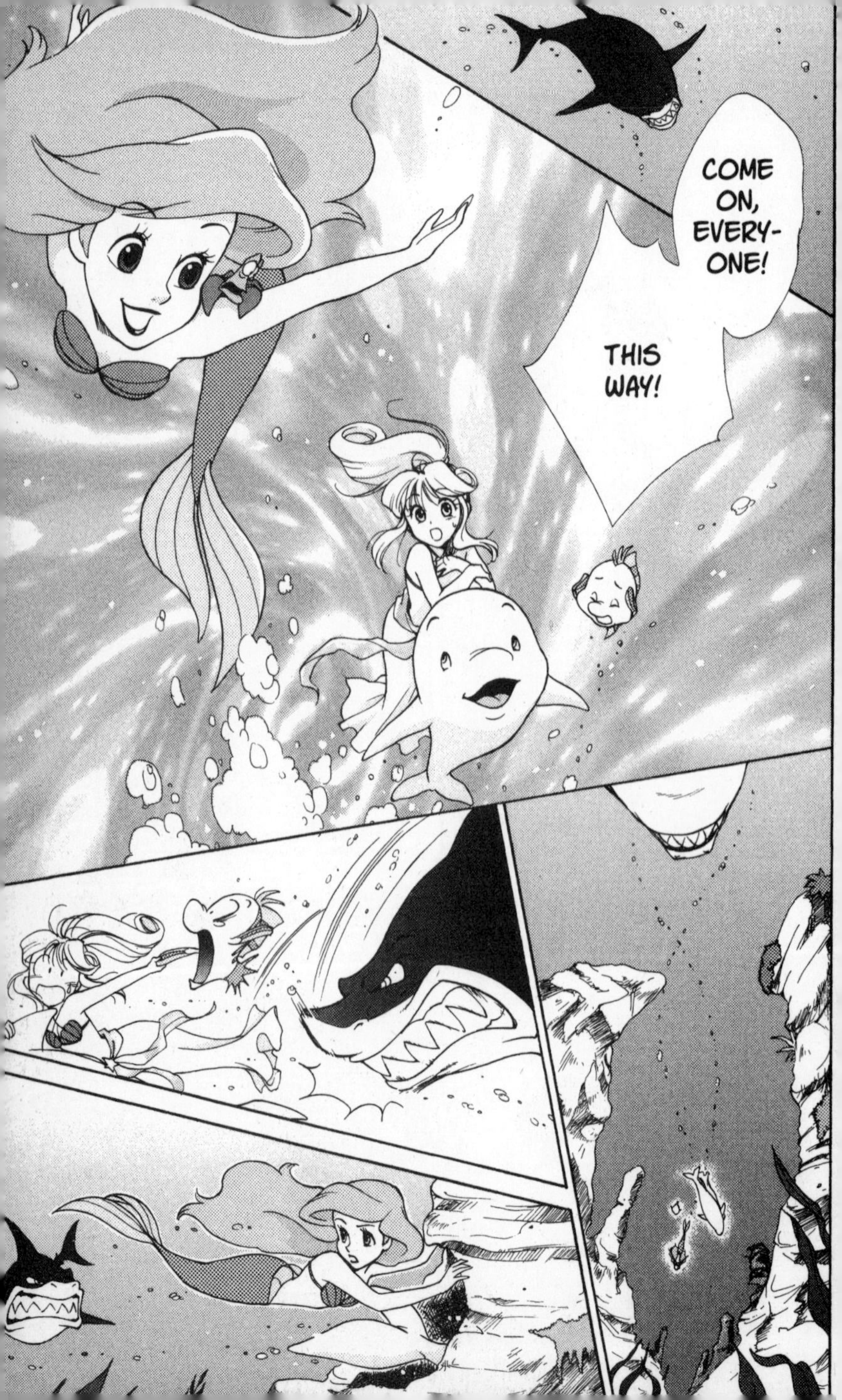
COME ON, EVERY-ONE!
THIS WAY!

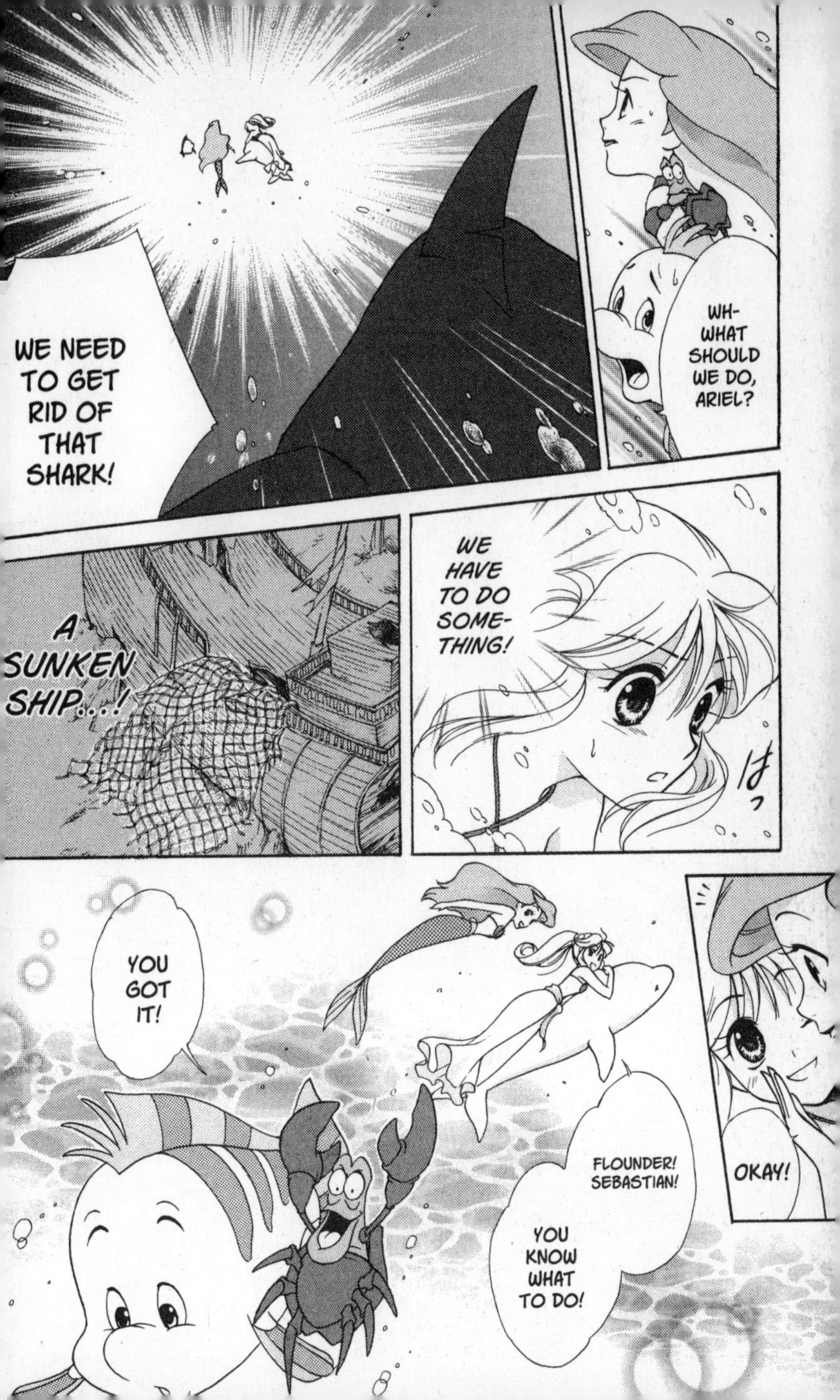
WH-WHAT SHOULD WE DO, ARIEL?
WE NEED TO GET RID OF THAT SHARK!
WE HAVE TO DO SOME-THING!
はっ
A SUNKEN SHIP...!
OKAY!
FLOUNDER! SEBASTIAN!
YOU KNOW WHAT TO DO!
YOU GOT IT!

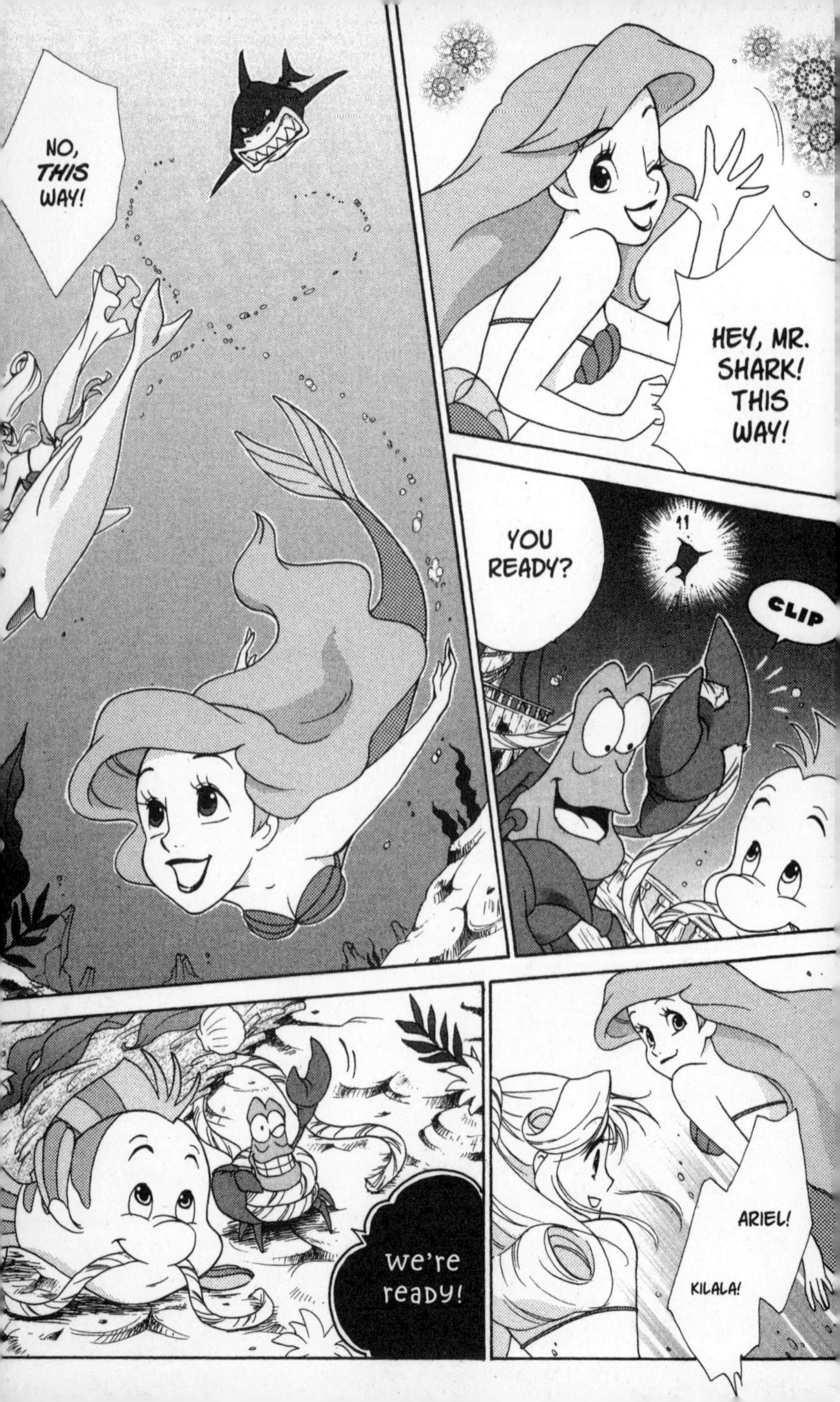
HEY, MR. SHARK! THIS WAY!
YOU READY?
CLIP
NO, THIS WAY!
ARIEL!
KILALA!
we're ready!

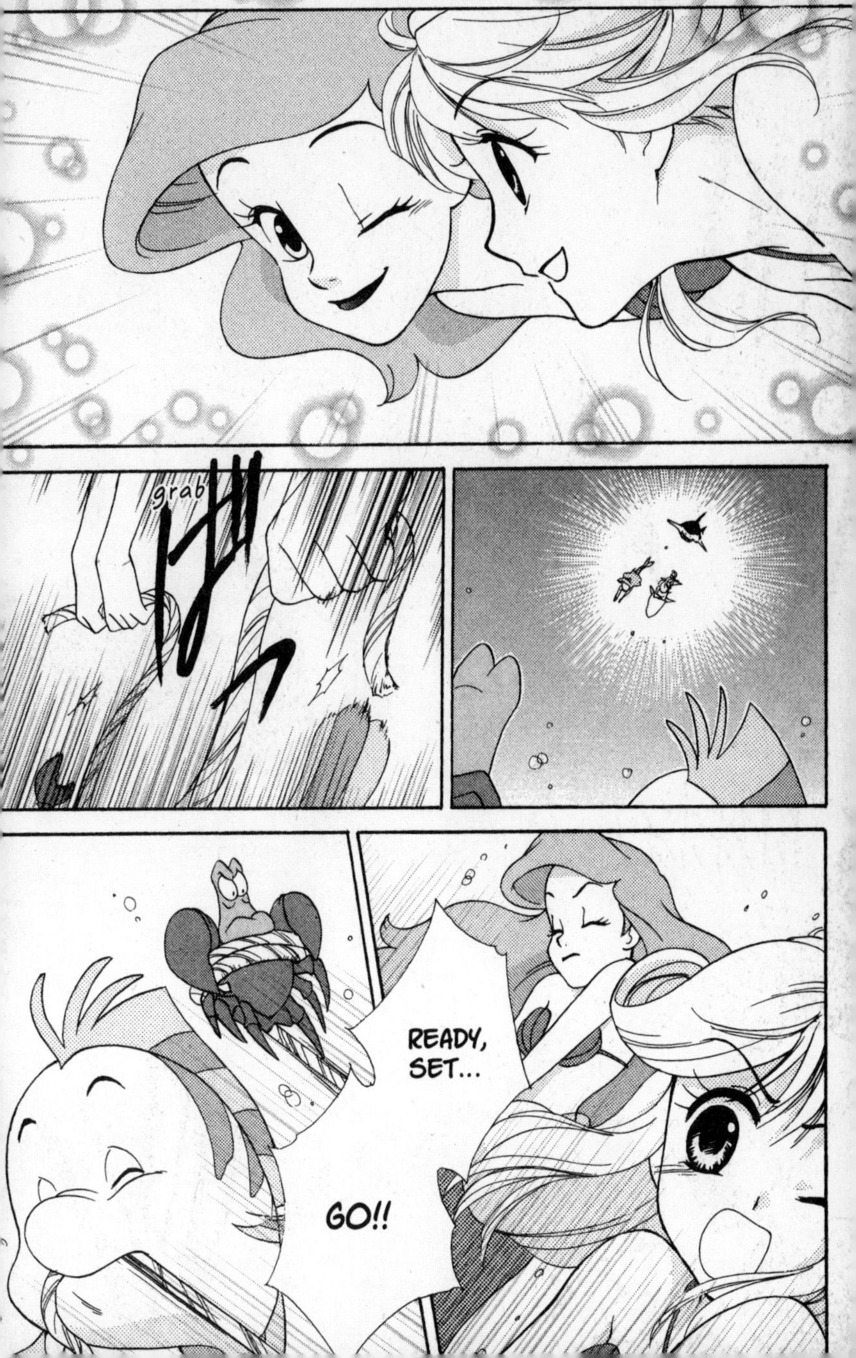
grab
READY, SET...
GO!!

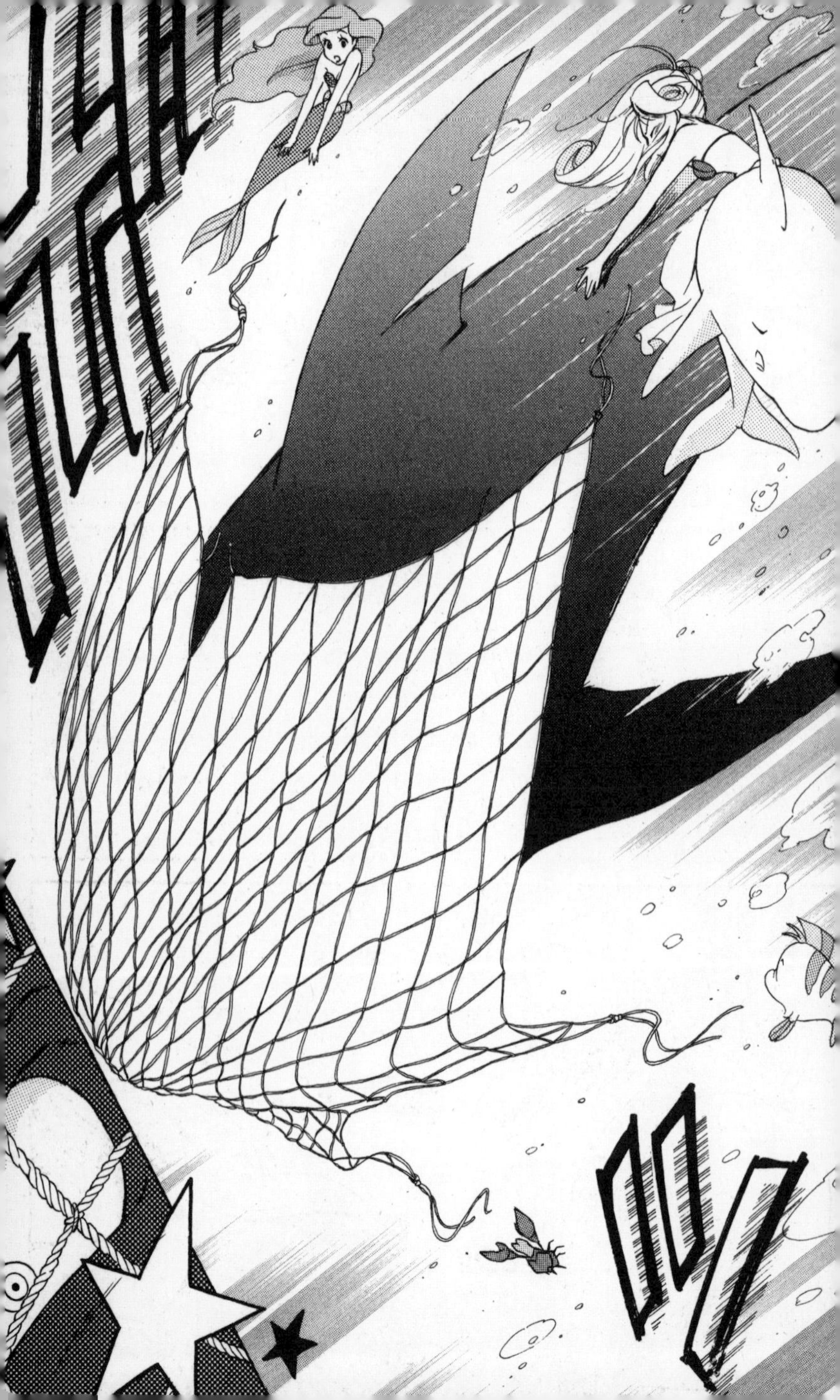

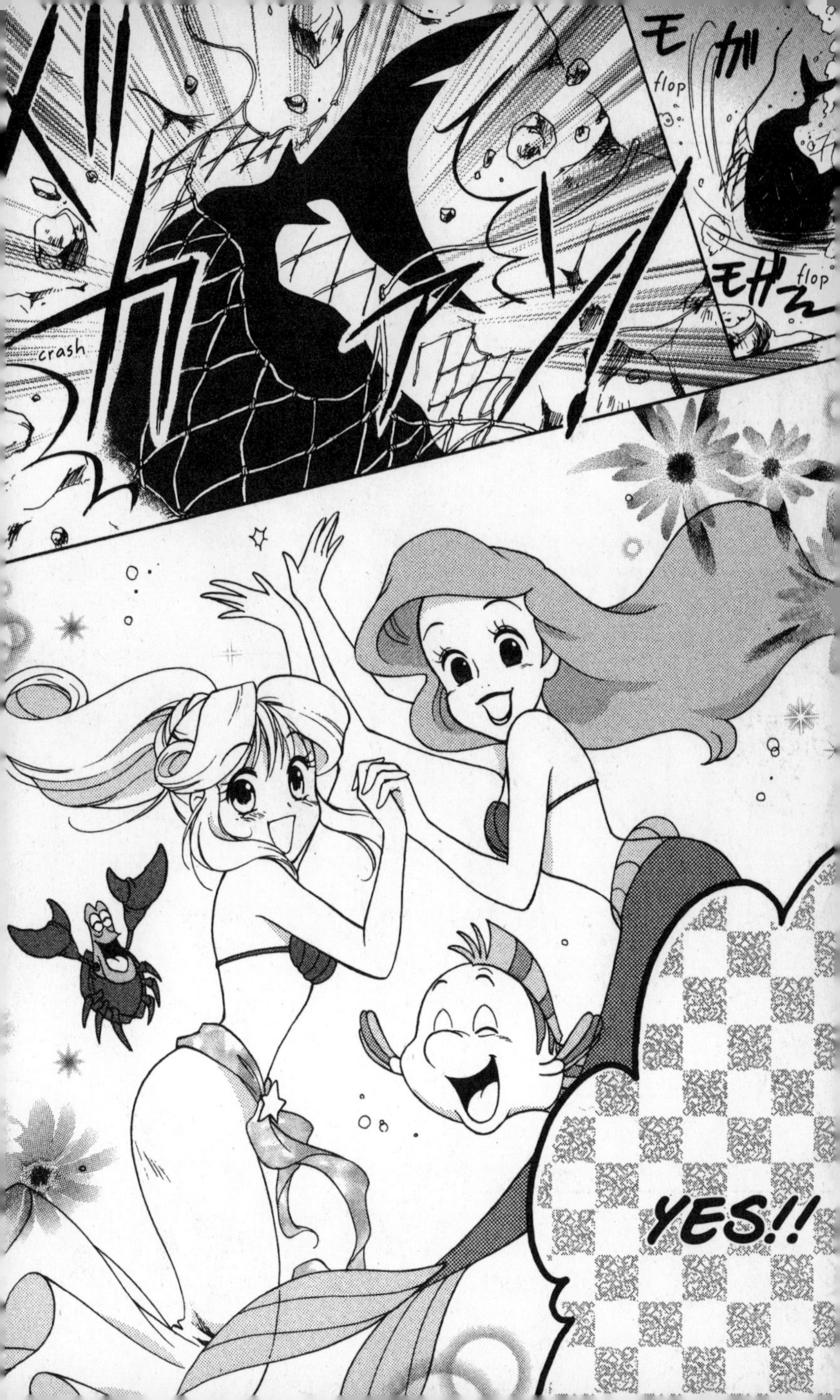
モガ
flop
モガ〜
flop
crash
YES!!

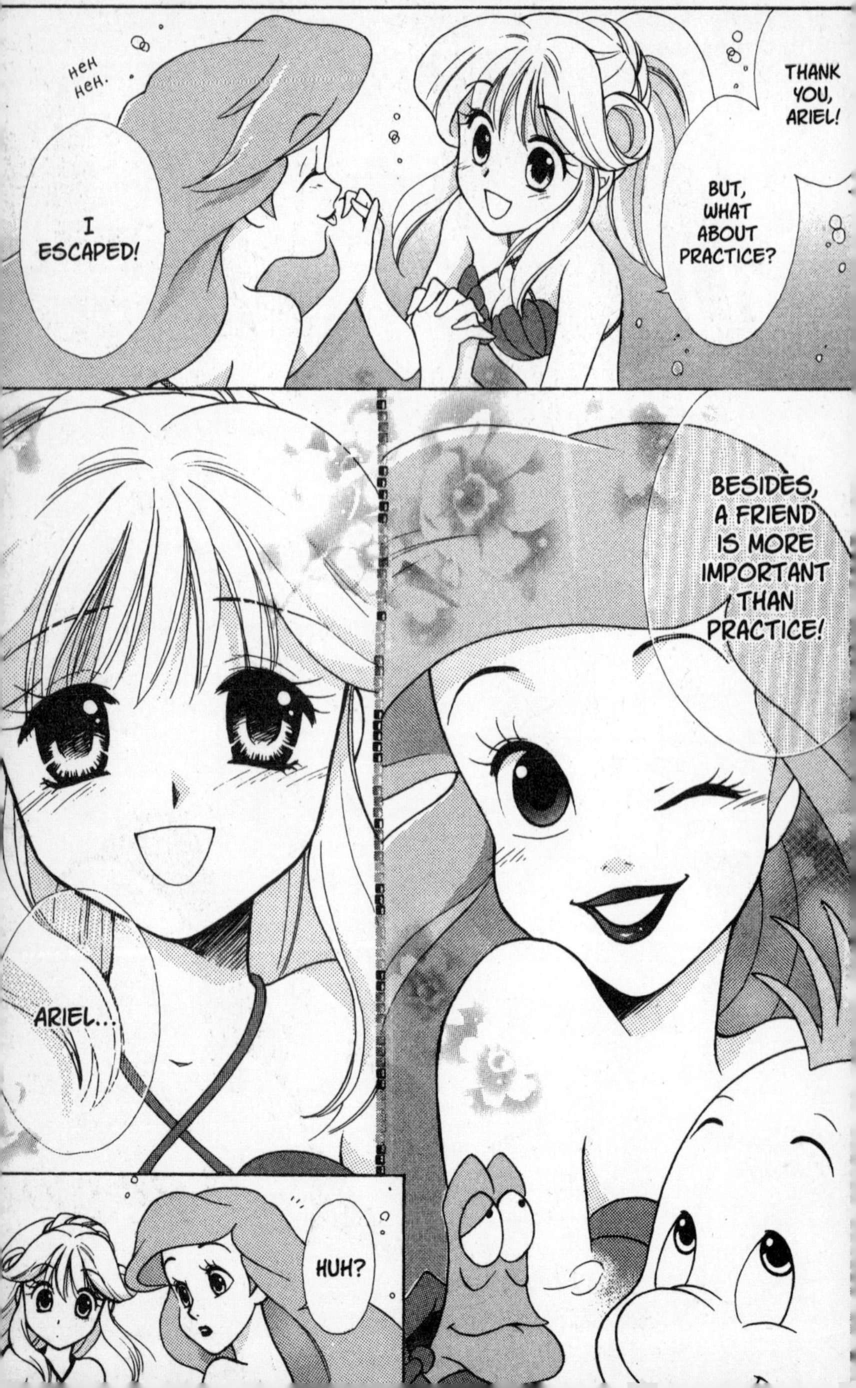
THANK YOU, ARIEL!
BUT, WHAT ABOUT PRACTICE?
HEH HEH.
I ESCAPED!
BESIDES, A FRIEND IS MORE IMPORTANT THAN PRACTICE!
ARIEL...
HUH?

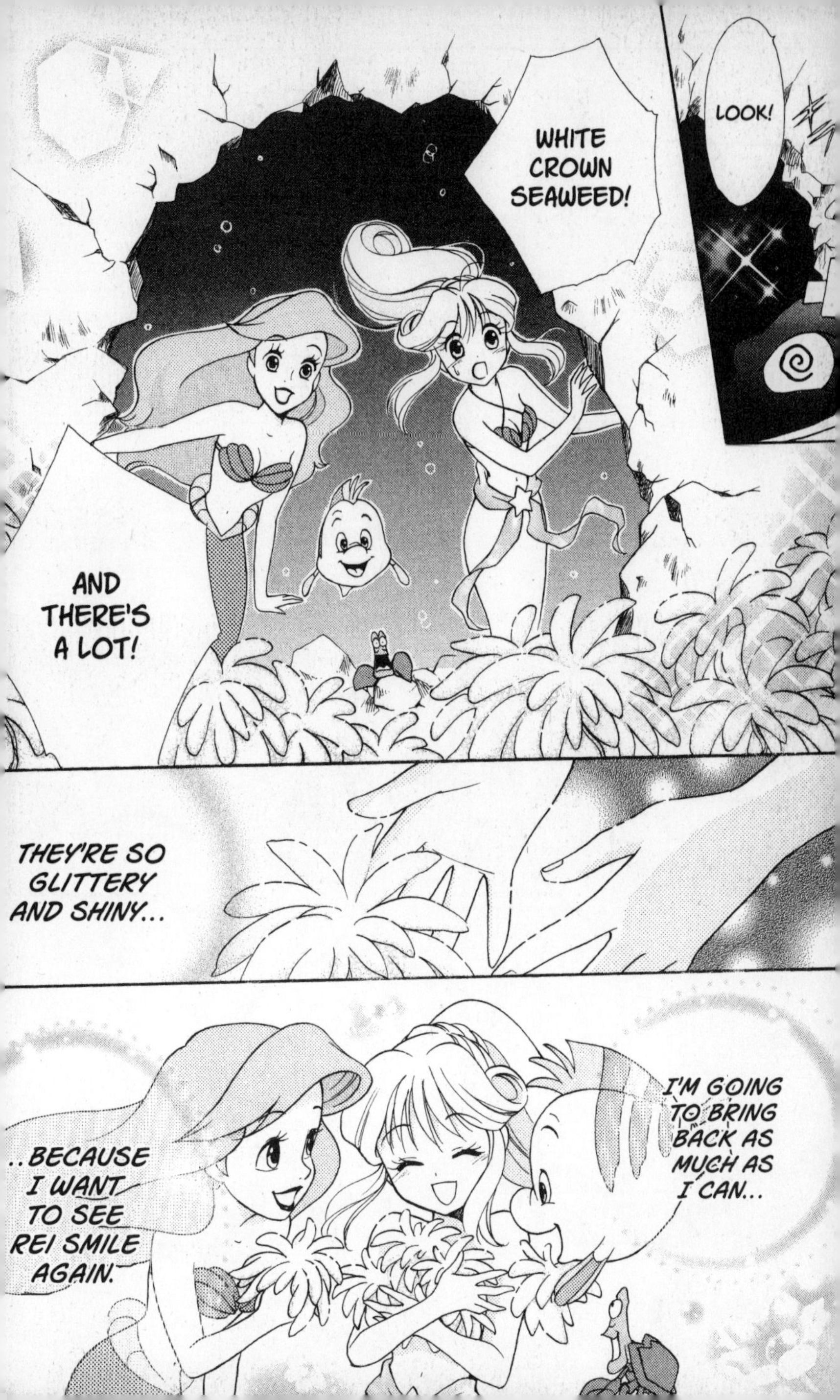

LOOK!
WHITE CROWN SEAWEED!
AND THERE'S A LOT!
THEY'RE SO GLITTERY AND SHINY...
I'M GOING TO BRING BACK AS MUCH AS I CAN...
...BECAUSE I WANT TO SEE REI SMILE AGAIN.

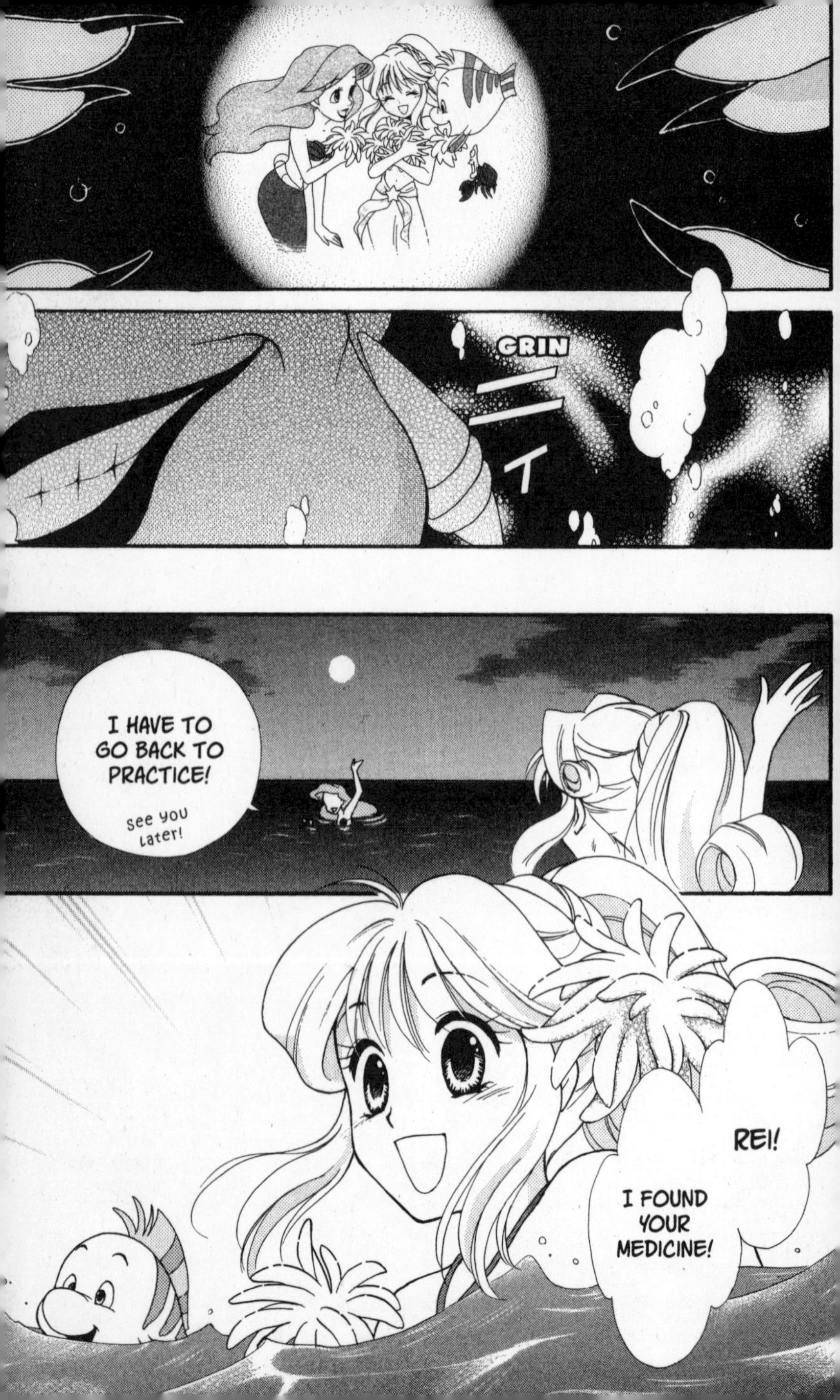
GRIN
I HAVE TO GO BACK TO PRACTICE!
See you later!
REI!
I FOUND YOUR MEDICINE!

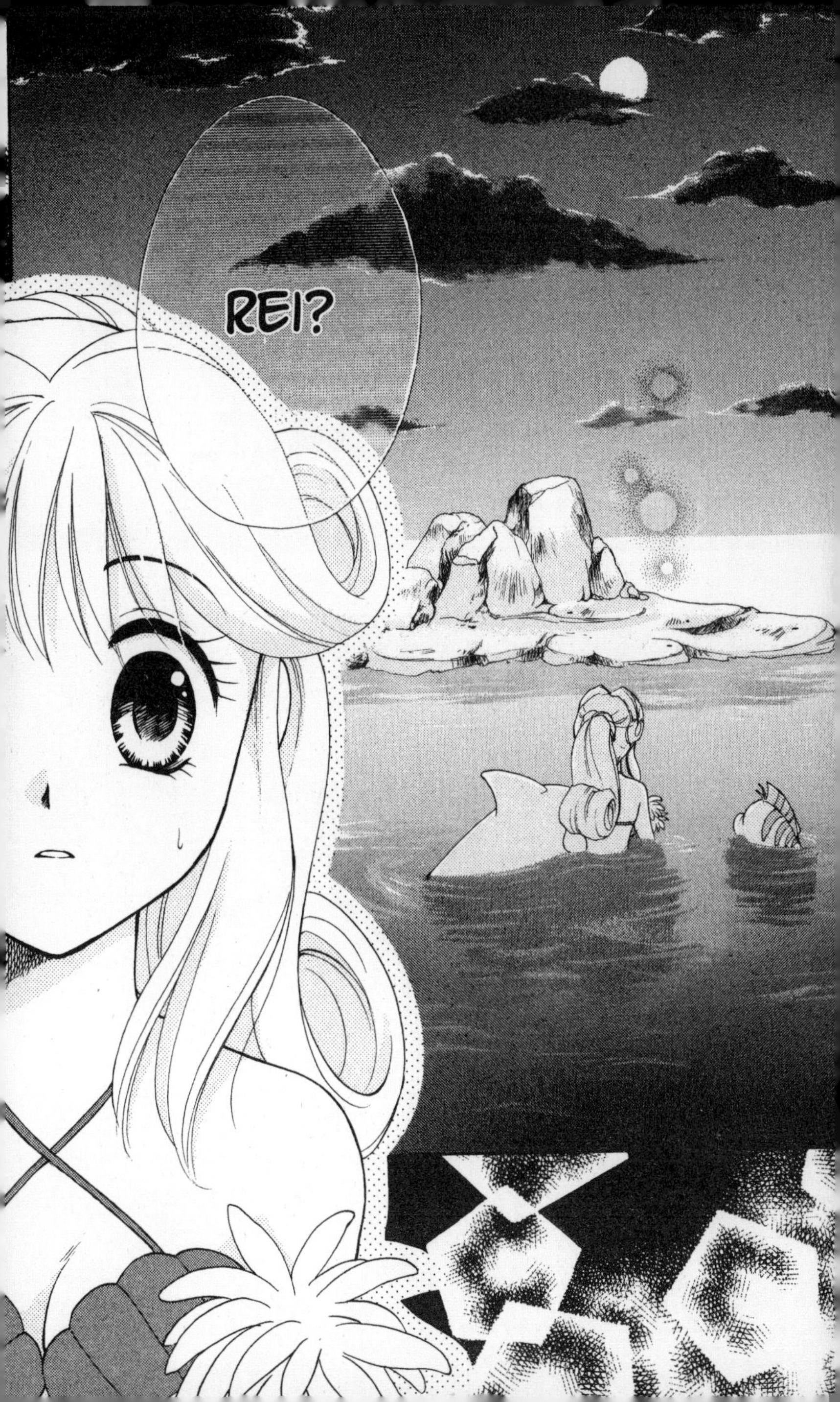
REI?

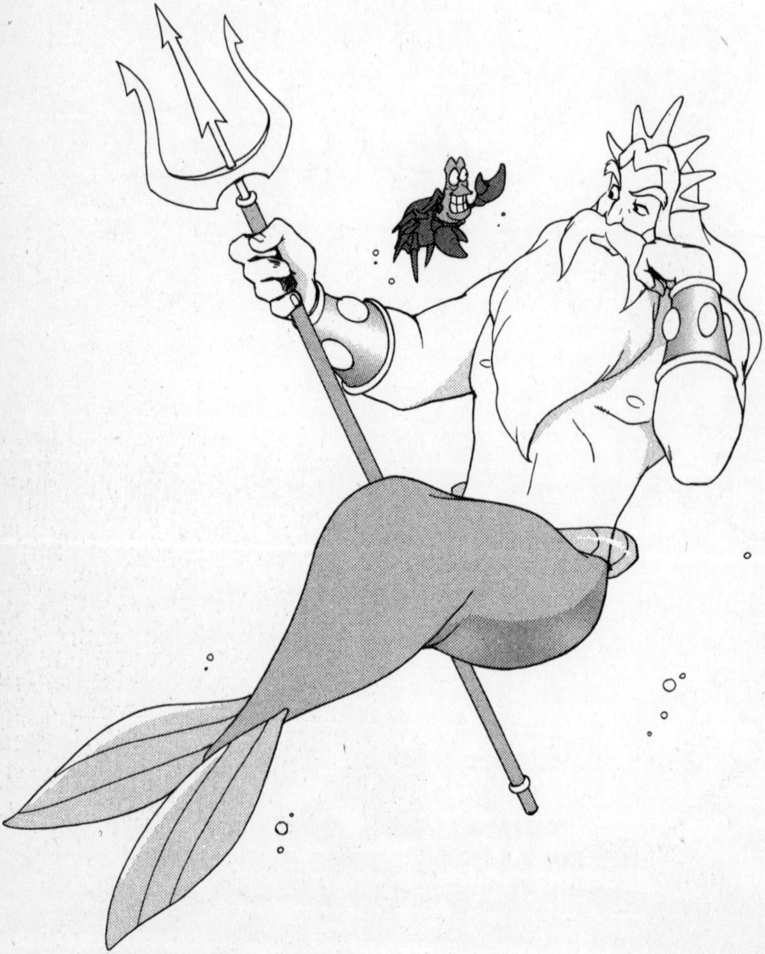

IN THE NEXT VOLUME OF

DISNEY's Kilala Princess

Ursula wants to crown herself
queen with the power of the
tiara. There's just one catch:
she'll have to marry Rei first!

**JOIN KILALA AND THE
DISNEY PRINCESSES FOR MORE
ADVENTURES IN VOLUME 4!**

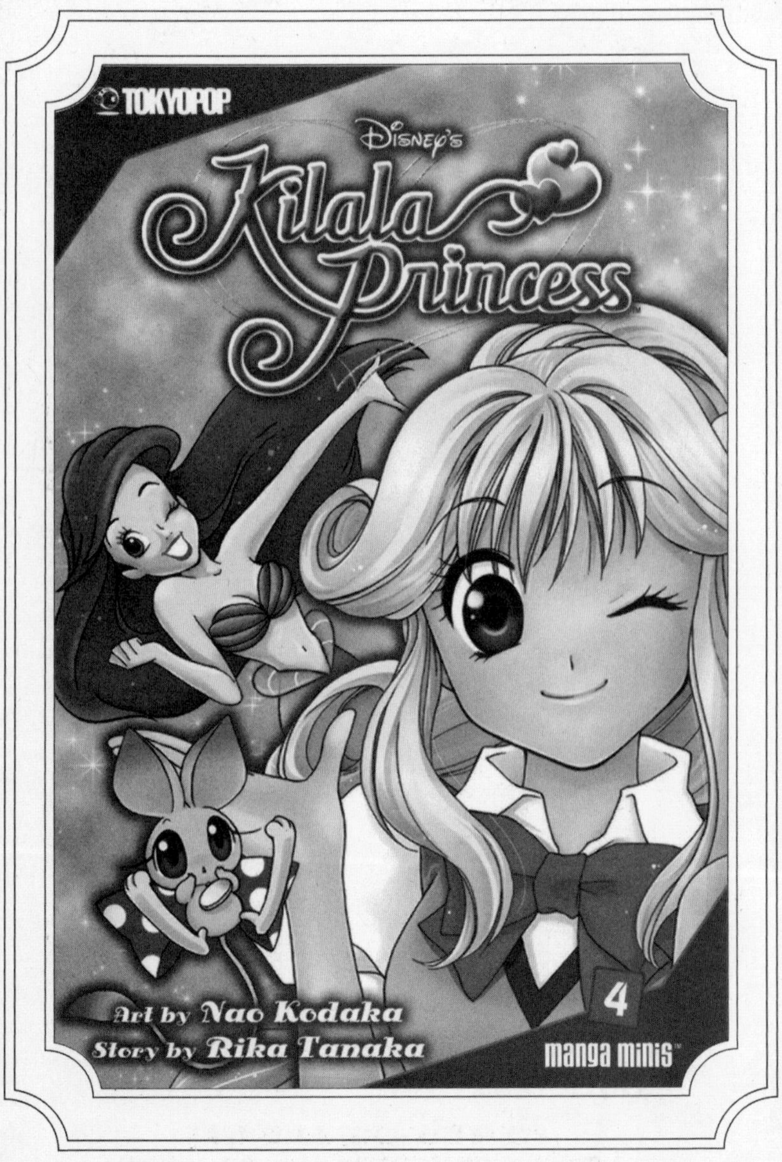
TOKYOPOP
Disney's
Kilala Princess
4
Art by Nao Kodaka
Story by Rika Tanaka
manga minis™

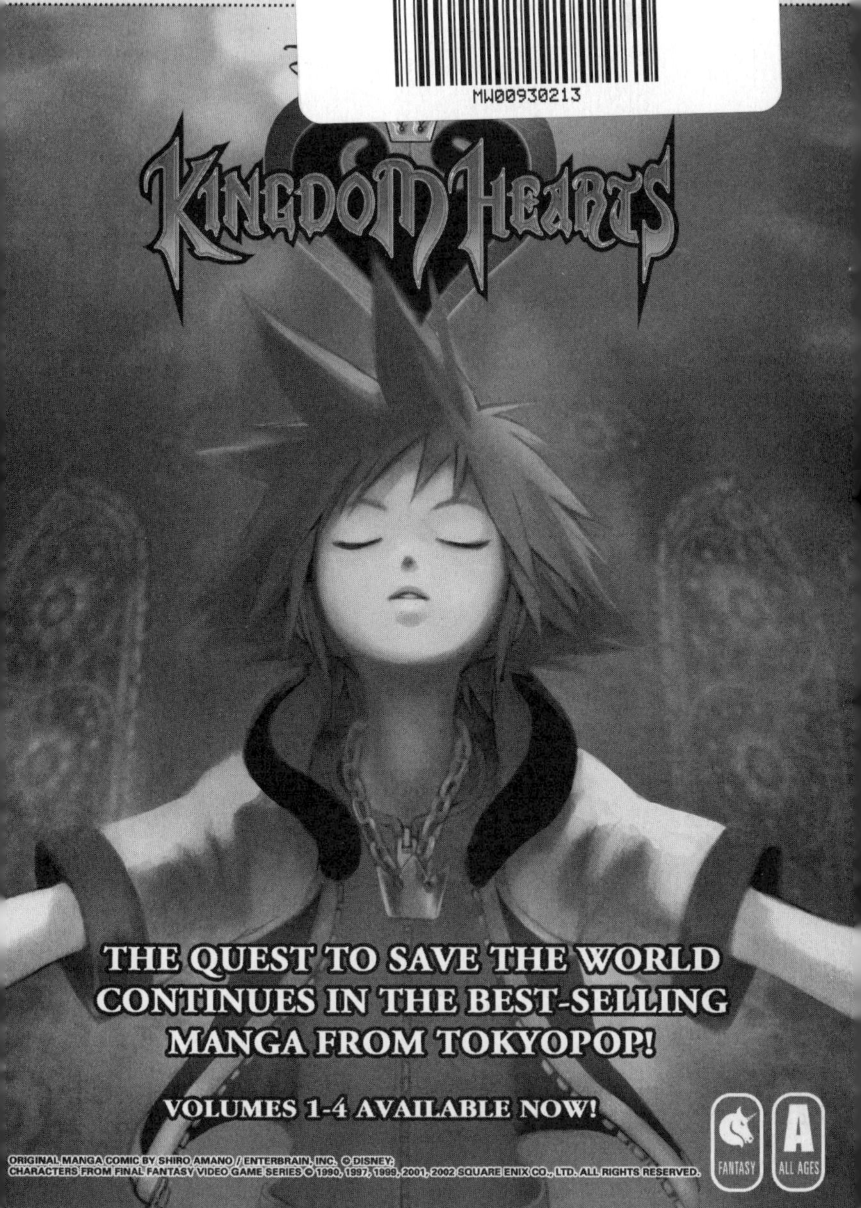
KINGDOM HEARTS
THE QUEST TO SAVE THE WORLD CONTINUES IN THE BEST-SELLING MANGA FROM TOKYOPOP!
VOLUMES 1-4 AVAILABLE NOW!
ORIGINAL MANGA COMIC BY SHIRO AMANO / ENTERBRAIN, INC. © DISNEY;
CHARACTERS FROM FINAL FANTASY VIDEO GAME SERIES © 1990, 1997, 1999, 2001, 2002 SQUARE ENIX CO., LTD. ALL RIGHTS RESERVED.
FANTASY
A
ALL AGES